Tenderness
Kindness
Forgiveness

Raymond T. O'Donnell

ISBN 978-1-0980-7499-9 (paperback)
ISBN 978-1-0980-7500-2 (digital)

Christian Faith Publishing, Inc.
832 Park Avenue
Meadville, PA 16335
www.christianfaithpublishing.com

Printed in the United States of America

Contents

Concepts

This book is about religion, family, and politics, partly inspired by a lady standing alone outside the Saint Ann Church in Hamilton, Ohio, in 1968 and said softly, within hearing distance, "There is no hell." When I heard her radical words, as she stood there, I believed it couldn't be further from the truth. However, she has remained in the back of my thoughts, especially in 2016 when I understood Jesus to say, "His Father has given Him all humanity and he doesn't want to lose any one." That statement by Jesus is absolutely profound, and that goes into my core.

I thought years later, she must have been forgiven for her horrendous sins in order to love our Lord as she seemed standing there. Her voice was foremost inside her; she didn't say anything else but the love Jesus showed her. I love Him too for the forgiveness given to me, but that doesn't mean there is no hell. There is a hell for those that reject God's love of Jesus Christ in the end. I hope by showing you spiritual and worldly examples, that Christ wants us with Him in heaven, even those who were responsible for His suffering and crucifying Him. He even asked the Father to forgive them. *He wants us all.*[a] For now, I'll take you on a seventy-eight-year journey to know God and find He is real.

Why can't I convince all the people of the world into believing in Christ? After all, this book is my attempt to achieve it, and it seems I struggle getting to the next phase that that requires more super efforts from my brain or heart. How do we get super efforts? Hopefully, you'll understand in the next ten chapters.

---

[a] Luke 23–34.

It is like the story of three children, waiting in the dark for a bus near their home in Indiana, in late October 2018, and were killed by a young girl driver veering ever so slightly off the road during the time a school bus was stopped, and her auto drove into the children. Later it was reported that even the highway patrol officers were crying at the scene. What happened? Was the driver distracted by texting? We don't know at this time, *but* let's say that's how it went down. If the story does go down that way, think of how many warnings we've had concerning texting and driving, and a few of us continue driving and texting without regard to the warnings. That, I think, is similar to an analogy of people hearing the Word of God and continue not paying attention to the warnings and nudges seriously. We'll see God someday, and then I wonder, when we see Him, if we'll find out how we could not have seen what is in our hearts during our stay on earth. That's the objective—we are made free to search or not search our hearts during our life challengers, storms, and nudges, and there are many as we begin to see. We were cast into this world to figure it out, with help if we ask. And the mystery, do we figure it out? Different from plant and animal classifications to survive, we are challenged, not just to live on bread alone but to find truth. And God is love.

Steps Backward

I have to tell you that what I've recorded in the following chapters is from following my own steps back in time and warn you that the steps aren't necessarily in the same *chronological time sequence at times*, but what I've seen and heard that flows in my thoughts, in the following chapters, for the past seventy-eight years. And thinking even now, as I write, I wonder if I can finish this book before it is time; I would continue waking up three to four o'clock in the morning and type in crucial notes to be included in my writings. I didn't mind the sleep interference; I knew it was from deep inside me and my inners was to keep on writing what I know as spiritual inspirations. Also you'll see after some statements, there may be a small letter indicating a reference at the end of that particular paragraph. Example, go below for the reference "b."[a]

Note: Also, I make no distinction when writing concerning the Old Testament, among Jews, Israel, and/or Judah; I call them Israelites throughout my writings.

The TWOS

Hopefully as I write this, I can communicate to you what is inside me, an enthusiasm of faith and discovering the fantastic *TWOS* while I was teaching a two-year Bible class to Catholics parishioners in Portage, Michigan, during that time Barbara and I were documenting incidents before and after my youngest son's death. The TWOS became the main motivation for the inception of this book. I found the TWOS throughout Scripture after Michael, my son, passed, and you should know that such things as TWOS exist in our world. The TWOS are two incidences showing the beginning in the first part and a final second part of a related happening. As an example, we see the beginning of the world and the end of the world in the Old Testament, and another beginning in the Old Testament and the final end in the New Testament. Both incidents show a beginning and a final, and finally TWOS aren't recognized immediately in Scripture as the threes, sevens, twelves and so forth are. The other reasons for writing this book is to help me and the world know God better, and maybe—just maybe—we can help save our world from destruction. Also a tidbit, after more than fifty years of Bible study, I found that animals and trees know God, and maybe they know of God—as I have found indications they do—and maybe more than a few humans do.

---

[a] *Kalamazoo Gazette*, March 12, 2017.

Not Always

It wasn't all tenderness, kindness, or forgiveness on my part. It's almost been too long of a journey, attempting to clean my head and heart; and when I look back, I wonder how I could have come thus far—or have I? I did it by confessing my sins, trying to be honest by questioning myself, and have a strong tendency to be on the literal side when reading Scripture.[a] I began reading Scripture in the late ''60s, over sixty years ago, soon after completing military service. You'll see, throughout this book, my attempt to bring religion, politics, and family together in harmony and in truth.

Early 1940s

You'll see that all of the challenges beginning in the early 1940s, the concerns, witnessing events or problems are now stories that have to be told, or I would burst with chest and stomach tightness and pain. All the lessons and disciplines that were given to me were always given with tenderness and kindness, even when our son, Michael, died; there was a gentle kindness consoling Barbara and me. My intent for writing this book is for the world to know that the struggle of getting closer to our heart is worth the challenges and storms we face in life. What have I truly learned from getting closer to God beginning in the 1960s? Whenever I threw up my hands in failure and asked God for help or a favor, He always gave us what we needed, especially when both Barbara and I asked God together. Barbara and I continue thanking Him for daily occurrences. And Barbara, my wife of almost sixty years, is my witness.

---

[a] CCC 101 through133, *Jesus of Nazareth*, by Joseph Ratzinger, suggested that when we first begin reading Scripture, that reading it literally was better to understand Scripture unless proven otherwise by the church. I felt free reading the Bible, if I first took it literally.

TENDERNESS, KINDNESS, FORGIVENESS

When the rubber hits the road, how can man be kind, tender, and forgiving all at once? And what about nature, does nature have the same traits of having to be forgiven like man? And I ask myself, "Why do we need to be forgiven, and why do we need to forgive?" And I always find the same answer. I did something that wasn't of God, and my heart warned me. I see man as the only creature needing forgiveness from the Lord, and as you continue reading, you will hopefully understand why I write that only man needs forgiveness. Right from the beginning of Scripture in Genesis through the end in Revelation, we see forgiveness is what God does for us. Forgiveness is not deceptive, and the more we can forgive, the more we find God's love, the stronger we become. It is through Jesus Christ that we begin to understand forgiveness.

What I Thought

Kindness was not my thing. I'd rather not show a weak side, I'd rather stay firm and be tough and cogent. I could never be tender as my wife, and I really didn't think it was in my best interest to do so. Forgive, I thought, erroneously, it all depends how much the other guy warrants my forgiveness.[a] And meanwhile, I'll keep my guard up, so I thought, but it only made me more of a fearing person, until I

---

[a] Matthew 18:21–35.

became more dependent on our Lord, and subsequently a stronger man depending on Him.

You'll See

Little by little, from following His footsteps, you'll see in the following pages how my insides turned upside down, and I began to love in order to forgive and be kind and tender. It takes a powerful God to begin changing what was deep inside of me. It was a mountain of frustration and turmoil and I was determined my mountain could not be budged; I would not give in to loving the rest of the world, especially the enemies of America and the unjust of the world for years to come. Besides I was familiar with me, and I would not go where it was strange, uncomfortable, indifferent, and take away my ego-proud person. It was, as I now see, difficult getting out of my tough comfort zone. After all, I joined the army when I was seventeen to get away from home and rid armies from enslaving the world. Later I could see how foolish my pride was, and how that same pride made a lot of trouble for me in understanding who the real slave masters of the world were. During the time of spending a tour in South Korea, I found what personal enslavement was and how I began learning to forgive to get that heavy burden off of me.

But there was something else about what forgiving does. It creates a deep assurance of self-being, conviction, and peace from fear.

Book Prayer

To the breath of life, a love letter pouring out with sobs, and to my wife, my ever-forgiving wife, and our eight children—those that are here—and Michael, my eighth child who is with our Lord.

I See Warnings

What I see from the beginning of written human history are warnings, understandings we have inside of us that we should not go against. History shows, without a doubt, many civilizations that went opposite of what was created into them from the beginning failed miserably.

> I love my country and I see it crumbling as God is becoming less depended upon, while many citizens can no longer see that which is coming."

The Crux

The crux of the entire Bible is, I think, 1 Kings 6:12–14, "If you follow my statutes and obey my ordinances and faithfully follow my commandments, I will fulfil that promise I made about you to your father David. And I will make my home among the sons of Israel, and never forsake Israel my people" (we are Israel).

Introduction

Oxgoad as a Spiritual Weapon

Shamgar Ox-goad

I'm Catholic, a perfected remnant of Israel,[a] and I made an eight-foot grapevine replica of an oxgoad as a reminder to fight sin.[b] The oxgoad is to help me create true impressions concerning our Father (our Maker) by prodding to incite action. I honestly have abilities to disperse many misunderstandings of Scripture and Christianity when you hear what I have to say.[c]

---

[a] Romans 4:18–25, Jesus of Nazareth
[b] Judges 3:31; Ecclesiastes 12:11; I will gladly send a photo of it, if you wish.
[c] John 20:30–31, CCC 80, 83, 102, and 103, believe in the holy Bible as the divine Word written; however, I also know there were many more Spirit-filled words spoken that couldn't be contained in the Bible.

By the way, the oxgoad is an ancient weapon used by Shamgar, an Israelite judge about 1100 BC. The oxgoad is intended for me as a spiritual weapon, helping me rid evil from my mouth, hands, feet, and heart, only such as is good for edifying and fits the occasion, that it may impart grace[a] to those who hear me.[b] February 3, 2017

---

[a] CCC 2000–2005.
[b] Ephesians 4:29–30.

Review of Chapter 1

Michael, Dreams, Visions, and the TWOS

We'll commence this chapter jumping ahead from the 1940's, when my son Michael was born in Michigan, in the summer of 1980, and went home thirty-two years later, on May 19, 2014. He was our eighth child, and he had six sisters and one brother. Some of his siblings, but not all, lived at home during his teenage-developing years. We'll include in this book later information from when I was a kid in the 1940s, a time line later beginning in chapter 8, a Grass Man episode and, in chapter 9, discuss how history's actual secular architectural building designs indicated the rise and fall of major nations throughout world history.

Chapter 1

A Parent Shouldn't Have to Bury Their Child

To begin, in 1981, when Mike was born, it was an evening in Grand Haven, Michigan, after Michael was about a week old, and the both of us were alone in the house; a strong desire came over me for him to be strong and close to God and to show my loving appreciation to God for having given Mike to us. I simply picked him up and held him over my head and offered him up to God our Father. Mike was a special baby, and he certainly was a gift. My *primary* responsibility as a parent was to ensure he and his siblings knew who God was. Michael had seven siblings: Guy, Susan, Ann, Denise, Janine, Myla and Colleen.

But First, Recording of the TWOS

Throughout this chapter is Mike's story of happiness, accomplishments, hardships, and his last days with us and various spiritual happenings; but first, we'll step back to 1946 when my aunt Catherine Meegan died, and at that time, an unknown event of *TWOS* occurred that signaled many more to come, especially during the period of Michael's passing when it became clear, sixty-seven years after Catherine passed.

Our Dreams, Visions, and Hearings

The main motivation for writing this chapter was for you to become familiar with the newly discovered *TWOS* as a real happening and continuing in our own lives and view the many sensitive happenings before and after my son Mike's death. The other reason was to tell you exactly what spiritual happenings were around me and others that knew Mike.

The concept of *TWOS* is something I have never seen in all fifty or so years studying and teaching the Bible until recently, when I found it by accident in many areas of Scripture not readily exposed.

Aunt Catherine Has First TWOS

As told by my cousin Larry Meegan, our aunt Catherine died of throat cancer, supposedly caused from a World War II war factory that she worked at in Queens, New York. Catherine worked at the war factory in the 1940s, and during that time, she came down with cancer of the throat and died in 1945, at the age of twenty.

The war factory made glow-in-the-dark dials for WWII fighter planes. Her job was to use a small paintbrush, paint the letters on aircraft instrument dials. When the paintbrush began to flatten, workers would put the tip of the brush between her lips and make it sharp again in order to paint the unfamiliar radioactive glow in the dark liquid onto the small letter or numbered impressions. That is what we think caused her death.

Then it happened, an evening after her death in 1945, when she was laid to rest in a local funeral home, and her mother and her brother were sitting on the living room couch on the first floor, when they heard Catherine's voice come from upstairs. The voice said, "Mom, Mom." And that night was the last time the voice was heard. This incident was the first of the *TWOS* we recognized today but did not recognize it as such seventy-five years ago.

Catherine's mother, my grandmother Mary Meegan, had thirteen children and lost six before they reached middle age. Living conditions were tough in those days, during and previous to World War II, and each child had to work or carry their own weight in the '30s and '40s. Medical care wasn't readily available as it is today nor did citizens have a high understanding of dangerous chemicals. However, I don't think they could have cured Catherine's cancer, but maybe, just maybe, science could have comforted her advancing disease.

Discovery of the TWOS

I've taught the Bible since the late 1960s, and what I found during one of the Bible classes in 2016, after Michael, my youngest son, had passed were two similar related events happening that were followed by other separate *two*-type events. The second *two* of particular events was noted as being a final event, not to be continued again. Besides our immediate family recognizing *two* events, we found the *TWOS* throughout Scripture and not just personal happenings around us. As we go on, you'll see more of the *two* events witnessed by Barbara and myself as we kept careful notes as to what experiences were taking place just before and after our son passed. Because of those notes, we developed the first chapter of this book. We noticed, after discovering the *TWOS* in Scripture and later went back to the notes that were kept of Michael, the *TWOS* were happenings at all life key events without fail.

Other examples: Scripture doesn't mention *TWOS* like it mentions threes, sixes, sevens, tens, twelves, twenties, and forties. The *TWOS* seem to just happen with certain events and not readily noticeable until you see it, and then other events become obvious. However, I began to see many patterns of two events, like the two dreams of the Egyptian Pharaoh of fat cows and skinny cows,[a] two children of Joseph belonging to Jacob,[b] two long enslavement peri-

---

[a] Genesis 41:1–7.
[b] Genesis 48:1–22.

ods of Israel,[a] and[b] the beginning of the first world[c] and the second world.[d] The two water crossings, the first in Egypt[e] and the second going into the Promise Land,[f] the Old Testament and the New Testament, Israel's ark of the covenant that contained the Word, and later Mary, similar to the ark carrying the Word, bad and good, and most of all the death of the human race, with all dying in Adam, and a final in Christ, all will live,[g] and the pairs of *TWOS* go on and on throughout the Bible, indicating what I think is the assurance of the beginning and final episode of those similar events from God. Note: If you wish, I will send you more about the TWOS list, if you will send a self-address envelope with postage on it for several sheets of paper. My address is in the back of the book.

Bible TWOS

I began to see examples of *TWOS* in the Bible and in Mike's story sometime in 2016, and decided to write this book after good friends Shawn and Theresa McFall commented favorably on the original record we kept and the surrounding people and their experiences. All of the individuals mentioned later in this book that had actual experience and particular incidences were verified and recorded.

My Son Michael Patrick O'Donnell

Suspected but unbeknownst to me for many years, Mike's story began in 1964 in South Korea, sixteen years before he was born. I was sitting on my bunk, in an old military Quonset hut one after-

---

[a] Exodus 2:23–25, 3:1–20.
[b] Baruch 6:1–6.
[c] Genesis 1:1–31.
[d] Revelation 21–22.
[e] Exodus 14.
[f] Joshua 3, 4.
[g] First Corinthians 15:20–26, 28.

noon, when a fellow soldier, whom I have lost recollection of his name, came and sat down on the bunk across from me and told me he knows how many children I was going to have. "Is that right?" I responded.

He continued with an absolute gesture and began looking at my hand; and I became suspicious he may not be of God. He proceeded to tell me I was going to have eight children, and one would pass away. He hesitated just a little and said with extra kindness that everything will be all right. As it were, I had eight children and one passed. How did I know later that soldier was a true messenger, giving two real happenings? We'll get into that in a later chapter. You have to know that guardian angels are all around us, and so is evil here.

I wasn't shocked; I wondered why he told me that, and I kept it in the back of my thoughts and only remembering what he said several times after Mike, our eighth child, was born, and I never told Barbara about that conversation. Several times, through the course of years, I wondered if I would really lose a child and who it would be. I didn't dwell on it much; I knew all our children were on loan to us, and I have to trust our Father of what happens. I knew when my eighth child was born, they all belonged to God, and I knew it with every fiber in my body. Don't ask me where that faith came from, it was just there. I guess it was always there, even as a tough New York City kid, I knew back then we were God's children. It may have come from the nuns in the lower grades of Catholic school.

First TWOS Since the '40s

Unbeknownst to me at the time, when I was still in the army in Wilmington, Ohio, I experienced the first part of the TWOS traveling to our missile base. I received a phone call at our military housing complex, which was ten miles from the missile base. The call was from the military to report back to the site immediately and receive further instructions when I arrive. The road back was a two-lane country road with many hills and curves that should keep a careful driver from going over the speed limit. But that day was different, and I had to go faster to what seemed to be an emergency. I was about halfway there, near the bottom of a hill, when I got an awful *loud screeching* in my right ear, making it impossible to drive and necessary to pull over to the side of the road and stop. As I pulled over, I noticed two cars coming over the hill, the hill that I was about to negotiate. One car was passing another car in my lane, coming at a high rate of speed, and I remember thinking at the time, I was lucky to be pulled over and away from both cars racing. The driver in my lane looked at me when he was passing by with a *frightful-eyed* expression. After that, I was a little shaken and proceeded to my base, feeling very lucky to have missed a terrible accident and only thinking slightly of the noise that was in my ear for several minutes.

The Second Final Two

The other incident of the final *two* happened when I was a recent veteran, just out of the military service about four years after the first incident, attending night college under the veteran's GI Bill. It was a rainy night, getting out of class, and my friend and I were trying to get across the middle of a busy four-lane dark street to get to our cars. The rain was coming down like cats and dogs, and there weren't any cars coming on our left, and we proceeded across to the middle of the street and stopped just short of the double yellow line to allow a blurred-looking car to pass us coming from our right. But it happened again, a high-pitched *loud screeching* started sounding off in my right ear, making me look to the right, at a car not too far away. As I looked, with rain hitting my face, all I could see were big car headlights almost upon us, and at that instant, I reached back with my left arm and grabbed my friend, making him fall backward as I was already doing. I noticed the driver passing us, looking with *frightful eyes* at us and then disappeared into the dark rain. My friend began yelling very loud that, "He tried to kill us, he tried to kill us."

I nervously laughed, getting up and said to him, "We almost did it to ourselves."

That was a close call, and I remembered the close encounter with the car coming over the hill several years earlier in Wilmington, Ohio. And years later, I remembered when I uncovered more about the *TWOS* and of guardian angels being there. I was sure later that God wanted me to understand it was by no accident why I'm here today, and it certainly wasn't because of my own cognizance. Good or bad, we exist because God allows us to exist.

At this time, I have to say something what I think. I've read the Bible for the last fifty years, reread, prayed, taught religion classes, wondered about the world surroundings, why my life is the way it is, and why others meet life challenges knowingly or unknowingly. Most of all, why does God grant me my breath to go on, and how come He always forgives, even before I know I need forgiveness? Our Father knows ahead of time what we need, and most of all, He knows we'll ask Him for forgiveness centuries before it comes to pass.

Does that mean our lives are predestined? No, not at all. God knows everything and plans everything; He knew when He made us what we would do on our own cognizance. He made us to have a free will, to do whatever we want, but not without pain and the truth being available. Unlike animals and trees, that He set in their limited unique senses to know Him, instead He gave us various opportunities to find and know Him. However, it is known to Him only what courses in life we decide to take. He knows what we need even before we ask, and He certainly knows before we forgive that we do so. It's a struggle, folks, and I wrestle with the fine points of this doctrine less and less lately.

What I find when reading Scripture is the Old Testament is the creation of the law for earlier man to use searching for God and the New Testament is the Word planted into our hearts to gain salvation through faith. Also before I forget, it seems when Jesus left us for those three days after He was crucified, He recovered the people who died before His coming. I believe it was a purgatory.[a] Remember, that is my comparison, and maybe you'll define it differently. I'd love to hear your thoughts. God, knowing what we want before we know

---

[a] CCC 1030–1031.

what we want, is a little of what I'm going to pass on to you in the following chapters. Keep in mind, God is all-knowing.

Another Two

During one of the years while teaching at Saint Johns in Mattawan, Michigan, in the 1990s, there was a teenager named Joey Tetreau in the class. Joey was kind of hyper and not too willing to listen to the religious lessons in the beginning of the season, but slowly began to sit still as the year went by and began listening intently to every word I spoke. I hardly ever read directly from a book but paraphrased everything I knew about God from the assigned topic, and Joey seemed to like listening when I paraphrased from the lessons and stories as it came from within me and seemed to go into him. I reflected back in those moments when a beautiful nun in the 1950s touched my heart in a religion class, when I was in the fourth grade, and she spoke from her heart to my heart. But for now, this confirmation class was in its fourth month, nearing the end of preparation, when Joey visually began listening and questioning intensely to the words I spoke. During the class prior to him becoming confirmed, Joey came to me and said he believed in Jesus, and he was glad he found God.

The sad and bittersweet thing for me and his family was that Joey died a few months later, riding his dirt bike. I didn't find out about his passing until several weeks after the funeral. I remembered what he told me about believing in Christ, and I made a point to convey it to his mother, Mary Tetreau. I met her at church and told her that Joey is okay. Mary then told me that a lady at the funeral told her the same thing, that "Joey was okay." Joey's mom did not know the lady that told her Joey was okay (did you notice the *two* okays?). Joey's death reminded me to wonder again of the soldier in South Korea that told me about losing a child too.

Extra Effort

Months later, after Confirmation classes were completed, I began teaching adults the Bible at Saint Johns; and during those classes, we decided to create a church organization to help needy parishioners sometime in the mid-1990s. The Bible study group organized and developed the program to the point that we needed to communicate those endeavors to all our parishioners to gain more support. The organization was called Grace and Beyond, and we were attempting to recruit enough people to help all present and future spiritual and financial needs in the parish. During and at that time, we developed a concept to create a used clothing store to help finance defaulting home mortgages in the parish.

As it was, Michigan was again beginning to go through hard economic times, and this time, there were indications of people losing their homes, and it appeared to be becoming a national problem too. The newly formed group we called Grace and Beyond was to help prevent financial disasters from happening to anyone in the parish and possibly grow further into the community. I was elected by the group to speak at all the masses to gain support and volunteers in hopes of recruiting generous and energetic people.

It was a success; we recruited over forty parishioners and immediately began designing a used clothing store concept to help support the needed revenues and organized various activities to help support the needy.

However, disappointment struck, and the organization failed to grow or continue due to two reluctant leaders and became what seemed their determination to disband the group. Can you believe it? I certainly went into full-fighting mode against a few, and it was similar to going up against a thick block wall. In frustration and desperation, I wrote the Vatican newspaper what was happening and spoke to the acting Kalamazoo bishop to no avail, that I know of. I was angry and finally gave up and left the church in Mattawan to find, as mentioned in the first chapter of this book, Saint Catherine of Siena.

Later, around 2010, when I learned about how badly Father Solanus Casey, an up-and-coming saint, was treated by his peers, I related to him and his troubles that he went through with his peers. You'll see Father Casey in a chapter to come. It took all my strength about four years to forgive the Catholic Mattawan Church leaders, and once the healing process began, I could see why we locked horns. I thought maybe because the main leader, a priest that came from a poor country like India, knew all too well what the real poor of the world were like, he just couldn't find it in his heart to support an endeavor of the up-and-coming American poor. Whereas in my experience, I knew American poor was nowhere near to be compared to the world's poor; but no matter, it was a very different poor we were dealing with in America, a loss was a loss no matter what country you were in. In fact, America had different types of poor—they were more spiritually poor. In any case, realizing later we are in God's hands to be judged by Him alone, it was easier to let go of the difference between us. I was glad to get rid of my anger, and unbeknownst to me, it was a great stroke of grace to forgive them because of the spiritual energy that was needed in other encounters I would soon have to submit to in order to be adequately stronger.

Michael and Joanie before the Hard Times Above

Mike and Joanie tied the knot and married right out of high school in 1998 and soon began raising a family while Mike attended college, working toward a mechanical engineering degree.

During that time, we had forty acres of hills, hardwood trees, Christmas trees, and a large garden in Lawton, Michigan, we called home. Our kids knew that each of them would eventually get five acres as part of our gift to them. Well, Mike and Joanie asked for the five acres to live on in 2001 to be closer to us, and as Mike wished, it was to be near us and possibly take care of Barbara and me if need be. We gave both of them the five acres, along the county road next to our home, to help in their purchase of a home. Mike and I shovel-dug the footer foundations in order to set a modular home onto the concrete piers for Joan and the boys to be raised. We could not imagine that Mike would pass in about sixteen years from that time. I would pray sixteen years later and thank God the day Mike passed that he wasn't in a war far from home but in Lawton, in a hospital, where I held his warm neck at my side for four hours, wondering if I should pray for him to come back to life.

Going Back a Little, Finding a Church

In May of 2012, before Michael passed, I had a deep need to find a church from which I would be buried at. I found that peace in Saint Catherine of Siena Church in Portage, Michigan, as the place to have my last rites said. But instead, a year later, we buried our son Michael at Saint Catherine. It was a kind of peaceful feeling that my boy was buried at the church I held as close to heaven as any other structure on earth.

Just Before Passing

On May 16, 2014, several days before Mike passed, we were at our dining room table when Mike told me he wants to be just like me.[a] I didn't know what to say. I just didn't expect any of my boys would admit to wanting to be like me. I didn't know what to say to him except, "You can't be like me because I'm an artist and you're an engineer." Why, why, did I say that? I thought at the moment that I can refine what I said later. It was so clumsy of me, but later never came.

Two Days before Passing

On May 17, 2014, two days before Mike passed, I fantasized and dreamed of creating a religious diverse singing group. The group

---

[a]   CCC 2214.

would be made up of Catholic, Protestant, Jewish, and Islamic singers praising God. During this time of fantasizing about the group, I kept hearing over and over my favorite song of the 1950s titled "He Has the Whole World in His Hands" (*first* indication of the song). Also I daydreamed that this could be a unique way of uniting God's people by forming one chorus, attempting to unite man in one spirit. The diverse group would sing songs in the language of the country they performed in. I began writing my thoughts down in case I ever had the opportunity to begin a project like it.

Mike Passing on May 19

On Sunday morning of May 19, we celebrated Pentecost,[a] the second holiest day of the year (the Holy Spirit coming into the world to help fulfill the churches' mission). Mike was outside that morning, taking pictures of his colorful chickens, and he wrote on his mobile phone that, "This might be the best part of waking up early so far. If you have ever sat outside on a cool morning, wrapped yourself in a blanket, watched the sunrise, and just enjoyed the quiet around you? You know what I am talking about. If you haven't, this is what I imagine heaven to be like." Mike was outside his home in Lawton when he wrote this caption, just hours prior to his passing before a marathon practice run on our county road. Michael died a sudden death a short time later while practicing for the upcoming marathon race; he was about a mile and a half from home when a kind neighbor found him, lying alongside of the road, and called 911.

Phone Message, 2014

When Barbara and I got home, we had a message on the phone to come to the hospital, that Michael was hurt. He wasn't just hurt; Michael had passed away just an hour before on the side of the county

---

[a] Acts 2:1–4 and CCC 767.

road he often made his practice runs on. We arrived at the hospital, and I could see my son-in-law Troy Johnson sitting outside the emergency room, on the curb, with his head down. I thought the worst seeing him there, and Barbara and I went straight into the emergency room. Mike had passed and was lying on a stretcher in his running clothes, with his neck and face exposed. The hospital allowed Mike's body to stay there for about four hours, at which time I held my hand onto his warm neck and prayed until I could smell death.

I couldn't bawl or cry, it was too real and natural or something. His face was beautiful, and I kept kissing his hair and his neck while warm, and I kept my hand there until he was taken away. However, during a period of those four hours, when the room was empty, I thought of praying to the Holy Spirit and asking God to raise him from the dead; but as I began to pray, I did not know if I questioned my faith or if I just couldn't do it, or did I have enough faith to believe God could bring him back, or maybe Mike would be disappointed that he came back. I stopped praying, I let him go, thinking why should I pray to bring him back to this mess when he is now in Jesus's bosom, content and with our relatives. In any case, God wanted him now, and I would have to hope and wait to be with my children, wife, and relatives someday too. The state coroner spent weeks of extra time and could not find evidence why Michael passed. Nevertheless, God consoles our family's loss and friends after his death as you'll see other happenings as you read on.

Voices, Dreams, Sightings, Reoccurrences

My oldest son, Guy, came to stay with us during the funeral preparations, and the morning before the funeral mass, he couldn't sleep and woke me up at about 3:00 a.m. and began discussing the big bang theory. I was attentive and wondered what was going on, and I knew something important was about to be discussed; and besides, this may be what God wanted heard, I'll listen and participate. After all, it was the early morning hours, and that is when our faith is stronger and understood more than any other hour. These hours in the mornings are truly God's time for us.

Guy is a metallurgist engineer graduate and studied the big bang theory in college, and it became a challenge to his faith during those days and for an additional ten years after that. However, later after that struggle, Guy found the answer between science and religion. He came away with a firm belief in God making the universe, and that religion and science should work closer together to find the truth.

We began celebrating Mike's Mass of the Resurrection (the raising of the righteous who will live forever with the risen Christ on the last day)[a] at church the very same morning, at about nine o'clock, after Guy and I discussed the big bang theory just hours before Mass service. The opening of Mass begins with an Old Testament and two New Testament readings. After the readings, before the meal, the celebrant, Father Stanley, began his homily with a story about the big bang theory. *What did he just say?* He was saying what my son Guy and I were discussing hours before at home and is now being discussed by the priest[b] as our homily.

I became spiritually filled knowing Guy and I discussed the big bang theory just hours before, and I began listening intensely to every word Father Stanley spoke of. It was comforting knowing the Spirit was there, and now this wonderful loving priest was discussing it a second time, to our amazement, hours after Guy and I went deep into ourselves discussing it (notice the *TWOS* coming up once more?). Father Stanley went on to explain that science made much effort in looking at the small particles of what they think may have caused the universe to form, and they failed to prove the big bang made the universe. Some scientists may have come to the conclusion that it was still a mystery, but others hopefully came to the conclusion that God's ways are a mystery too,[c] and we just aren't capable of fully understanding all of His ways. It's a mystery why God called Mike to be with our Lord,[d] and hopefully we too will be with Him someday.

---

[a] CCC 997, Resurrection of the dead.
[b] CCC 688.
[c] Genesis 1, 2; CCC 287.
[d]

After the homily and preparing for the end of the Mass, I was again comforted and in awe when the choir sang the song that I was daydreaming and humming about a few days before. The song they sang was "He Has the Whole World in His Hands." That song is not a typical Catholic song you would expect to hear at masses, but it reminded me of how the Holy Spirit was softening my pain, and pain it could have been. I thanked God for allowing the final song to remind me that He has the whole world in his hands and knowing that Mike is with Him (notice the song the choir sang was a *final two*).

Go Way Back to the '60s in Ohio

For many years, after being discharged from the army in 1966, my observations were that America turned their backs on their soldiers, and I would not allow our children to go into military service because of the bitterness I harbored. I prayed often that God would keep them out of military service and be near and safe with Barbara and me. However, some close calls cropped up, especially when Ann, our third child, and Mike both expressed a desire to go into the military. However, after we had some thoughtful discussions, they changed their minds. I was determined that none of my children would experience the violation of American people turning their backs on me. That experience was serving our country, even at the cost of my life.

How could a nation become so selfish or cowardly in the '60s that the young men that were to protect them were being turned against? I was bitter and wanted nothing more than to watch America sink in their selfishness, and when my military enlistment was up after seven years, I left the army, only to struggle financially for years to come. I could actually see America sinking into despair when many of our leaders of all walks of life showed their ugly moral degradations, taking hold in the 1970s, and progressively worse, it was affecting daily American attitudes that continues to this day. And I wondered if the corrupt leaders were a reflection of us or we of them. I determined they were a reflection of us, and I'll discuss this phenomenon in chapter 4 in detail.

Garden and Voice, May 2014

A couple of days after Mike's Mass of the Resurrection, I was in our home garden at about 7:30 a.m., setting tomato stakes, and about the same time, eleven-year-old Ethan (Mike's son) was feeding Mike's chickens next-door at his home. The home Michael and I had built the foundations for about sixteen years earlier. Ethan seemed alarmed, and I heard him calling out "Grandpa" from the other side of the woods near his home, about four hundred feet away. I answered him, and he came trotting on the pathway through the woods toward me in the garden. He stood there, looking at me for a moment, and then asked if I was calling him (Ethan and I spent many hours together in the garden during planting and harvest times, so he was familiar with me being there). I knew, by the way Ethan spoke, that something significant happened. He asked if I was calling him, and I said no, I didn't call and asked him why. Ethan's response was his dad said, "Hello, Ethan. Hello, Ethan" (at this time, I was not yet familiar or firm with the *TWOS* episodes). Still I knew this message was from God and not from Mike. I hugged Ethan while I cried, at the same time, telling him that God allowed him to hear his dad's voice and for me to know my son was okay.

Unbeknownst to me, at the same time when Ethan and I were in the garden, sixteen-year-old Christopher, Mike's oldest son, also heard his dad's voice. The voice said, "I'm okay, I'm okay."

Again as I look back to my accounts of spiritual episodes since 1945, there were always *TWOS*, and it seemed the second was the final episode as it is in Scripture writings too. A short time later, Myla, my sixth child, reported that thirteen-year-old Andrew, Mike's second son, had a vision as he was in an automobile driving past where Michael died, and he saw three men in whitish clothes standing with his dad.

Accounts of Dreams and Visions

It was later in the week after Mike passed, and both Myla and Joanie told me about a dream Jessica had. Jessica is Joanie's niece, and she was close to Mike and told Joanie about the dream. She dreamt she was in Mike's house, at the kitchen sink, when someone opened the refrigerator door and was stooping down, looking in. She looked down to see who it was, and it was Mike. She was startled to see him and asked what he was doing here. She noticed Christopher sitting on the high stool in the kitchen and Joanie on the living room couch, checking what was left of their finances. Mike responded by saying, "What do you mean why am I here?"

And Jessica said to him that he wasn't supposed to be there, that he had died. Mike felt his shoulders and upper body and apologized, saying twice, "I'm so sorry, I'm so sorry" (*TWOS*). And he walked out the door.

Mike's Son Christopher's Dream

Four months after Michael went to our Lord, Christopher dreamed he was coming out of his room when he saw brightness and his dad, sitting on the couch, smiling and radiant and said to Christopher, "I'm fine, I'm fine" (*TWOS*).

Christopher's Second Dream

In July 2014, Christopher had a powerful dream, what seemed even more real than the one before. He saw his dad smiling at him and asked his dad, "How'd you come back?"

Michael, smiling at Christopher said, "I don't know" (as far as I have determined, the "I don't know" was said only once). Just to let you know again, Christopher was the oldest son, and Mike and he were involved in many types of activities together, and they were close as brothers.

Christopher's Third Dream

In September 2014, Christopher dreamed that he was hugging his father. He went on to say that his dad's hugs were strong and powerful. After Christopher told us about the dream, he seemed to be more at peace with God.

Ann's Dream

Ann, Mike's sister, was a runner as Mike was, and she dreamed sometime later that she was at the Santa Clause Run in Paw Paw, and it was on the race starting line when she saw Michael, and his face, radiant and smiling at her from a distance.

Ann's Second Dream

Another dream occurred around September 2016, with Ann when she dreamt that she and Mike were goofing around on a boat dock when Mike threatened to throw her into the water. Ann responded back that he too was going to go into the water with her. Mike lunged toward Ann, and she jumped up while holding her arms and legs around Mike, making both of them fall into the water. Ann commented that she understood angels sometimes cause dreams like that, and when I told her that they may come in *TWOS*, she was disappointed and said she hopes the dreams never stop.

Michael's Snapshot

Me, I had reoccurring dreams that seemed to take place many years ago, what seemed to be during the 1970s, but not recently. The dreams were of a long winding barren road with trees on both sides that seemed to be part of a fearful place. I thought in the dream, it was a lonely road in Arizona. I remembered about those dreams when we developed the last photograph Mike had taken from his camera only seconds before he passed. By the way, we knew it was the last few seconds before his death because he was wearing a runner's watch that tracked time, and his heartbeat which was correlated to his phone camera. The photo was taken on a section of our county road he was running on, and it showed the similar winding barren road with trees on both sides, similar to what I dreamed about that seemed like years ago. We have that photo in our living room as with others. We think Michael observed something while he was running and snapped his camera at it, but the picture shows only a road and trees as below. However, many of us have heard of people that were near death in bed and would open their eyes and lift up their arms, pointing at something at the ceiling. Barbara's sister, Claire, pointed to something just before she passed in 2017.

Dreams and Now Vision Accounts Too

About two weeks after Mike's passing, four of our grandchildren, Elijah, Christopher, Andrew, and Ethan, were participating in a soccer tournament in Toledo, Ohio, when another spiritual event took place. This episode was the *second* vision incident for Ann in many years. The first spiritual event I'll mention later, but for now, the four soccer teams from our side of the state were wearing black armbands, and all the kids knew why they wore them, given to them. They were given to them by Ann through the permission of the league's soccer management. Mike was a soccer coach in the same league for several years, and the soccer management wanted and approved of the armbands to be worn.

Elijah, my grandson, Ann's boy, was one of the players, with two of Mike's boys who were still highly distressed over Mike's death. Elijah was very close to Mike and loved him like a brother. Ann was sitting in the stands when a woman that never sat next to her, and they hardly ever had words to say, said excitedly, "Look at that!"

What they looked at was a halo around the sun that lasted several hours while the game was going on. About one thousand fans could see the halo. You know it can be said that the halos were acts of nature, but for it to happen *twice*—once when a good man passed decades ago and the other when my son passed—doesn't make it a coincidence or act of nature for us. *Twice*, Ann had seen similar halos around the sun after *two* major death incidences.

The next day, Ann came home with the kids and told me about the halo they had seen. I reflected back about forty-five years earlier, when a good man, Bishop Liebole, a newly appointed young bishop of the Cincinnati Diocese and already loved by our family and many other parishioners, died suddenly.

On the afternoon of the bishop's death, about forty-five years earlier, we noticed a large halo around the sun that remained for hours in the area for everyone to see, while the haze kept the sun from hurting our eyes. I even called the Hamilton, Ohio, newspaper, asking them to take pictures of the halo, and they didn't want anything to do with me and gently hung up. At the same time, we were looking at the halo, my daughter Ann and her friends were a mile away at Saint Ann's School playground when they saw the halo around the sun too. Some places in America, people see halos often, but here, this was unusual.

Note: Barbara and I did not have dreams and visions like others around us after Mike passed. However, just hearing their stories were messages from God and gave us more hope that Michael is with our Lord.

More TWOS

Barbara went to Mike's grave site one day, during the first winter after his death, to adjust a waterproof photo of him in order to make the site more visible. The headstone wasn't set yet because of the winter weather in 2014, and we had various items sticking out of the ground above the snow to locate the exact site of where he lay. After a while, Barbara tried to locate the photo, but the snow was too deep, and she left without doing what she wanted. She came back the second time a week later, but the snow still covered the ground; but this time, it had a thick crust layer of ice, and she was only able to walk on top of it.

As Barbara walked toward the markers, she realized the snow was still too deep and now frozen. She said to herself, "Well, Mike, I guess I won't be able to get your picture this time either." And within the next instant, the hard crust gave way from under her foot and exposed Mike's photograph. Barbara bent down, picked up the photo from the ground while exposing its long attachment prongs, and simply reset it on top of the hard snow for visitors to see.

Note: Whenever Barbara and I gave up on a situation close to our heart, we prayed. God always helped us.

Second Time to Fall

In October 2014, Christopher visited his dad's grave a second time, and as he was getting near, he felt a sudden deep calmness and peace swelling inside of him that made him fall to his knees (again *TWOS*, this is the second time Christopher fell on his knees. The first time was when he was leaving the church as a pallbearer, and my son Guy grabbed him to steady him). As he got close and fell to the grave site, Christopher stayed on his knees while absorbing a complete sense of peace through his whole being while at the grave at the site. We noticed Christopher remained happy and energy-filled for many days after that. And this morning, April 5, 2020, as I edit this book, Christopher remains close to God.

Janine's Dream

On November 25, 2016, my daughter Janine, our fifth child, dreamed of Michael, and the dream inspired her to go to his grave site and have a friend take her picture while she was there. From there, Janine went to Joanie's (Mike's wife) house to tell her about the dream and show her the picture. Joanie added that she dreams of Mike every week. In her dreams, she could see Mike just watching and not saying a word of anything at all. Janine then looked around Joanie's living room and could see all the family pictures several years later, still on the walls, showing Mike and family. I loved writing about Joanie still remembering Michael.

Our Friend Sharon Experienced TWOS of Her Own Grief

In 2014, a lady in our Bible class, Sharon Stevens, told me she lost her son who was struck by a van when he was five and asked if I was ever mad at God when Mike died. I thought a second and told her no, and she replied that she wasn't angry either. She couldn't be mad because she needed all the strength from God to get through the ordeal. I wondered if that was what happened to Barbara and me, needing all our strength to get by. We both knew inside ourselves that we had to take care of each other, along with the other children and grandchildren. We just couldn't fall to pieces, we had to stay alert and be there for them too.

I think when we know who created us, our biggest hope is that when we die, we'll be with Him; I don't think we can really get mad or angry. It just seems natural but frightful to think of dying, and hopefully we will all be with God someday. Sad, we are, terribly sad, wishing we could hug and kiss our son; miss him, yes; knowing he is with our Lord, and hopefully someday, we'll be there, yes, we hope.

Also Sharon's letter concerning the death of her son Paul is below. I asked Sharon to write her story, hoping to paraphrase her writings; but upon reading it, it was more than I anticipated, and I included her entire letter as is and indicated below.

Sharon's Letter

My son, Paul Daniel Stevens, was the third son of our four boys. He was born into our family on March 10, 1976 and born into eternal life on June 11, 1981 at the tender age of 5 years. In his short life he touched the hearts of many people with his beautiful smile, his zest for life and his tender heart. He was wise beyond his years when it came to loving others and his belief in Jesus. I remember walking into the kitchen and witnessing him putting the dishes away in cupboard and singing Yes Jesus Loves Me, or when he wrapped one of his prized possessions as a gift for a friend's birthday. He often asked to stop by Saint Mary's Church in Spring Lake, Michigan when we went for a walk so he could light a votive candle and pray in church. He liked to ask and re ask questions about the statue of The Pieta[a] that was located outdoors in the rose garden. He would sit next to me and hold my rosary as we prayed the family rosary. It was always my intention to buy a rosary for him, but, unfortunately, I never got around to it.

---

[a] A representation of the Virgin Mary, mourning over the dead body of Christ.

Pieta

Before I tucked the boys into bed at night, we would pray the Angel of God prayer together. One night before tucking Paul into bed, we heard crying coming from his room. We rushed to his side wondering what was wrong. He was inconsolable. I tried to calm him by telling him that God gave him a mom and dad to protect him and, although he couldn't see her, God gave him a Guardian Angel to protect him. He looked at me so seriously and said "What if mine flies away?" For the life of me I don't remember what my response was. I couldn't help remember this incident three months later when he was hit by a van and killed while crossing the street with his older brother, Chris who was nine. What did he know? Did he know his life on earth was short? Is this why he has such an interest in Jesus, praying, loving others and asking questions of faith at such a young age?

In Bible Study, Raymond the author and I have talked about our sons and the *TWOS*. I've covered the first ones but there are many more. It was the last of school and I left my boys in the care of a sitter so I could attend the appreciation luncheon for mothers who volunteered at Saint Mary's School during the year. It was just a block down the street from our home and this is where I received the news of Paul's accident. Our Pastor, Fr. Joe Malewitz, was in attendance and drove me to the hospital. It was a comfort to me that he would be able to see Paul and give his blessing. Chris Mastenbrook, who lived across the street from us, gave Paul CPR and road with him in the ambulance. She stayed with me until my husband, Ken, arrived and they broke the news that Paul had died. Everyone was so sorry, but the hospital wouldn't grant me my request to see Paul. I was too numb to insist or be angry. All I wanted was to hug him and kiss him one last time. In the two years to follow, Paul visited me Twice in my dreams. In these dreams I knew he was just visiting, but I was given the chance to hug him and kiss him goodbye. They were happy visits and did a lot to help heal a broken heart.

Paul was 18 months old when Andrew was born and in no way, was Paul ready to abdicate his position as The Baby of the family and let it be known in various ways. When Andrew turned six, Paul visited me for the last time. In my dream he was sitting talking to us with a big smile and excited to tell us "Now I'm the baby of the family and always will be." That's why I know when I see him again; he will be that little five-year-old boy that I love so much.

When we came home from the hospital, we had the difficult task of telling our boys that their brother had died and that he was an "angel" in Heaven with Jesus. Three-year-old Andrew climbed up on my lap and said "Paul is a green angel, because green is his favorite color." Over the years I have collected and received many green angles that in one way or another portray a story of Paul's life. When I was expecting Paul, we decided if the baby was a girl, we would name her Angela and call her Angel. Wow! Can you believe it? I did get "My Angel" and it turned out to be a boy!

Twenty years ago, just after my Dad passed away, my oldest son, Scott, was crossing the street at night and saw the reflection of headlights coming over a hill. He heard a voice telling him to go limp. He says he did and then was hit and thrown over a pickup truck. He received no serious injuries but, while he was laying in the street waiting for help to arrive, he heard my dad say "Tell everyone I'm happy." And he heard Paul say "Tell Chris that I love him." Remember, Chris was crossing the street with his younger brother Paul when he was hit by a van. Unbeknownst to us, Chris still had deep seeded guilt about the accident. I'm sure Paul's message to him was meant to help heal those feelings of guilt.

I have one more TWOS to share. Twenty-three years ago, my Mom called me home to Grand Rapids as it became apparent that my Dad, who was ill for some time, was close to death. That night when I kissed my Dad goodnight, I prayed that God would send His Holy Angels to take Dad home to be with him. Soon after I went to sleep, Mom woke me because she thought Dad had passed. After checking on him, I went to make the necessary phone calls. When I returned to the bedroom, I found Mom holding my Dad's hand. She looked at me and said "I hear Singing". I told her the prayer I had prayed and that she must be hearing the Angels sing. I had no doubt that my prayer had been answered that night and that God was giving my Mom a beautiful gift of witnessing a little of what my Dad was experiencing at that exact moment— "The Angel's Song".

Like Raymond, I am a Believer. God is a God of love. None of what I have relayed is in any way coincidence, but proof that He loves us unconditionally and He only asks us to love Him in return. Amen." Sharon Stevens

Christopher and Spiritual Gifts

About 1995, Joey Tetreau and Michael were in my confirmation class, and years later, Mike's son Christopher was too. It was imperative to me that all students understand that we as parents were responsible for their infant children to enter the church at baptism; and when they became adults, it was their responsibly to make their own confirmation with faith and knowledge to accept our Lord.[a] The kids absorbed everything and understood how they related to God. They knew about the Spirit being among them and within us and angels being around us as messengers of God too. They all seemed excited and wanted more during those classes.

Lifted Christopher

When Christopher was a baby, Michael and Joanie weren't able to be with Christopher during the day, and Christopher was left with us. Barbara and I took care of him during the day while Michael and

---

[a]   CCC 1285.

Joanie finished high school. Christopher and I were alone, and an inspiration came over me for him to be close to God. Like Michael, I lifted Christopher up over my head and offered him up to the Father to show appreciation for God giving him to us as a precious gift. Like Mike, Christopher also has high regard being close to God. I could see love inside both of them; I could see God. Perhaps most of all, their spirit went deep.

College Advantage

During the time Mike's son Christopher was in high school, we were worried and concerned that Christopher may not have college advantages, as other kids have, without a father. Christopher was an excellent student and a state wrestler, but he nor his widowed mother had finances for him to go further in higher education.

Barbara and I threw our hands up and then prayed together each night while our two sons-in-law, Jody and Jacob, made contacts with ROTC college officials in hopes of Christopher being helped and becoming an air force reservist candidate. Great news came, and Christopher had an appointment to see air force captain Livingston. His initial appointment went well, and next he was to meet with a board of officers who would verbally evaluate him. Christopher remembers the first question that was asked of him. It was *integrity*, and what does it mean? He was stunned, he had heard the word before but did not know the definition nor did he ever use it. He thought about it for a long moment and figured he was going to blow this one. But I myself heard and used the word *integrity* many times during the 1960s, while serving in the army, and always felt the word was close to sacred. *Integrity* was one of my favorite military words, and I never used it again for the next fifty years as a civilian, until Christopher came home after the interview that day and told his story.

Well, anyway Christopher went deep inside himself at the board meeting and told them the following, "*Integrity* means the state of being entirely honest, upright, and whole." He could tell from the faces of officers that he nailed it, but he wondered, where inside of him did that come from?

Christopher presented himself well, understood that the Holy Spirit was with him, and this is what he was supposed to do. Later Chris was awarded a full scholarship to any college with an ROTC program with housing, meals, and an income from the US Air Force Reserves. The above gifts from God, some may call miracles, but to Barbara and me, they are almost everyday occurrence after throwing up our hands and asking God for a favor. You know, with nineteen grandchildren, there is always something going on. Cameron, another grandson, now is in a dangerous military job, but during his high school years, he was involved in sports and was a state wrestler too. That was less fun for Barbara when we saw kids getting hurt. We know from experience now how fragile life is. It is a constant daily prayer that we cannot let go of for their safety.

Review of Chapter 2

Animals Know God

Nothing, absolutely nothing, is wasted with the words of Scripture. Every sentence, if we see it, is meaningful and impacts our lives. What some people think are codes in the Bible, I know is the Holy Spirit leading us into deeper understanding. Besides it's fantastic and exciting to read and think outside the box and see what another good things God has for us.[a] Some of the best teaching skills come from looking for additional meanings in verses that the prophets and apostles wrote about.[b] For me to get excited of what mysteries God has in store for us keeps my inners and thirst for learning alive and young. One example was when I was studying the book of Job years ago, for the thirtieth time or so, I ran across a passage I've never seen before concerning "animals know God"[c] and "trees know God."[d] And in another Old Testament book, there was a verse indicating stones recorded conversations.[e] Now do you think the stones recording conversations are literal or not? And we see enemies of God's anointed king David being defeated by tree activity more than by swords.[f] I take Scripture literally and wonder how it is until proven otherwise. And I believe that the stones recorded conversations too. I don't have

---

[a] First Corinthians 2:6–16; *Jesus of Nazareth*, 78; CCC 243.
[b] John 3:1–33.
[c] Job 12:7–10, 38:36, 38:41; Psalm 77:16; 1 Kings 17:4–5; Ecclesiasticus 42:15.
[d] Genesis 31:52.
[e] Ezekiel 17:22–24.
[f] Second Samuel 5:24, 18:8.

a clue how, but I think the answer is in various books for the Spirit to reveal and left for science to prove. Maybe someone looking for the so-called codes may find it if they ask God the right questions. So do you see my excitement?

Chapter 2

Animals Know God

As mentioned above, I found in the book of Job years ago that animals know God. *How can that be? Are they set in their ways? Do they do exactly how God made them?* I asked myself. Animals can't think, they don't pray. Animals don't show any indication they know God, or do they? I now think animals know God, and so do trees, plants, the weather, and oceans are also included in knowing God; and a big wonder to me now are how stones act like recorders.[a] Also God speaks in Revelation about having all people and creatures come to Him at the end of time. And I ask myself, what are creatures? I'm a hunter, and almost every time in the last few years I went out hunting, that verse in Revelation often went with me. It went on for seven years with that in the back of my brain, thinking and searching for some sort of explanation. And finally the answer was found in a 2016 Bible class I was leading at Saint Catherine of Siena Parish in Portage, Michigan.

God Is Love

One night in Bible class, many weeks after we studied the book of Job, a class member, Jim Lennox, brought into the class an article and photo from the *San Francisco Chronicle*, dated December 14, 2005, that illustrated the Pacific Ocean and people in a small boat removing a tangled fishing net from a whale. The whale kept its head

---

[a] Joshua 24:27–28.

above the water and steadied itself next to the small boat. It seemed like hours to the boat crew and the divers cutting and untangling the net, as shown below, but was only about an hour that had passed when they eventually freed her.

Whale Rescue

Sometime during a lull in the class, Jim showed the printed article to the class, and it reminded us of when we studied the book of Job, about six months earlier, that animals know God. But how in the world on God's green earth can animals know God, I truly wondered. We finished the rest of the class, discussing the whale story and questioned how animals know God. But how did they know was still a burning question? They can't think like us nor sing or talk to him, right? Right, they can't think or sing praises like us, but they must have something we were all born with to help us to know God. The other amazing thing that happened after the whale was freed, it was reported to have jumped in and out of the water, swimming around the small boat several times.

The class was over before we knew it, and we began packing to leave when Jim asked if I wanted a copy of the whale news article, and I accepted it. I put the article in my carrying bag and went home, ate dinner, watched the news, and went to sleep. I suddenly woke up around midnight, thinking of the whale being rescued, and I instantly knew *exactly* how animals, trees, bugs, and *all* of creation know God. Who is God? I asked. "*God* is *love*,"[a] and everything in the world knows love. Treat a person, animal, plant, or anything badly, and they will wither away; but show them love, and they prosper. That's the main reason He made us, to love and obey Him, and everything prospers when we love and obey God. That's the way it has been for God's people, plants, and creatures since Adam and Eve, and especially Israel and America when they were tuned toward God's love. How could I have missed it all those years studying the Bible? It was the time and place to reveal it to me. And I asked myself, why now?

Even Trees Know God

It's a wonder to me how trees may know God,[b] but a little bit of information goes a long way, especially when I turned on a Public Broadcasting Nature television documentary the other day, in mid-August 2017. The channel had a segment on animals and trees located in the forest of the Austrian Alps.

PBS Documentary

The documentary was part of a 150-year-old spruce tree forest suffering through a severe drought in the Alps. It began with one tree being attacked by a couple of bark beetles and how the defense of

---

[a] First Corinthians 13:1–13.
[b] Job 12:1–10; Psalms 69:34; Daniel 3:52–90.

the tree began emitting its sap onto the first few beetles that began damaging the tree's bark. That sounds to be logical of a plant resisting damage, right? But the scientist evaluating the incident wondered what it was that made the tree begin using its sap to smother the beetles, and the researchers began to investigate.

Soon a whole army of bark beetles began attacking the same tree, and more sap was being produced by the tree to encase the insects in its sap and prevent further damage, but the beetles kept coming, and there were too many beetles overcoming the tree's ability to defend itself. But the researchers discovered something else. As the beetles began overtaking the first tree, the other trees surrounding the first tree began emitting sap even before a beetle came upon them. The research staff commented that the first affected tree sent out a chemical signal alerting the other trees of the beetles.[a] Now how can that be? I questioned the comments from science discoveries, as I do with Bible discoveries too. It's real and I think when science and religion come together, they will prosper as a team and find additional truths.

How Does Man Obtain Love?

How do we love? You know He created man to search and love Him, unlike animals and trees that He has *set permanently* to know Him. If that is real—and it is real—we will become more fulfilled as we learn to love; that I think is the reason why he made us—*to love Him.* That is a fact, we were made to love Him. Many others may hold worldly things dear to them in lieu of loving our Lord, and they may never achieve in their lifetime that which is inside, already stored for us to expose. However, our purpose is to love God and communicate the Word to others and allow the Spirit to foster love inside them, and hopefully, the person finding love will continue to discover more.

I have no doubt that there are trillions of connections in man to find God, and I don't pretend to know how to make anyone know or

---

[a] Job12:9–10, 38:36–41; Psalms 66:4, 145:10–11, 148.

love Him, I know only God can do that. It's like every person in the world must ponder their absolute one-of-a-kind human side once they hear the Word. As an example, what about the rich person in The Book of Matthew that Jesus said, "It is easier for a rich man to pass through the eye of a needle than for a rich man to enter the kingdom of heaven?"[a] Was that a warning to all rich people? Well, yes, to keep our hearts on God first, but much more was behind what Jesus said. But first, why did He make that comparison in the first place? When we go deeper with that remark, we conclude it is a message for all mankind to know sins prevent us from loving God and can prevent us from obtaining graces and going to heaven. Sin, in fact, is a turning away from God. However, since sin is so overpowering, some of the disciples asked, "Who can be saved?"

And Jesus replied that "For God everything is possible." And in that whole testament of Jesus, it shows God the Father sending His only Son to earth to offer man forgiveness of their sins. So His story wasn't just about the rich man being dependent on riches but all sin that make us dependent in lieu of depending on God. Remember, God wants us to prosper, and it is not a sin to be rich; the only sin is to think riches can satisfy our hunger of our soul.

Loving Is Easier Said than Done

Loving God is easier said than done. Each time I advance to love God more, I often fall short because of not *ridding* my heart of petty baggage, which I held high as my personality and was reluctant to lose that part of me. I soon found what I was saying—I love God—was just a surface reality, and I didn't know the deepest meaning as I see now—love is deeper and endless. I had a gut feeling that finding more love was going to be difficult, and part of that work was to go deeper into myself which had to be done. And realizing, I may have to ask God to take something of my old self and help me to remove it didn't sit well with me. In any case for me to get closer,

---

[a]   Matthew 19:24.

it had to be (1) timely, (2) the right place or location, and (3) sincere when I asked for help.

To sum it up, it was best to get on a conversation with our Lord in the early morning and in a place that was quiet; and most of all, it had to be the highest priority of the day, nothing should distract me. Like now, editing this book in the early hours. Nothing, absolutely nothing, for me could be done without the above three points being achieved. That doesn't mean the spur of the moment to speak to God couldn't happen anytime, it means what I'm calculating to do daily, I need to do in a special quiet place. Meanwhile I had to continue learning to truly love my neighbor and stop my petty sinning, which was, by the way, high on my priority list. What I found if things are to go further toward Him, I had to appreciate what was currently happening around me. It included, for the most part, not harboring bad attitudes toward adverse relationships, and especially getting rid of my anger toward lying politicians, nonthinking automobile drivers, and sports referees. The only way I could ease up on my anger was to turn it over to God. I had to pray to ease my anxiety, knowing all the time the Father appoints world leaders and for me to trust Him. Discovering that the Father appoints our leaders was easy for my faith to accept but difficult to understand watching political leader actions as well as watching inconsistent sports referees.

I can't say love is elusive; it's more of a challenge that my heart is still not completely there yet. I keep thinking God is challenging me to get rid of the things that prevent me from getting closer to Him. We're all challenged daily. I find my only recourse is to talk to God directly concerning my inadequacies and not the other person's inadequacies. After truly talking to the Father and not babbling on, I feel secure, a sense of release, and all I do is ask God in earnest and hope that He shows me grace in order for His kindness to come. What did I just say? I have to ask for His kindness. Yep, He wants us to ask, it isn't the other way around. He'll prompt, challenge, and nudge us, but the whole thing of getting to God is in our corner, our responsibility.

When Did I Truly Love God?

I was a restless fourth grader in New York Catholic schools in the 1950s and would often get scolded for not listening to the nuns during religion classes. I couldn't stand the reprimands, and I soon learned how to appear as if I was listening during religion classes, while all the time I was daydreaming of something else with my eyes opened.

You see, most nuns would come into our religion hour class and read the laws and rules from the catechism or the Bible. That was too much to ask of me, to stay awake attempting to memorize the lesson while listening to their perfect not-skipping-a-beat monotone voices. So I faked it; I began pretending to be listening to all of the religion classes. Except one day, when a beautiful, warm, soft-looking, pleasant nun came into the classroom to give us religion class. I settled in like any other day to turn her off and prepare myself to daydream. Well, it didn't last but for a few seconds when my whole being became energized at hearing her voice. The nun left her book on the desk and began telling us in her own words about a blind man being cured by Jesus.[a] I glanced at that nun as the most beautiful person I had ever seen and heard while she tapped at my heart as she spoke. It was wonderful and exciting to hear from her heart, what God could do and did to cure the blind man, but it didn't last long. She was a visiting nun, and it was the last time the class heard her again.

Soon after that, my sister and I were transferred to a newly built William Floyd Public School just blocks away from our home in Shirley, Long Island. I would never again experience the excitement in my heart until that night about seventeen years later, when I came home exhausted from night college classes and experienced a supposedly near-death situation explained in chapter 3, under "Stress Free."

---

[a]   Mark 8:22–26.

Can Love Be Solely a Universal Language?

How can we communicate with no lips? A better question is, can we communicate efficiently without making a sound or writing a word? I think heaven may be that way; however, we may be able to do it if the other person is spirit-filled too, but in order to go out and speak to most of the world, the Word of the Lord should be communicated verbally first. Now let us go back to the thought of communicating without sound for a minute. I think we have to obtain more of God's love without some kind of scientific breakthrough, but one thing I noticed was that the older I get, the less verbal communication I have with Barbara. We seem to know some of what each other is thinking and don't need extra energy to talk. Well, I could interpret it by saying we've been around each other for so long that we know each other's thoughts. Yes, it could be, but it goes further than just being around each other all these years. After all, humans have been around for thousands of years, and they cannot completely communicate love to all persons. We are still fumbling, and the opposite of love, I'd say, is to care less about our surrounding circumstances.

No Cost

You'd think since it doesn't cost to love but makes things better in returns, that humanity would pick up on it. However, it appears that humanity and the world economic wizards may find cooperation by spreading the dollar around. It appears the process may be more profitable and thereby ensure future peace working for a common goal. I think our world leaders see how to make profits, but what happens later when, through attrition, profits belong only to a few? Will the goal still be the same, or will the competition of a few turn into violent greed as history suggests? There may be big trouble, and maybe we should write the rules down now, preventing that from happening, but can we trust by writing them down that it will be adhered to?

As an example, we presently see what political movements attempt to do to our basic sacred national rules in the US Constitution or how a simple book called *Fifty Shades of Gray* can delude almost the entire world and begin causing serious worldly trouble. I'd say it takes trust, faith, and charity to get to that point, and I'm not sure the world can think in those concepts entirely, especially with present higher education and manufacturing systems being highly materialist. If they were to exercise their desires, I am convinced they have to blend it in with good morals to be more successful, like promoting the Marshall Plan after WWII as discussed in a later chapter. And what costs less besides love? It reminds me of that old saying, "you get what you pay for." That old saying, "you get what you pay for" is true as proven in history.

Barbara and I, like many other people, are paying nothing by searching our hearts to acquire a smidge more of love that works and much more is gained free. So again, the old saying is right in that we get what we pay for. If we pay for drugs, we get what we pay for, and if we don't have the drug money, we suffer needlessly. If we pay for war, we get what we pay for, and if we don't have enough weapons but the other guy does, we become the prize. If we take the time to get close to our Lord, we live without any expense for it, except to wonder, *How could I have stayed away for so long?* Are men capable of true love? Not without God, can we express true love? Feelings are not necessarily love.

Idolatry

How did I find more of God's love? I paid by ridding myself of familiar worldly thinking, of wanting more material things, of allowing my eye not to linger, and I can go on and on. Each time I prayed not to have more of what interfered with finding the truth, I found inner relief, or as some folks like to say, they have peace for various time. Since receiving a little smidge of love, my world is simple and not as complex and is kept that way in prayer and weekly celebrating the Eucharist, a way of physically bringing the Lord into me.[a] No matter what, we all have to find self-peace and worth, and we can't find it by adoring people, money, and pride to satisfy our appetites or may become dormant looking for more of the same in all the wrong places. I see these wants as feelings.

Why can't we get to God by adoring people, money, and power? Because He is in our hearts, and adoring other than God is a self-creating road block we can't pass to get to His graces. And what are graces?[b] God shares His life and friendship with us. It is a gift of love that I find worth more than all the silver and gold in the world. Look at the Hebrew and Israelite nations after giving up idolatry practices and soon received life-giving rewards.[c] Time after time, in history, we see the Israelites gain graces or lose them when they strayed from our Father's true meaning of life. Their easy inner worldly self followed crash courses unknowingly.

---

[a]   Matthew 26:26–29; Mark 14:22–25; Luke 22:19–20.
[b]   CCC 1996–1999.
[c]   Second Chronicles 15:1–7.

Review of Chapter 3

Asking Makes Things Happen

I found that it took constant prayers on my part, the difference between asking God for a favor and really asking God for a favor. Example, when I prayed for something, how deep did my faith go or how much did I need the favor? Experiencing a serious problem and praying about it, I always got some type of a response from the Lord. Remember when I mentioned taking the Bible literally, especially when it said "all we have to do is ask?"[a] Well, there were times I prayed, and nothing happened; nothing happened at that time or even later. However, it wasn't long that I noticed when I was down and out, or when I threw up my hands, giving up trying to do something impossible, that I found my prayers were answered. Even trivial annoying requests that I could not take care of, I would sincerely offer them up, and they were taken care of when it was turned over to God.

So the first step, I later found, to my prayers being answered, was when *I was hopelessly dependent on our Lord.* Just like the example of the needed six girl coats discussed later in this chapter, I could not do anything worldly to remedy the problem. I had to reluctantly say to myself, I can't do it and turn it over to prayer. The second step was to make it a habit each day of asking and thanking God for my breath and allowing me to get up and look around. I no longer take it for granted that I can function property; after all, I am seventy-eight, you know. Praying was so successful in asking for favors that I find myself constantly asking or thanking Him daily for something,

---

[a]   John 15:7.

and that is not deceptive. Most everyday now, I ask to help rid my bad thoughts of those that hurt others or annoy me, and the prayers work. And because it is working, I am not hindered, and I have more abilities to get closer to our Maker. And by getting closer, it brings more insight, mental and physical comfort, and security.

However, I found some of my prayers were answered before I even prayed for it. As an example, Barbara and I would pray for something in the evening, only to find it was already done prior to praying. How do I know it wasn't just a coincidence? It happens all the time, and Barbara is my witness. God certainly knows how my heart has changed toward Him. Our Lord knows what we need even before we know it. That makes sense to me because God knows what we're doing in the future. So what if I forget to pray today, I know God already has me covered, especially when I naturally trust Him. He knows I would pray sometime in the future when I finally remembered. We just have to remember God isn't a candy god, and He loves us deeply, and His blessings give us favors even when we don't deserve it. After all, look how sinful the world can become, and God continues to bless it. Seriously, look around and close your eyes.

But then again, if I take the Bible literally—which I do—the verse that says all I have to do is pray and my faith will make it happen.[a] So I asked myself, as I reasoned I have a bunch of kids, if that is true, then we can pray to win a million dollars, and we'll get it, right? Go ahead, pray for a million, and if you need it, I'm sure you'll receive a million; but in my case, I didn't need a million, it was just wishful thinking, and it would only distract from what I had to do later. It was just wishing, and the million dollars just didn't come about. Yeah, I wished for a million dollars often but to no avail. So can I still take the Bible literally? Yes, indeed, it was my heart that knew I didn't need a million even though my thinking was wanting it. So my thinking was easy to find, but my heart would be a challenge all my days. And—it's a big *and*—your heart is where you'll find peace, not your brain.

---

[a] Matthew 18:19–20.

However, in those struggling days, raising our family, we always got what we needed. If at any time, while raising the kids, that was the time to win the lottery, but we never got close to it, and I discovered that playing the lottery only put me in a position depending less on God, and that, my friends, is a major cause that leads to sin. And sin is a cancer that keeps us from loving God.

Chapter 3

Asking Makes Things Happen

Back Up Now, Way Back When We Got Married

Oh, I forgot, let me back up first when Barbara and I were thinking about marriage in the early 1960s. I wanted to get married by the justice of the peace, and Barbara wouldn't hear anything about that. She said we're getting married in the Catholic Church, so I said to God later, "Well, if I get married in the Catholic Church and do what the church wants, *then you're gonna have to help me with all the kids we have*" (it was known Catholics had a lot of kids). And years later, as the kids were coming along—all eight of them—He was there taking care of us, even though I had the audacity to talk that way to Him earlier; but it must have been okay because it was truly a sincere throwing my hands up in gesture. We didn't have riches, but we had all our basic needs taken care of. And that was a big deal, and especially noticing that when we didn't have much in material goods, we could see we had more to be thankful for by clinging onto each other. We were happy. However, when I began to succeed at my job and have some extra cash in my pocket and feel great and on top of the world was when I faulted. I didn't need God when success came, not that I rejected Him, I just didn't need to ask anymore. I took care of things myself. I was on top of my game. Like Israel, when she was on top of the world, and later, time showed negative results happening, and I plunged into darkness like Israel and sin while depending solely on myself.

How could this happen? It was pure pride, fantasies, and temptation all around me that I succumbed to. Nothing made me do the things I did. I allowed, little by little, evil to take the place of God. What I think most people do when they fail is leave God out of their lives for their own desirable time.

How did I pick myself up before I destroyed the family? I confessed my sins[a] and began recovery, not that I was perfect, but the struggle going back into the confessional with a priest again and again gave strength each time to fight off my bad intentions. So you might ask, what the heck, Ray went to see the priest and confessed his sins, and it didn't seem to do any good? It did a lot of good; I kept going back, confessing my sins, until I had enough spiritual strength to fight back. I think that is why Jesus wanted us to confess our sins. Not only confessing your sins seven times seven but being able to, little by little, reject the sin, thereby rejecting Satan and all anxiety pulling us down.

Ohio, Michigan, Back to Late 1960s

Don't forget we are in chapter 3, "Asking God." When my second army enlistment was up in 1966, and I got out of the army, we had three children: Guy, Susan, and Ann. We purchased a home in Hamilton, Ohio, where the next four children were born: Denise, Janine, Myla, and Colleen. Barbara was a stay-at-home mom, and I worked in an architect's office doing drafting work while attending the University of Cincinnati evening college. Using the GI Bill, attending evening college, I obtained an associate's degree in fine arts (architecture) and stayed in the architectural field until I switched jobs to become an industry construction and maintenance manager. Later in 1979, while working for a company in Cincinnati, Ohio, I was promoted and relocated to Grand Haven, Michigan, where we had our eighth child; but for now, we'll stay in Ohio for this story until the evening college is complete under the GI Bill.

---

[a] CCC 1446; James 5:16.

Stomach, Chest Pain, and Stress Free

One stressful night in 1971, while attending night college in Cincinnati, I would go to class four nights per week and study those many nights, while working a full-time job during the days. When I got home one night from night classes and sat down on the couch to study for exams, a profound lifetime experience happened that should be told to others. I was exhausted and was limited to how much time I could study. I was limited in that I had to wake up early each morning to go to work, and after work, I would travel twenty miles into Cincinnati to attend class. What wasn't so familiar that night was Barbara had become Catholic a couple of weeks earlier, and I gave her a large recently published Jerusalem Bible as a gift and put it on the nightstand next to the couch, where it remained unviewed until that very eventful evening. But before we get into the next paragraph, I want you to know that anytime I opened up a Bible to read, I would soon put it down, becoming tired or bored to death. Although the New Jerusalem Bible was in modern-day English, which I appreciated, I still couldn't finish a sentence without falling asleep. Sort of like being in my lower grades when nuns gave dry religion classes, reading from a text.

On that evening after class, I sat down and began studying college homework, and soon, I was experiencing stomach and chest pains. At first the pain was uncomfortable, but soon it became fierce, so fierce that I began bending over in pain and wondering if this was a heart attack. I began thinking Barbara would become a widow, and my children would be without a father. The kids were upstairs sleeping, and Barbara was in the next room, on the same bedroom floor, sleeping, and I began trying to yell but couldn't get loud enough; it hurt my insides to get louder. I figured this was it and pretty much gave up, and I was convinced I would soon die. The next instant, I was truly desperate and desired only to understand God's words before I passed. I did not ask God to save me from dying, I really thought dying was now, and this was it—I wouldn't see tomorrow. And I asked the Father to help me understand His words before I died. I had only *one desire* at that moment, and that was to know God before passing. I reached over and picked up the Bible and opened it up and looked down into the book. *The words actually began coming out of the pages and flowing into my mouth.* I just froze, wondering what was happening, I thought I was going crazy. I began to get nervous as the words kept flowing, and I thought I was going out of my mind and working too hard; and at that instant, I slammed the book shut. I waited for a moment, looking at the book, and finally began *opening it up* and wondering if the words would continue flowing out of the pages again. It didn't happen, it didn't flow back into my mouth, and hasn't happened again. But something amazing began to happen to my inners.

Now after that episode, I began looking at the pages. I began to read and understood and could interpret almost every verse that night. I was happy and excited; I no longer got tired or bored reading Scripture, and I became full of energy reading Scripture to this very day. Again I'm seventy-eight, folks, and it is still early in the morning, and this writing continues. Why, what for? For you.

Matter of fact, that evening, I was set free of stress and no longer crammed in my studies anymore, and my grades improved. After that, I had more time for the family and volunteered to teach religion to high school teens on the weekends. As I taught the kids their religion lessons relating a great deal to the Bible, the words just flowed out of my mouth with hardly any effort. The kids were alert, and I made sure after each class that we prayed and thanked God together that the class was clear and stimulating. Today, fifty years later, the same Spirit helps to make things happen in Bible study class for adults.

Asking Winter Coats for the Girls

This is a drama of how Barbara and I struggled financially and did not have enough money to buy winter coats for our girls while living in Ohio. It was several years prior to moving to Michigan.

The story begins when Barbara mentioned to me on a fall Saturday evening that the girls needed coats for the up-and-coming winter. I thought for a second and knew we didn't have enough money to buy coats for all the girls. I was a recent veteran and had a low-paying architectural drafting job at the time and scraping each month to survive was a common way of life. I was worried, it was my responsibility to keep the kids housed, clothed, and fed. We had less than one hundred dollars in the bank, and credit cards weren't readily available in those days. We just had the shirts on our backs, our children, car, and a veteran GI home mortgage.

I had no choice and did the only thing I could do. We held each other's hand that Saturday evening, and we prayed for six coats for the girls. By the way, I don't think the prayer exceeded two minutes in duration. Later that night, we slept without a hitch and woke up the next morning not remembering what we prayed for the night before. On that morning, when we were getting ready for Sunday Mass (church service), and later while at Mass, both Barbara and I still didn't give it a thought that we had prayed for the girls' coats eight or so hours before. After about an hour, the Mass was over, and we began heading toward the Narthex to exit the church when a beautiful wealthy lady with six girls of her own stood in front of us as we were leaving.

She asked us at what seemed to be an apology, with one arm holding the other arm behind her back and looking frightened and asked if we could use six girl coats. At that moment, I remembered our prayer, and I responded that we just prayed last night for six coats; and with a lot of enthusiasm, I gave a big yes, that we needed the coats. The lady, Mrs. Zettler, looked relieved, probably because I didn't snap back negatively in pride, knowing we have to be good givers and good receivers too. The other kicker was that the coats were wool, and the coats weren't from local discount stores but a highly regarded store in Cincinnati. Needless to say, the coats were of such good quality that Barbara continued passing them down to the younger girls through the years. And that is the end of this story with more ministories to follow.

Trip from Hamilton to Joliet, Illinois

There was another time we had help from the Lord when we lived in Ohio, around the time we had the seven children, and we got a phone call from my great-uncle, a priest in Joliet, Illinois, asking if we would like to go to his twenty-fifth anniversary of becoming a priest. Our history with my uncle was that he came to Fort Bliss, Texas, to meet Barbara and to marry us in 1961. So when we got the invitation call to join him in Joliet, Barbara and I had a strong desire to return his kindness for making the trip to Fort Bliss years earlier. Also we had another reason for going there, we were the only relatives close enough to be at his anniversary, but our finances were a problem, and our car needed a tune-up, and the tires were just okay to travel the 250 miles, and especially in the winter, we just didn't have the cash available. So Barbara and I did the only thing we knew what to do, and that was to pray, holding hands, and ask for help to be with my uncle for his anniversary. That very afternoon, we had a call from a local home building contractor, asking if I could design a home for him to obtain a building permit, and he would give $100 in exchange for the minimum three plans.

I accepted, knowing I could make house plans for a building permit in eight hours, and when finished, I received the money to buy and install tune-up parts for our dated Chevy II wagon, enough money to fill it with gas and put the kids in the back; but before we left, I noticed the gas tank was about three-eighths full.

We got to Joliet that evening, and my uncle invited us to stay; but the next day was school day, and we had to get back. Besides we didn't plan nor did we have enough money left from the building plan money to stay overnight if we stayed in a hotel. It was late when the reception was over, and we began our trip back to Hamilton. We had unexpected bad news getting into the car and turning the radio on. The weather person announced a sudden winter storm was coming from the West as we were headed South back to Ohio, across Indiana. You have to know that Indiana Interstates 65 and 75 are terrible roads during winter storms, especially when a West wind whips across the north to south flatlands of both interstate roads, and we had to travel back using those highways. Our car tires weren't the best, and the snow was heavy, and the wind began and icy conditions were everywhere.

As we began passing trucks and cars off the side of the road, I wondered how the car we were driving could be better than those stuck on the side of the road. Barbara and I were very concerned while traveling through the storm while the kids slept in back. We wondered several times, how was it that we could keep from being blown off onto the side of the road and not be in a ditch ourselves. We made it back to Hamilton without a problem, and before I turned the ignition off, I noticed the tank was three-eighths full, just like when we started; and to top it off, there wasn't a penny left in my pocket from the building plan money. Barbara and I wondered if we prayed while on the Indiana highways, and we couldn't recall today. But as we discovered later, God was always with us and you too. You have to know, humans cannot live without God being in us. It's our soul that keeps us alive.

As you may now know, God was with us, gave what we needed, even though I may not have been the perfect person that you'd think would get favors from Him. I was not the ideal person. I wasn't a do-goodie person either, and I certainly had my hang-ups, but never have I ever felt in my life, no matter what may have happened, that there wasn't a God, that knowing was always there. God loves you and me, but the question was how much do we love Him? It's when we obey that we find how much we love and how close we are. I have to find more of Him, and that is the kicker, it isn't easy for me, but then the struggle of finding our Lord takes patience, is exciting, and knowing my sins were always forgivable is worth all the money and gold we could accumulate.[a]

---

[a] Proverbs 28:13.

Now Back in Michigan, We Found More Time for the Kids

It was in Grand Haven, Michigan, in the early 1980s, that our family began to shrink at home, and the older kids began attending various colleges, and the remainder of our family were stay-at-homers. We found more time as a family to spend with the remaining younger kids. I was asked by my older children why their younger sisters and brother weren't treated as strictly as they were. Simply put, I learned to handle a larger family, and it was a priest that got to my inners on how not to raise a family. He (Father Ratterman) and I were having a casual conversation about family when he said, "Children get an idea who God is by watching their father." If their father is overly strict, that could be how they perceive God; but if their father is kind and loving, that is what God is like. I melted, to think, I treated the kids somewhat like when I was in the military, simply because I wanted order. I was shaken to think I could influence them into thinking something else other than what God is. To this day, that understanding haunts me.

Michigan was about the outdoors, and the family took up camping, cross-country skiing, fishing, and hunting. Michael was born in Grand Haven, and as soon as he could, he did everything with us in his young abilities. He was game for anything and proved to be an exceptional student, skier, and fisherman. In his early years, when Mike went salmon pier fishing with us on Lake Michigan, we would tie a heavy rope around his waist onto the pier structure, and he'd fish. His hand movement wasn't entirely restricted, and he could still hold onto the small fishing pole with ease while a rope tied around his waist kept him from being blown over the pier by an unsuspected wave coming from the lake.

What a sight we must have been to the Chicago tourist walking up and down the pier while we fished for salmon. I always felt someone would call the cops on us for child abuse, but we escaped that scrutiny, and they weren't called. Mike loved hearing those old-time stories, especially when he was two, a story about him catching a baby painted turtle. He was studying the baby closely when he attempted to kiss it, and the turtle bit him on the lower lip. The turtle hung on for dear life, and Michael bawled for dear life. It seemed like hours to Mike until the turtle released its grip from Mike's lip. Needless to say, the turtle was the only thing he caught that day.

Do Not Kiss Turtles

Things got bad with the Michigan economy during the late 1980s, and my job was terminated. I found another job, about seventy-five miles from Grand Haven, in Kalamazoo, Michigan, where we purchased a home and a forty-acre wooded and tillable farm near the town of Lawton. Barbara and I both knew the property, and our possessions were gifts to us. We did not want to let the land sit and do nothing with it, so we began growing Christmas trees for a future home business to help with college tuition, but it would take eight years to gain a profit from mature trees. In the meantime, we raised sheep, cattle, and cultivated gardens to help make our food intake healthier. As we were getting settled, Barbara and I joined Saint John Bosco Church in Mattawan where I began as a volunteer, teaching confirmation classes for high school students that eventually included Michael.

Michael graduated from Lawton High School, married, and began raising a family to include Christopher, his firstborn, while going to college for mechanical engineering. Nothing was easy for him in those days, raising a growing family, going to school, and working. And I often look back and wonder how much more I could have done to help him with his endeavors. It gets painful, folks, when you lose a child and wonder and wonder what more you could have done. It was only through faith and prayers that I believe God has everything in His hands, and I received some sort of peace. The tendencies to feel guilty is absolutely terrible and must be avoided in order to continue normal relationships with the rest of the family and friends. Maybe what kept us going was that Mike left a widow and three young boys, and it wasn't long before Mike's siblings began helping too.

Guy's Son Patrick Was High on Our Prayers

My grandson Patrick, about the same age as Christopher, was diagnosed with autism. It appeared he would be dependent on his family and the state forever. We understood, at the time, there were no cures, only repetitive type of training to help make him function better in life. It became obvious to us, years later, Patrick needed extra help. When Barbara and I realized we had no other options but to pray, we had no choice; none of the doctors gave any positive reports that Patrick could be cured. We threw up our hands and asked Guy and Maureen, who lived several hours away, if Barbara and I could pray for Patrick to be cured of autism, and they agreed. Barbara and I began praying for Patrick, and it was sometime later within a year, things took a turn for the better, and he was rediagnosed to not having autism. However, Patrick, at the time, we felt was immature for his age but highly sensitive, fearful, and very intelligent.

A couple of summers, he would spend time on the farm with us and help with chores. Some of the chores were gathering of chicken eggs from the egg nests or helping me cut trees into logs, splitting them, and stacking the logs for winter heat. He was smart, and if Patrick was left on his own, he was like any other boy; he would get lazy, and it would require stronger motivation to get him to finish the job. Pat soon caught onto my bag of motivational tricks, and I had to resort to forceful army tactics. He didn't like it, but the tactics achieved the objective. Huh, Patrick was more like a city kid and not like a strong active farm kid; he preferred sitting around either at school and or at home on his computer, and that did not sit well with me. Everybody had to work and do their share of chores, especially Patrick, he had to learn work is what we do.

No Way Sports

Sports or physical activities was not Patrick's thing, which didn't sit well with other boys. When his cousins got a soccer or football game going, he would often quit halfway through the match and just take it easy. The boys, mostly his cousins, were considerate toward him, and he would be the boy not wanting to be active in their activity. He would get bored watching the kids on the sidelines, and next he could be found on his computer or snooping through our refrigerator. One night, while staying over with us, hours before most of his cousins were coming over for breakfast and a fantastic desert in the morning, he came downstairs during the early morning hours and went straight for the refrigerator and began eating the remaining cheesecake Barbara left for the kids to have after breakfast. The next morning, we had a bunch of his cousins over for breakfast, and after the big breakfast, we would eat the desert Barbara made. It didn't happen—the cake was missing; and when we were questioning what happened to the cake, Patrick finally confessed he ate the whole thing. It's funny now, but back then, the best desert ever made was gone, and his cousins took it in stride, knowing Patrick just couldn't resist a midnight snack. I didn't take it in stride, he heard from me and heard it loud and clear. I would not treat him different than the other kids but was ever watchful of a better approach.

Later in high school, Patrick began having seizures that deeply concerned all of us. How we came to know about how bad the seizures were was when Guy, his father, made a phone video of Patrick going through a seizure as a passenger in Guy's car. Guy videoed

Patrick leaning back, stretched out on the passenger seat, quivering and going through sporadic jerks with his body. The next thing you could see was Patrick's eyes rolling back and foam or spittle coming out of his mouth. It was nothing I had ever witnessed before, and it was not a sight I wanted to look at again.

Stress and Seizures

What Barbara and I surmised that caused most of the seizures during this time period was Patrick's involvement on the Internet. We found he often got onto fundamental religious sites, and he discovered the book of Revelation and what I call want-to-be computer preachers. The Revelation sites portrayed extreme fearful views of people suffering concerning the end of the world. Patrick picked up on the deep fear and the intended emotions that come with the fundamental type of interpretations and went into deep despair when he self-evaluated himself. The authors of those extreme interpretations may or may not know how damaging it could be playing on fear, but worse yet, they think they know the message without realizing there is much more to Revelation than fear. I get the impression from these fundamentalist people, they think God is all about fear and to scare nonbelievers is the only thing they do. Maybe, but without fully knowing the entire message themselves of the book of Revelation, they may cause others to adopt wrong understanding of God and His Word. After all, Christians should ask themselves, why did the Lord Jesus Christ come in the world in the first place, was it mainly fear or love? I find Christ came to show us the face of God, and God's face is *love*.[a]

It is a shame Patrick became extremely depressed from the fear they posted on the Internet. It was awful to watch a kid's body going through convulsions and rolling his eyes up into his head, along with foam-like spit frothing from his mouth in the video. It took praying and time for me to forgive the people that promoted that type of

---

[a] *Jesus of Nazareth*, 3–8.

God. Since the age of the New Testament teaching began, we should change from fear to love. And case in point, you can see the progression the centuries the Israelites went through to help make that change easier. I finally forgive them but haven't forgotten, and Patrick eventually limited himself of the ongoing seizures after our many conversations concerning God's forgiveness and medical help. He knows that if it's kind, tender, and forgiving, it is a priority from God. I think Patrick suspects that Revelation is more of a book of hope for followers of Christ rather than of fear. Catholics even say several or more prayers during Mass, asking for the end to come.[a] It's not mournful, it's plane ole faith that we hope to be with our Lord when He comes the second time, when we consider the end of the world.

Patrick graduated from high school and was later accepted into Michigan Career Technical Institute located in Plainwell, Michigan, for people with disabilities (he was on record at that time as having learning disabilities but not autism). He selected culinary studies and received a certificate of culinary after completing the course; however, cooking just didn't materialize and wasn't in his heart. During his times in culinary classes, he was faced with unknowns that were known to instructors and not to him. Patrick was oversensitive after he fumbled with those unknowns and would became disorientated and frazzled and have bad moments and days.

Unbeknownst to me at this time, in culinary school, Pat was having difficulties when I just happened to call him. It was on a Thursday, and we set up a time when we could have lunch together on Friday and receive a tour by him of the dining room and kitchen. I was looking forward to this time to spend with him. Well, the next day before I got there, he opened up—by mistake—an extremely stinky grease trapdoor and got a chewing out, but worse, his peers laughed at him. The chewing out frazzled him to the point he forgot about the luncheon date we had with each other and went into hiding somewhere. At about that time, I traveled for an hour in winding back roads to get there, and when I arrived, he wasn't anywhere to be found, even the adult monitor's paging could not locate him. When I finally

---

[a]　Prayer of Our Father, Creed and the Eucharist Prayer.

found him, he was despondent and embarrassed, and his enthusiasm to become a cook was lost. I felt bad that Patrick was down again and taking a couple of steps backward to his old self, but the best part was that he did not go into seizures. Patrick continues reading the Internet religious postings less, and now he has begun seeing God for what he is and slowly becoming a self-independent young man.

Cooking Mishap

Keep Asking

Barbara and I continue asking God to help Patrick with his life each evening. One weekend after culinary class, Patrick stayed overnight in our house, in Michael's old room. And Pat, born with a computer nose, found an old hidden Nintendo computer game that once belonged to Mike when he was a teenager. He proudly determined it to be an antique and worth a lot of money, and he told us that certain people search for this old type of computer game components on the Internet all the time. In the excitement of him finding it, I wondered how he knew those things and was he on the road to recovery. Anyway Pat quickly asked if he could have it. The computer didn't work, but he assured us he would fix it. I wondered how he would do that, he never seemed to have any mechanical or electronic abilities, and sadly I wasn't happy giving away Mike's belongings without a good purpose.

We gave Pat the computer components before he went back to culinary class in Plainwell but with a stern comment that he was supposed to fix it. His first attempt to fix the so-called valuable equipment was to get it into an electronic repair shop in Kalamazoo, but he soon found it was too expensive and difficult getting it to the repair shop and back. Besides I followed up with him about reminding him that he would fix it and not have someone else do it.

He began looking at various ways of how to repair it, including contacting the school maintenance staff, asking them to help him fix it, but having the maintenance people do it was to no avail. He knew he had to do something; after all, he was convinced it would be a valuable asset once it was working. His next option, if he wanted this piece of equipment to work, was to repair it himself (finally he was getting the idea). Patrick went online and found various fixes to the equipment, and he proceeded with the help of his roommate to repair it. Both of them, together, accomplished repairing it, and for the first time ever, a week later, we heard a sparkle in his voice due to his new and maybe only electronic achievement thus far. We thought the little insignificant repair he accomplished could be a start of an independent life for him and his partner. If he continued to pray, which he better, he should find his potential in life.

Several months later, after graduating from culinary school, Patrick found a job near his home in Forest Hills, Michigan, and hopefully that was the start for Pat to be somewhat self-sufficient. By the way, this was supposed to happen since it came to pass, I can say as I do in the following chapters that this was God's plan or His allowing it to happen. In any case, God knows what happens, and further, nothing happens in the world without God allowing it to happen. I also know all of us take our next breath because God allows us to take a breath.

So you may say to yourselves, I don't like the above breath statement, and I don't feel comfortable allowing my thoughts to think that I'm not in control of my own breath. Then who is in control? It certainly isn't us, and I know from what I can figure out, there are at least six thousand years of documented history showing failure after failure of man attempting to be in control, only to lose.

And so, I say to myself, is putting aside the Ten Commandments the main obstacle of not understanding God? Yes, but the obstacle in our world is a lack of faith of not accepting Jesus as our Savior. And how in the world do I accept Jesus? For me, it takes searching my heart each day. However, to prove to ourselves we love God, we follow His commandments.

Prayers for Vincent, Another Grandson

We got a frantic call from my daughter Myla that Vincent, her son, a cancer survivor away at college, was being taken by his roommate to the emergency room. Once a child has a near-death situation, the causes linger on in parents for possibly our entire life. Vincent was experiencing severe right abdominal pains, so severe that the ER sent him to the hospital. The hospital had to wait until Vincent could digest his lunch before having an ultrasound done. In the meantime, Vincent was being evaluated, but nothing outstanding like an appendix problem or other abnormalities could be found.

The test results came back the next morning, and our prayers were answered favorably. Vincent had a strong case of anxiety from taking on additional classes and doing too much at school. Unbeknownst to us, Vincent added three more credit hours to his curriculum that may have been the start of his anxiety, and he quickly found out the hard way that he caused his own problems overloading himself. Was it self-induced? Yes, and should we still have taken the time to pray and be thankful? Absolutely, the more we depend on God, the stronger we become, even if it's only seemly minor problems.

Myla had the worst of it that night and morning since it was Vincent that survived leukemia as a child. All those old memories were lingering in us again, especially in her. Praying for both Vincent and Myla were essential.

Back to Vincent's Leukemia Days

The leukemia was in Vin-Ray's body for many years before he was free of it, and during that time, Barbara and I and his aunts and uncles prayed and hoped, asking God to cure Vincent. Myla never said she quit, and she kept knocking in those days, asking God for help. Sometime during that period, she found various foods were cancer fighters and put Vincent on a strict diet to help counter the severe medical treatment. She began giving him only wheat grass, carrots, broccoli, and pineapple juice to fight not only the effects from the medicine but the cancer too. And we believe because of the special foods Vin-Ray ate, he began having fewer medical problems than other sick children with the same sicknesses around his age. Later Vin-Ray's doctor of six years asked Myla for a list of what she gave Vincent in order to help further their research in curing cancer. We can now see from above, the start of Vincent and his college anxiety that he was able to figure things out and to get himself back to normal, but his brother Paul was experiencing serious problem failures too, attempting to get high scores on his ACT test for entry into certain colleges.

Paul Kept Knocking

Paul, Myla's second son, failed to achieve his goal five times to make higher ACT scores and was frustrated and ready to call it quits. He wanted more than anything to be accepted into Michigan Technological University (MTU), and it was too much for him to think it may not happen. He was also remembering his grade school years of seriously failing with his grades and just wasn't feeling good about himself at the moment. He was on his bed, showing signs of despair, when his parents, Myla and Jacob, sat down with him and asked what was wrong. Paul went on to say he was finished with college and further taking tests to get into MTU.

As quickly as he said that, his mother got into his face and began chewing him out, asking if he was a quitter. Myla wasn't a quitter; she was resolved and wasn't going to allow her teenager to just give up, and she began telling him quitters don't get near what they want in life. We have to keep knocking on the door to get what we want, she said. Understand what Myla went through; she went through pure hell thinking she could lose her boy Vincent to cancer and what she can do to prevent him from dying. But somewhere she reached in for faith, knowledge, and determination and got smarter and tougher inside.

Anyway Paul had good support and a real reason to take the test again, and this time when he took it, he passed and was accepted into the college of his choice. The icing on the cake came about two weeks later for Paul, after being on the Kalamazoo Robotics Team throughout his four years at Mattawan High School, the team was now making great strides competing against other teams and schools nationally.

The team from Kalamazoo is called Stryke Force Robotics. Paul and his robotics team just achieved *world-class* recognition while at the Saint Joseph, Michigan, robotic tournament in March 2017. Several of his friends who have been accepted into MTU were also on the team when they achieved the world recognition. It was no easy feat since the Asian teams, especially China, Korea, and Japan were eating our lunches in the industrial robotics field and were competing at the world competition too. I remembered, and we'll say more about this in later chapters concerning the South Koreans in the 1960s being poor and having a world-education level equal to the worst countries in the entire world. The poor Koreans are the same kids beating us in industrial technology and have just begun showing themselves as worthy competitors. You've got to wonder, what is going on with America throwing all that money, all these years at education, and when competing with kids from less-fortunate countries that didn't throw money at their kids like we did. It's not money, its heart, culture, and family living, and that is something many higher educated leaders in America don't seem to grasp or have the faith ability to ask God and to fix it.

However, Paul and his robotics team were able to show some of the stuff they are made of on April 28, 2017. After three days of grueling work, he and his team finally came up against the remaining final five world-class teams in the competition, and his team went on to win the World Robotic Championship in Missouri on April 29, 2017.

Without a hitch, the night prior to the world robotics finals, Barbara and I held hands and prayed for Paul and his team to do the best they could. Please understand, we asked for the best they could be, not be the best. This prayer was special; I did feel God's comfort around me, and it wasn't just for Paul that we prayed for but for him to understand how God comes into our lives when we ask from our hearts. And later we discovered Paul prayed too.

Note: Reminder we are still in the chapter asking God for help.

Elderberry Tonic Footsteps

Barbara and I have been making an elderberry mixture for eleven years now, and after successfully giving our children and grandchildren the tonic as a medicinal liquid to rid the flu and congestion, we decided to create our own elderberry business and share it with others outside the family.

I'll start from the beginning and end with how God provided something special for us. It began about the time we came to Michigan, thirty-five or so years ago. However, eleven years ago, I consulted a doctor for the last time because of my reoccurring annual coughing, hacking, stomach muscle pain from the deep coughs, and just felt miserable day and night attempting to sleep but couldn't. Often in those days, prior to eleven years ago, I either developed a bad case of bronchitis or pneumonia. I asked the doctor at that time, in frustration, what was wrong with me, what caused this, and why am I affected like this each year? His answer was simple—it was allergies. What? I said, "I've suffered for years using expensive prescription drugs, and it's only allergies?"

Searching

Soon Barbara began searching the Internet for ways to help keep us from purchasing the expensive Medicare pharmaceutical insurance and learned that elderberry extract would help prevent coming down with congestion, colds, and the flu, and it appeared to be a high immune booster. After investigating the elderberry qualities, we went into Kalamazoo, to a local health food store, and purchased an ounce bottle of the elderberry extract. I remember it well, it cost $15 for an ounce. As soon as we got home, I took eight drops on my tongue, and within two hours, my congestion and cough were completely gone. *I said gone.* It was a miracle; all these years I suffered and all the prescribed medicines I took were wasteful, but worse yet, the undesirable prescribed medicine was going into my body and causing other unknown harmful effects. I thanked God for the natural relief. But it isn't over yet, there is more to this story.

Wild Elderberry

We decided to plant our own elderberry shrubs to avoid the expense of the condensed elderberries. We planted six shrubs the first year and anticipated a three-year wait until the first harvest. It appeared months from our first harvest, we would have more than enough berries for the family and decided to create our own business in our perception of having an extra harvest of berries. We guessed that we would have more than enough and thought about the extra we could make additional tonic and sell it to the surrounding communities. We prayed for the business to be a success and waited for nature to do its thing.

In June of that year, before the first harvest, we observed for the first time in three years buds on the small shrubs and immediately estimated there would be more than enough berries in September to harvest for our family and the new business. We quickly decided a business name and to obtain a business permit. With that in hand, we began making large outdoor signs for our road advertisement and ordered raw materials to accomplish the building and making tonic for the new business. It was in mid-July that we observed the highly unusual *scented* tiny white blossoms were more than plentiful and to start preparing further to pick the fruit in several weeks. I thanked God that it appeared our home business was going to get off to a fantastic first start in anticipating the first plentiful harvest. Time went by fast while we waited, and several days prior to picking the crop, it looked and smelled great.

On the anticipated day, I got buckets and ladders and went straight for the ripened fruit and was stopped dead in my tracks. I looked up, and the dark-purple ripened berries were not to be found. I kept looking at bare fruit branches and not seeing purple fruit, thinking at my age that maybe my eyes and eye glasses have something to do with what I didn't see. I didn't see one ripened berry, and I was beginning to panic and immediately went back in the house, asking Barbara to verify what I had seen. Maybe, just maybe, I could not see the ripened color of purple, and things would continue on as anticipated. Barbara had seen what I had seen—a lack of berries that we verified last week ripening. However, not one ripened berry was on the small trees nor on the ground, and I was completely speechless, hopeless, and feeling devastated. I was shocked and wondered what has just happened and wondered deeply if God did not approve of this new adventure.

We soon discovered it was an unusual high number of purple finches hanging around that were the culprits. Now I believe this—God made us free to do whatever we wish; however, animals were created with more restrictions than we have and follow God's instructions to the tee, and the birds did what they were supposed to do—they ate the fruit as normal. So I did the only thing I know what to do when I'm down, especially being devastated, hopeless, and throwing up my hands; I had to talk to God. Now you have to understand, I don't have long conversations with Him. I always keep my conversations short and to the point. As an example, I was devastated and said, "God, if this is what you want of Barbara and me, not to go into the elderberry tonic business, it will hurt, but we accept you know best."

I walked back into the middle of our property which is a hollow wooded area, about 500'×500', and it was a quiet area. I often went to be alone in the past to think and pray. I sat down on the ground with my back up against a tree, and in an instant, I was amazed, I smelled the highly *scented* fragrance of the one-of-a-kind blossoming elderberry flowers. I looked up and around and wondered, where the heck was that amazing *sweet scent* coming from? The shrubs we planted, were presently too far away, and nearer to our home for the scent to be here in our hollow, and I looked up across from where I was sitting. I spotted an elderberry tree half in blossom and with half-ripened berries. I looked at other areas and spotted several more elderberry trees, and further looking around, I counted a total of thirty-three wild ripening elderberry shrubs around me. All I could think of was that we were back in business, and God had a hand in this outcome again. To me, *miracle* is the word, and it seems to be the better thing to say here. I think, *God had a hand in this outcome*, and it is the better to write about. After all, we have a lot of people now depending on the elderberry tonic including nurses, teachers, high school athletes, moms, and most recently, the next person to try its effects was our mechanic, Nick.

Nick called the other day to let us know we have additional problems with our old car he is attempting to repair. When he was explaining the auto problem, he sounded congested and broke into his own conversation and said, "I can't believe how bad this congestion is for me, and worse, my family has it too." I told him about the elderberry tonic we have, and it should clear his congestion and his family's. As soon as they took the special processed elderberry tonic, they were well again. But now thinking of God always knowing what is in the past, present, and future, I began to think the elderberry tonic may counter this coronavirus thing we're experiencing in 2020, and we haven't had flu shots or the flu since taking elderberry.

Back to the Purple Finch Story—Could It Be a Miracle

Well, I could think two separate incidents that happened when I prayed and looked up in the hollow: God put the shrubs there, or I could determine, as I do now, the trees have been there for many years, and I never recognized what they were. Not recognizing things is what I do, especially with relationships that I could have helped, and I blew good relationships away. It's the story of my life, folks, I'm partially blinded until I ask God for help. As I age and become less dependent on myself, I continue looking to the Lord more for help, and I see more. I also see an alarming number of people not able to see what I see and what is ahead of them, especially in world events, world sport soccer events, and even on everyday television episodes. I try not to look too deep in a weakened state at any one time for fear I would become lost in a maze of evil. Similar to the monsters that plagued Israel's history and in the book of Revelation.

Ecstasy

In the Old Testament, men seemed to go into a state of ecstasy, trying to pray and speak God's language in order to build upon his rich spiritual kingdom, but I think it wasn't physical enough to convince the Israelites and may be the reason why it was not recognized as a deep spiritual way of praying, as it is today. Oh, the Israelites seemed to respect the holy men at times, and that is all. It would be centuries later, when Jesus comes into the world, that the world would again see spiritual disciples speak in tongues (ecstasy).[a] Why would I relate ecstasy in 1 Samuel to speaking in God's language or in tongues as today? Samuel knew, all Israel knew, what they had to do was pray and believe, but their population seemed stuck or not interested as do some believers and nonbelievers today. How unfortunate Israel was when they forgot to talk to God, and their enemies marched into their lives and slaughtered them, time after time after time. Then I look into my own life, with my stumbling blocks, and realized I had not prayed enough either. I depended on myself; after all, I'm smart, educated, and I thought I knew God well enough. Israel also thought they knew God before they got sacked while not depending on Him, like me, the biggest fool of all to criticize Israel for being unfortunate when that fool was me all these years. Years ago, I didn't need God; after all, I didn't have an army coming after me, and I was on top of my game with my job, extra money in my pocket, and just didn't need to ask God for anything. However, similar to the Babel builders of the Old Testament, I failed to recognize my inadequacies until I became exhausted and crashed. No one caused the problem except myself.

Confirmation Class Ecstasy

Don't forget, we're still in prayer asking God. While teaching about the seven spiritual gifts at a confirmation class in Mattawan, a girl student told us that her family quietly prayed in tongues each week during the Mass (church service). Her explanation of speaking in tongues was a fantastic learning experience for me and the kids that were present and later to be confirmed by the Holy Spirit. They should believe in the Spirit as part of the Trinity and "become true witnesses of Christ, obliged to spread and defend the faith by word and deed."[b] I asked the girl who spoke in tongues, what was it like

---

[a]   First Samuel 19:18–24; Acts 2:1–2.
[b]   CCC 1285.

to pray in tongues? And she told us it was pure *ecstasy*, praying to God. Hence this is why I interpreted Samuel's ecstasy to speaking in tongues and needed to share Samuel with you. To let you know, in case you don't know, there are many spiritual gifts available to us, worth more than gold and silver to our well-being.[a]

Meditation/Spirit

How shall I write this concerning recent self-meditation awareness information? It is wonderful that we can learn to free our minds of unnecessary clutter, and most importantly, science is presently proving that we are capable to self-meditate and improve our mental and physical abilities. All we have to do as shown on a TV segment about five years ago is to simply sit down, close our eyes, fold our legs, shut out the world, and think various positive thoughts that benefit us. Even the USA National Football League is taking notice that science is proving its value, and they are watching their players improve their game. But we have to add that which I discovered years ago was the same type of meditation the NFL is attempting to do, and it was an excellent effort on my part to go inside myself, while pushing all the rubble inside me aside. Just what I needed as a young father of a large family. *But*—this is a big *but*—I was doing it for my own amazing self-awareness, and soon learned there was *a limit* of self-discovery, and I was stopped in my tracks from advancing further. How could that be, I asked, and soon found that the Holy Spirit went beyond my self-awareness limits and gave me additional graces that went beyond what I could achieve myself. I felt complete, sharing this with the Holy Spirit. I was more alive than of the human power I discovered. Even though we have fantastic human powers waiting to be tapped, there is more beyond ourselves.[b] That self-tapping is limited in us and is simply a self-awareness of ourselves, but it may not be our God being asked to enter into us directly as the spiritual gifts from the Holy Spirit. The

---

[a] Isaiah 11:1–3; CCC 1830–183.
[b] CCC 154–158; 1 Corinthians 12:31, 13, 14:1–5.

only requirement is to ask the Father through Jesus Christ, and if we don't ask, we may not achieve higher gifts as God has intended for us.

An example two-thousand-plus years ago was when the apostles of Jesus took notice and observed someone that was not part of their circle curing people of health issues. The apostles asked Jesus, how could that be? Jesus replied and told them to allow the person do what he is doing, if he isn't against them, he is for them. From that verse, I understood Jesus indicating we have fantastic human powers waiting to be tapped, *but* we're told to use that power in the name of Jesus for the glory of God, the Father. And I have discovered going to the Father is ecstasy.

So what is prayer? We hear words to pray, and sometimes it sounds like a household word or just something nice to say. *Prayer is when we actually talk to God.*

Priests, Father Ken and Father Bill

I thought the above "Meditation/Spirit" was the end of this chapter, but because of the following new story being verified, I decided to add it to this chapter. Matter of fact, I just put the finishing final sentence on the end of this book when my friend John Byrnes relayed to me the following story concerning Father Bill and Father Ken of Saint Catherine of Siena Parish, Portage, Michigan.

John and I were having a cup of coffee, and he mentioned that Father Bill, a seventy-four-year-old priest had a stroke on April 27, 17, and was paralyzed from the neck down, barely able to speak, see, or hear and wasn't able to walk without medical assistance. Bill's prognosis was not good as he was lying on a hospital bed. His visitor, Father Ken, the pastor, was at his side at ten o'clock in the evening when Bill communicated to Father to "go home and rest. You can't do anything here."

Ken declined and continued sitting next to his bed when at two o'clock in the morning, Ken noticed Bill's toes moving and screamed, "Your toes are moving." That began Bill's recovery.

When John finished telling me this, I assumed Ken may have prayed, and the Holy Spirit began curing Bill. I had no intention of writing about the above story based on that information alone, until better and stronger evidence to relate to you emerged. However, when a second story, almost a year to date, was verified and stronger, involving Father Ken at a conversion mass, I decided to write. As it were, I was a witness to several people experiencing the Holy Spirit, so I decided to communicate both above incidents involving Father Ken to you.

Hands on Allen's Head

On March 4, 2018, I was a member of the Rite of Christian Initiation of Adults celebrated at the five-o'clock evening Penitential Rite Mass for scrutinies (scrutinies are spiritual purpose rites reinforced by an exorcism for personal self-searching and repentance) of candidates coming into the Catholic Church. It was Allen Acker and Kati Kauffman in separate initiation processes to become Catholic. This day will be forever remembered.

Allen, Kati, and others were asked to go to the center front of the church, to have hands put on Allen's shoulders by other parishioners, while Father Ken placed his hands on Allen's head and prayed for Allen. A minute prior to Ken putting his hands on Allen, I put my hands on Allen's shoulder for the remaining five-to-seven-minute ceremony, I did not notice anything unusual. My faith was such that when two or more prayed in His name—and we were doing just that—I knew the Holy Spirit would be there, except I never experienced the Spirit as witnessed to me in a meeting room, as told by Allen, his wife, Narcia, and Kati about thirty minutes after the ceremony.

Meeting Room

Soon after the rite was completed, several of us left the main church for the small meeting room to discuss further with Allen and Kati two Bible readings and the gospel of the day, along with the responses from various books of the Bible. However, before we could get into the readings, Allen spoke up first and began telling us what happened to him during the ceremony that was performed in church. He began by telling us he felt the Holy Spirit enter him during the time Father Ken put his hands on his head. Allen explained his experience, while holding back tears, that he felt relieved and pure, as all his sins were gone from him and truly felt forgiven. I loved hearing his deep reflecting occurrence of those moments, as I was in awe. I felt the Spirit working in me many times but not like what Allen had described. But Allen wasn't the only person to experience the Spirit during that ceremony. Although Kati wasn't the center of the ceremony, she nevertheless experienced the power of the Spirit too.

Powerful Throughout

Kati Kauffman, another candidate for entrance into the church but not at the same level of understanding as Allen, gave us her story about when Allen received hands on from Father Ken and the other parishioners earlier. Kati also put her hands on Allen's shoulder. She told us more of the following experience when we were together in the meeting room after Mass. Kati announced, she felt the Holy Spirit in her and a sense of community while her hands were on Allen's shoulder. She felt unafraid and powerful, a power that came over her like nothing she ever experienced. To me, she appeared to be exhilarated. I would stay the remaining afternoon, if need be, to hear more of their testimonies.

Hold Up, There Is More

After both Allen and Kati told us about their experiences, Allen's wife, Narcia, entered the room. She spoke and went on to tell us that when she was watching Father Ken put his hands on Allen, she saw the Holy Spirit descend. Narcia had a special look on her face and in her eyes, and I loved being there to hear her words.

Now that was worth extending this chapter.

Review of Chapter 4

What has happened since 1945? Americans prayed for peace and helped win a nasty world war on two fronts. We became an even greater nation after the war, and we should continue to do so. We began to prosper; our factories were at high capacity partly due to the Marshall Plan in Europe, and our world trade policies helped not only Americans but other countries we traded with. However, little by little, we can look at current events, look back and see we are slowly replacing God, and the new world trading process may come into jeopardy. In any case, I intend to demonstrate the severe limitations we and our political leaders have and how to help put the whole world into true prosperity.

Chapter 4

We May Relive World History

The major causes that destroy nations was rejecting what natural good was put into their countrymen to be successful, but in time, many people slowly followed what seemed be a quick and easy path, not necessary the best way. Maybe fully unknown to the populace, or they just didn't realize, they fell into corruption little by little; and it was overpowering enough to reject what was the right thing to do.[a] We see a prophet, nearly 2,500 years ago, warning a great nation of their destruction, even during the brief second slave period of Israel, we realized it.[b] I began to see families in the 1950s taking adverse directions in their lives and wondered if the '50s was the beginning of the end for our nation. It was appearing America was on a slow engine heading toward her demise. The divorce rate was beginning to climb, and soon groups of young people were angry at America, and I wondered if those young people were product of divorces. I wondered how many people were being affected by family breakups. And still today, I wonder when I look at whole neighborhoods clustered together without husbands and fathers and wonder if a missing link is still appearing.

First Corruption

The first serious indication of a forced corruption was in my teenage years and a disappointment at how one person could be

---

[a]   Second Chronicles 36:14–21.
[b]   Ezekiel 31:1–18.

responsible for taking prayer out of the public schools. It wasn't Madelyn Murray taking prayer out of the schools so much as who was behind the scenes supporting her. She was not the only person responsible as we were led to believe, but there were multitudes of people that blamed her as the bad disrupted person. Think about it, how could one person be responsible for a major movement? The other alarm was our families, at the same time, were divorcing at an alarming rate as never before seen. Madelyn had her day, too, and she was an angry lady. So just like Communist propaganda was used in the past to blame others and to help disrupt societies, the anger began to grow in America. The convenience of divorcing was a helpful issue for the people wanting to destroy our way of life, and evil will pursue any disruption of life. And today the same pattern of techniques is being used in several of our national elections. As a teenager, I looked at Communism as corrupt as Nazi Germany. The Nazis wanted to control the world by taking God and freedom away from others to satisfy their indulgences of nontruth. It wasn't until I was stationed in South Korea did I see through both sides of the two opposite world regimes of Americans' sin and Communist propaganda. The deceptive propaganda continues today but with different titles.

My Army Days in Korea and Comparison

It was easy, I thought, to compare struggling South Korean people with their leaders taking advantage of their position by not having immediate accountability due to archaic technology available. It was impossible for all of the South Korean people to communicate their intentions in the 1960s mainly due to lack of communications systems and of a culture not conditioned to taking charge. But in America, communication is further ahead, yet our leaders don't communicate for one reason or another or to be truly transparent. Major examples of throwing out crumbs of information to the citizens of our nation are (1) Intentions of extreme relocating our lifeblood manufacturing to other countries while Americans had to accept welfare and/or lower wages erroneously to keep from drowning in the world markets. (2) And most hideous was the legal killing of the unborn. (3) The outrageous Obama Health Care conceived and developed secretly under the guise it will help the poor afford insurance. But the devil is in the details as doctors are discovering today. However, doctors are truly instructed to remain silent by their emerging corporate bosses concerning the health care law. Can you believe that? (4) And the idea to allow undocumented foreigners coming from a violent culture to enter this country without checking their credentials is atrocious, and worst, they are not being indoctrinated concerning our laws. The movement was rushed to razzle-dazzle us and not a word of caution from the investigative news media.

Similar to what Europeans experienced, our bad leaders wanted no interruption in the transition of even the undesirables into the country. Our leaders wanted them here as agreements with the existing world order organization to help balance world employment, maybe, and fill their pockets. In doing so, they were to replace the former USA higher wage breadwinner employees so as to compete economically with the rest of the world. It is sad, real sad, folks, that jobs that should give men good intentions and purpose in life but is now and systematically being destroyed and allowing more dangerous unemployment (Trump, when he became president, changed the onslaught attempting to keep order).

As a culture, we have to get away from the idea that throwing money around cures all. We should understand doing what is right is the thing to do. You may ask, what is the right thing to do? The right thing to do is for each individual to follow God's footsteps. One of the biggest mistakes is not providing meaningful jobs for men to help lead a family. Welfare and unemployment throw crumbs to people and continue to maintain *slavery* in modern times. If we continue doing this same half-hearted effort and not completely understanding this outcome, I have to wonder where our basic education system has gotten us? Something is wrong, and we're letting it continue, like doing the same thing over and over again that doesn't work. The ole saying for doing something bad over and over again is considered *madness*.

Korea Experience Once More

While I hiked through the small South Korean villages in the early 1960s, on my days off, I was disheartened to see the results of not enough food, especially kids wearing rags with protruding big bellies caused by hunger, illness, possibly by picking up snails or worms from the dirt roads and eating them raw. Also seeing their main mode of transferring what food they had was either pulling a cart with vegetables or using an ox to assist them. In the meantime, I discovered Korea was shipping out food to other nations while not fully taking care of their own first. It drove home to me that America, their guardians right now, may not be the land of the free and hope, even so, Korea was our responsibility. The war has been over for ten years, and we still have hungry people. They had no organized welfare system that I could see there in the countryside, nor did I see signs of them helping each other. It was a government, I compared, similar to the leaders of Russia, China, and Nazi Germany's totalitarian states. It was at that very moment, I could see bad for what it does, not just in aggressive nations but to see evil had a handle on all their lies, falsehoods, stealing, and power. I can no longer despise the various leaders and seemly bullies of being self-serving but possible instruments of discord if they refuse to walk in God's footsteps. Here is a truth: God appoints all leaders to serve Him.[a] And the leaders have it in them to be just.

International Rotary

Sometime after viewing the economic ills of the Korean people, I was asked to join the International Rotary to be a US Army representative in Seoul, the capital of South Korea, to help develop their economy. I first thought what I could do, and all I cared about was that maybe my observation input could help with the rotary group in Seoul. However, with the ability to look back and now see the people of South Korea with an improved economy and becoming a

---

[a] Romans 13:1–7.

major competitor in the world makes my heart soften as I followed God's footsteps being there. I trust good mixtures of people with good intentions and a drive to prosper and improving other lives around them. I can never ever forget the starving kids on the dirt roads. I had my chance to do something, and I followed what I think was good (but at the time, I did not have a clue I was following God's footsteps). Anyway sometimes a little bit goes a long way.

Second Corruption

The second worst corruption after the first removal of prayer was the breakup of marriages in America during the 1950s at a whopping 15 percent rate and would rise to 55 percent in the 1990s. From my perspective, even as a teenager, I could see a hurtful discord in families becoming worse. The lack of harmony, it seemed, was America becoming rich and preoccupied with themselves. I couldn't compare what was happening at that time, but I knew something was terribly wrong, for I viewed strangers and my friends coming out of those broken homes was hurtful, alarming, and unnecessary. The hurt and bitterness toward the world seemed to project from them into life in general. I wondered, later in the '60s and '70s, if the Vietnam protestors were the children of those bitter home divorces. And later in the 2000s, political leaders were acting similar to people of breakup marriages now in Washington, having less determination to hold onto American life and the constitution that helped and held us together. It seemed to me, it takes determination of commitments to adhere to a marriage and as well as with the US Constitution. When I look at divorced families, I don't judge the people for the unfortunate circumstances they have, but I can see from its effects on family, community, and a country that it isn't positive. Maybe we can get all leaders in the world to understand much stability comes from homegrown complete families that should be protected in all cultures. I see without a doubt abortion is the breakup of a family.

We Have Things

Families were working hard for material things, and we began losing each other in the process. Some of us understood the harm from marriage breakups but never realized the horror of it until the 1990s through 2020s. It is a historical fact, clear and a basic prosperity rule that a country is strong when the family is strong, and the fighting and tearing apart of one another promotes weakness and disunity within our whole population culture. The exception is when I visit the Amish farms to pick up chicken feed for our laying hens do I see successful solid normal families helping one another. I see major disunity days coming our way in America, and it doesn't appear it can stop without major disruptions. Don't think it is a strength of our nation when we see political leaders tearing each other up, thinking somehow it brings good diversity of ideas for us. It's not. Just look at your own life around you and see what bitterness causes broken relationships. Some of us think our way is the right way and often not giving a thought to, "What is the way God wants us to take?" We may say, "Oh, it's complicated." Not to me; modern man with modern pressures avoid the conversation. It's not modern; it's the same culture appearing that has been going on for thousands of years. It continues to prevent man from getting closer to our Maker and/or each other. And I see nothing new with what is happening to America, people, the same person causing their own destruction and not persevering in what is to be done to achieve self-peace.[a] I love reading Scripture because of the insights that can cause change of our natural selves and abilities to do great things helping others. And I ask myself, why can't everyone see what I see? However, it's no easy task, and I don't think it was meant to be easy, we must persevere to help change people's hearts, but until *God is ready to do so*, we continue working, and better yet, raise up our hands, asking for help.

---

[a]   Psalms 7:10–12.

Out of World War II

An example of a whole group of people doing great things was after WWII when America made its biggest strides as a nation. It was due to a large part of people understanding their surroundings and experiencing in their hearts the suffering around the world. But Americans too, at home, got to see and understand the problems overseas when movie house newsreels showed the aftermath of war-torn nations, especially Germany and Japan. The aftermath of people dying of hunger and disease as shown made us wonder and opened our hearts, even though a cruel and terrible war just ended. I remember watching a poorly dressed woman in rags somewhere in Germany, searching through garbage cans for a morsel of food. And later in the '60s in South Korea, I would be affected watching children eat snails off of the dirt roads. I truly remember as a preteenager the American churches were filled and the news media filled with hardship articles and photos of the world hunger and the suffering. As a nation, we truly wanted peace, and by the way, I just now wondered if my faith grew seeing and being with those people praying together asking God for peace?

News Media

Respect for one another went deep when I was a kid, and during WWII, the news media seemed responsible to write truth; but later, as we progressed, things changed, and the news media helped slant and divide the population. The news media seemed only interested in their type of political correctness, and many times, I could actually see them beginning to take political sides that slanted toward damaging American culture. They weren't interested in communicating truth but their own side and the news people seemed like puppets. As an example, the abortion issue clearly is wrong. It kills babies, causes hardships, and divides families, and not a word from the contemporary news media to do the right thing in lieu of a quick fix. The disconnect of avoiding telling the truth about abortion was a justification to remove undesirables from American communities. The Russians did it to their own people in the '50s and '60s and look what they got. And presently the Communist Party, like our political parties but one worse being worse than the other, have the same inner self condition as the news media has, and because they say it is okay or keep silent, that *doesn't make it okay*. Don't forget it only took 10 percent of the Russian Communists to gain control of their country, and they did it with their fake news media. They soon achieved their goal, and as fast as it occurred, it came to pass and their news media self-destructed in their own political deceit campaigns.

I have to tell you, we have similar stuff going on today. A simple understanding of hate, fear, and deception is the wedge the media put between the Democrats and Republicans and the people. It is no longer *truth or lies, good or evil*, it is *liberal or conservative*. So as an example, it could be a bad political thing to horde money by not sharing or a political thing to kill babies, and we may say, "It isn't me, they are the ones." People begin to feel less responsible knowing their leaders support immoral issues and fall deeper into false happiness of bliss. And that, my friend, is not an advantage of a position to be in. Just look at the German people staying silent, allowing Hitler to do his thing. Untruths just simply multiply untruths.

Good and Bad, Not Liberal or Conservative

How do I know I am right? I've researched Scripture for the last fifty years, compared advantage and disadvantage events for more than seventy-five years by looking around; and most of those insights have proven valuable but may not be as favorable for others wanting proof. I could stand on my head with proof and still not satisfy you or them. Simply put, love is good, and love is not bad, and killing is not love and is exactly what the world has been doing soon after it began. But there is a catch implanted in us, we have in us, to reject love and quite often take whatever is easier to benefit ourselves, and there lies the bump. So as another example, is it good or bad, liberal or conservative if a new mother doesn't care for her baby? Is it good or bad if a national leader attempts to destroy others? God loves us and, about four thousand years ago, arranged for a special people to show and help the world understand. He formed the Israelites and taught them good from evil. He gave them the Ten Commandments[a] to ensure they *would lead happy and prosperous lives*. They did indeed lead prosperous lives several times and even influenced the surrounding world, until they forgot who God was and failed miserably with each demise. Israel was the only great nation to fall and regain their standing in the world after asking God again and again and again. And as a sidenote here, Israel's enemies knew when Israel was without God and most certainly knew Israel was vulnerable as evil knows today of America. The Israelites continued, as we can see in Scripture, picking themselves up but to no avail, two thousand years ago, when the Father sent His only Son to help Israel pick themselves up.

Deceptions

Deceptions we see today coming from political parties, which I mentioned above, is deception because people can blame leaders, and we are not responsible. But we are responsible as a community, and it will affect us for sure. So if good and bad affects us, why would we want bad responsible leaders? We don't, but evil can be overpowering. Sort of like Nazi Germany proclaiming Jews were subhuman, and many people went along with it, creating actual laws permitting Jews to be hauled into gas chambers. Also how about those Islamist countries having laws to punish or destroy women and others that don't step up to their beliefs. Since when is it right to kill? So can you actually say live and let live? But then in the 1970s, America made a law to kill babies, and the news media was silent too. So now knowing what happened, what do we do about it? Allow our society to deteriorate or stop the madness of killing unborn babies? And how can we stop it? We certainly don't want an eye for an eye, instead we

---

[a] Deuteronomy 5, 6; Matthew 5.

should throw up our hands and ask our Father to help us rid this national and worldly affliction from around us.

When I am out on the sidewalk these days, in front of abortion centers, I do not hate the others calling out the F-bomb, finger bombs, or coughing near me, knowing full well about the coronavirus scare. I am sad that people have so much fear, malicious intent toward me or other medical greed that they have to allow the destruction of babies. I guess I truly understand a young woman's fear, especially when the father encourages her to have the abortion. Sadly it is documented that most women allow the termination of their baby because of their boyfriend not wanting the baby. What does that say about contemporary men? And I find women want to cling onto a good man and is already, in her young life, gravely disappointed.

So how shall I start in showing actual evil deception progressing? Could it be man saying, "Do as I say and not as I do?" Maybe. Just yesterday, it now seems, on April 11, 2017, a Trump news spokesman was upset about the Syrians gassing, injuring, and killing all ages of people, especially babies, and made a remark that Hitler wasn't as bad as the Syrians. Well, the outcry and another outbreak of negative criticism came spewing out of the news media that the spokesperson intentionally downplayed the Holocaust (political correctness or deception?). From there, the news was focused on the speaker, and the supposedly anti-Holocaust remark diluted the real problem of the Syrians killing innocents. Too bad but do you see the deception? Where did it come from all at once? We may find out when time of unbearableness comes. It is sort of the same thing facing us today with eliminating babies and attempting them to be downplayed. Too bad, the news media got it wrong, or did they get it wrong for the evil ones? We may be in a terrible state of affairs when evil sets the standard on political correctness, and worse yet from people supposedly in the know and should have higher morals that don't attempt to do the right thing.

My comment has always been that political correctness hides the truth. Now I don't care for Trump's personality, and most certainly, I don't care for Obama, for I think both of them and their parties have diluted thoughts of life—one party being worse than the other.

Obama's followers and Trump's followers continue without asking the simple question. Is it the US Constitution, justice, or is it against a political movement of the day? It'll keep getting worse. Both the Democrats and Republicans seem to resist trends in truth and seem to have more energy to call each other names. One party is worse than the other. What is scary and is difficult to stop is that they may be a reflection from our population? So if you scale up what these leaders do, you may see what is happening in the country as a whole and particularly within our families. We are being *moved* to be angry at certain parties and not trust their leaders. How can we trust them when we hate each other, sort of like Hitler propaganda against the Jews?

Unwittingly the news media is leading the charge in spewing hate to the populace, forcing people to take sides against each other in lieu of *good* and *bad*. That is bad and is not to be confused with expressing different positive ideas. So I ask myself what the definition of hate is, and I see it is the opposite of love, and love doesn't harm people; yet from a hateful act, almost sixty million babies have been harmed in America since 1973. And the news media is mum about that kind of death. That can't be love, unless of course you believe there is middle ground for murder. It's no wonder ISIS and other fundamentalist people of the world don't trust America, when we seemly are powerless to do basic justice in life ourselves. It's here, folks, and we are being conditioned to accept something other than truth and justice. There can be no middle ground when innocent lives are at stake, or we may assure ourselves a place in history similar to all the other fallen nations of the world. And I asked several years ago what is next, and it appears it's the new Obama Health Care system, or a better name is *selection*.

Okay, okay, I'll get off this abortion issue, but I sincerely want you to understand, the law that the Supreme Court passed could be an example of another beginning and of an end. It has to be alarming for you and me that a government can develop such physical and mental processes to include becoming a culture of death. But if you are so inclined to be passive, and if there are more passive people like you than us, then I guess the beat will continue getting louder.

It will for sure continue, and evil will become more brazen as shown throughout history, and the *beat may go on for how long?*

How Do We Fix Bad Feelings?

We can't fix bad feelings the conventional way, like being happy and pretend to be friends with one another. It'll just keep growing like it currently is because of being *nice*, politically correct with false intentions, and not for the *good*, loving others. A good example was all the billions of peace dollars—sorry, mistake—it was trillions we sent to various countries over the last few decades, only to find later it was corrupted. So we trusted highly educated politicians to do what they do best, and that was to spend our money. Was the money sent as a true gesture for peace or ill-conceived hush money? I think it was ill-conceived, like the ole saying goes, "money talks." Maybe because after all, if those same types of leaders can accept the self-destruction of part of their population, what makes them morally deep peace thinkers? Are they "bad to the bone," as another ole saying goes? As a nation, our only chance to understand and get out of our spiraling situation is to do something stronger. Or continue wasting time, making mistake after mistake in favor of secular expediency until we run out of money. We can for sure run out, you know! Maybe we can all turn the empty directional tide and begin on a different concept to love God first, and then a faraway second is money. You know loving God is the first commandment, and a close second is loving others.[a] None of us are justified nor is it healthy nor is it progressive to hate our neighbor, no matter who or what they are. Does that mean I have to like what is going on? No, we don't have to like what is going on. What we have to do is ask for guidance on how to handle the various situations before it consumes us, and we become the unfortunate ones.[b] Throwing dollars at a problem is counterproductive and isn't frugal.

---

[a] Luke 10:25–28.
[b] CCC 214.

Broken Marriages Hindering Us

Idols in our way—Our leaders seem to be paralyzed to even speak out against broken marriages or attempt to help make social changes, saying *no* to stop the deterioration of families, community, country, and the world. Centuries ago, the Catholic Church would not allow an English king to divorce his wife because he wanted to remarry his brother's wife, and when the church said no, the king formed his own church and got his own divorce and remarried his sister-in-law. It appears leaders are helpless and not informed, leading moral ways too. Or are they? God equipped them with the same heart as we have. And what did the good leaders of Israel do to bring their nation back to sensibility and to prosper again? They lead the way, asking for their nation to pray, and they prospered soon afterward. When they stopped praying is when they slowly deteriorated and later experienced terrible misfortunes. It appears obvious to me, "When you work for the best, things happen for the best" (Marjorie Lemke 1962). I think it is common sense what I just said about working, but unfortunately it may be rejected, and maybe the writing of this book is rejected. It doesn't matter, I have to write this book or my inners would burst.

The Catholic Church seems to avoid saying no out loud to divorce these days, and I think I know why. I wonder if attitudes of cannon law (Catholic law) was softened concerning divorce because of modern Catholics being bombarded by contemporary problems? Or worse yet, are they backing off a little and kicking the can down the road? The church knows America, along with the world, is on a truly decaying spiral, and they may be holding onto something, hoping eventually we will get back to values that help us and not destroy us. After all, the church knows it cannot judge and is primarily responsible to spread the Word to the world. And what I truly see the church doing now is loving more, especially the hurting brothers and sisters of these generations. You know similar to what Jesus said to Peter, "Here are the keys to the kingdom of Heaven, whatever you bind on earth shall be considered bound in heaven; whatever you lose on earth shall be considered loosed in heaven."[a]

When it was noted by Jesus that Moses gave dismissals for marriages, and it was because the people were not teachable. And I ask, what does that mean? It means they are not teachable. Remember, I take the Bible literally. However, God created male and female to be one, and nothing should separate that which God puts together as one.[b] Why the big fuss? Marriage goes deep and isn't to be taken lightly. Marriage builds nations, and our leaders can't do a thing about our epidemic of divorce, yet they are the ones that are supposed to be in the know. What a shame, they think they are politically correct but not having the power of truth to help moral situations.

Kids Going Wild

D-F Student

---

[a]   Matthew 16:18–20.
[b]   Matthew 19:1–12.

I looked into how second grade kids were doing in a low-class economy and the other in a higher-class school in 1999, I found many lower-class classrooms were disrupted by a couple of individual kids, and not much was permanently done to correct other adverse behaviors. They and the kids around them didn't get the full benefit of what our highly trained teaches are capable of teaching. The same teachers that went to at least sixteen years of education to get where they are at found that both the parents and their kids don't show respect for their surroundings. Many of the parents of these kids have uncontrollable problems of their own at home brought into the classroom. It's too bad, their own problems cause envy, resentment, and rebellious attitudes in themselves when they view others with good opportunities.

A good example of today that we can look at are the football millionaires taking a knee in front of the world, showing their disrespect to themselves and others. So it appears money doesn't make them happy, what a surprise. What can make them happy, I ask. Thinking at the same time, I wish I had their money but would money make me happy? Most of us realize that with money comes responsibility, and maybe, just maybe, those football millionaires don't understand their basic responsibility. As they seemed to accuse the rich people of basic irresponsibleness. They might look into a mirror someday and see they are the rich ones, and they may be acting like spoiled kids. And it may be that old saying I told you about earlier, "Do as I say and not as I do."

What about the European millionaire soccer players; they too are bending their knee in solidarity with the American football players, and when they were questioned later by news media and asked, in what way were they in solidarity with the American football players? They couldn't give an appropriate answer. They sounded unhappy; I say that because they complain, yet they have more material things compared to the average person. You'd think since they appear fortunate, they would be happy, but they don't seem to be. Do they want more riches? Would that make them happy? They have physical health, fame, and they are rich but cannot find the most important of all—and that is self-fulfilling ingredient from our Lord. It is there in themselves, but they can't find it. They might find it if they were determined to find it, as determined as when they go after a soccer goal.

Are We Gods? Book of Genesis

Recall what the serpent said to the woman in the garden when she looked at the fruit of tree of life and was being tempted. The serpent said to the woman, "No! You will not die! God knows in fact that on the day you eat it, your eyes will be opened and you will be *like gods*, knowing good and evil."[a] Now don't tell others that I said you'll be God, I said, "You'll be like gods," a big difference. Don't get me in trouble because as you know, I interpret the Bible literally at first. And the nonliteralist would love to get their hands on me. Ha ha, just kidding.

Possible TWOS

Also remember the story of the Tower of Babel in the book of Genesis when God made a single world language into a multitude of languages on earth?[b] Was that a story of that time only or could it be a sequel to another book? I think it was a story of the time and a possible present warning for man today. Seems far-fetched that we would have a second final world language again, but it appears that another one world language is just beginning to be another single world language today. Think about it, do you think a new world language is coming? Could a new world language be developing right under our noses? And if so, why does it seem to be building up and advancing without any notice or hesitation, probably like the early builders of Babel of the Old Testament; they didn't see it coming. I see computers having the characteristics to become a new world language. What will happen if they become a world language, or what

---

[a] Genesis 3:5.
[b] Genesis 11:5–9.

does it mean? I think it will bring human domination on earth as we can see examples of in Genesis. Human domination often became cruel in history, and you have to wonder why? In any case, it appears to me computers may be the final of *two* of one language, in its infancy.

Back up a little, do you think the people in Babel's time were evil? I think they are similar to people as today—proud depending on themselves and not depending on God. What do you think? I think they will pride themselves in this New World Order and will desire buildings to reach into heaven. Will they be stopped at a certain point from creating fantastic things with their own hands? Why did God stop the Babel Tower from being completed? Because man was becoming single-minded with a single language! And He further said there will be nothing too hard for man to do and purposely scattered them throughout the world. I suppose He stopped the construction as an example to us that they were becoming self-proclaimed people as today and not dependent on their Maker. God is a jealous God, and He won't have any other Gods before Him. Could there be another reason why He stopped the builders? He may have wanted us to see an example of how people can develop evil intentions by slowly depending on themselves, and He stopped it. Kind of reminds me of the end of the world story. That is all the Babel story may be about, men attempting to be gods. We should try to become like Jesus in love and fully understand we should depend on God first.

Review of Chapter 5

Leaders and Education

You'd think that good would be a natural priority for world *leaders* with all their knowledge, money, food stuffs at their fingertips, and material things they have compared to other populations. And as we have seen in the last chapter, we may have obtained stuff and given it away in vain. Barbara and I know it is true that when we give to our Lord to help others, we get back much more than what we've given. But that isn't the reason to give by getting back. The first time I noticed getting back more than we gave was when we had one hundred dollars in our bank account, and we gave it to God. It was given in desperation and having nothing left. Everything was hopeless, and it was at least a last-ditch effort to get God back into my life. I could not find Him, He vanished from me, it was a horrible experience, it was pure loneliness, it seemed I was floating in space and had nothing to grab onto and wondered if a drug could take this extreme empty feeling away. The hopeless feeling was a terrible loneliness that couldn't be brushed off, and it remained with me day and night for several weeks on end, until I hit an all-time low, with my hands up asking God for help. The next thing I knew, I attended an Oral Roberts Crusade rally in Dayton, Ohio, expecting a miracle. I went to the crusade without any hope, a last-ditch effort, and sat down, listened to Roberts, and understood I had to make a sacrifice to get back whatever was missing from my life, and I gave our last hundred dollars from our family savings to the Oral Roberts Crusade. Yes, our total savings—gone.

I drove back to Hamilton from Dayton, Ohio, on that Saturday afternoon, feeling a little better, but I had to tell Barbara I took the last one hundred dollars of our savings and gave it to God. When I told her, she didn't flinch; she trusted my decision, she accepted what I did, and she never brought up the subject again, and I was totally grateful she trusted me (it is the same ongoing theme of God expecting us to trust in Him. He expects us to trust Him with our hearts, and Barbara trusted me with her heart).

The weekend ended, and it was Monday morning, and while getting ready for work, there were no thoughts of what happened Saturday or what would happen today. I didn't do anything out of the ordinary at work. Monday was a normal day of drafting architectural buildings and details. However, just before quitting time, the owner, Cy Baxter, for the first time ever in the firm's history, passed out special bonus checks to all employees. He gave an envelope to me, and when I opened it, it was a check for $1,000. I realized that God just gave me back ten times the amount of what I had given a couple of days ago. I believed with all my whole being that He answered my prayers only because I went outside myself and made a sincere sacrifice in order to get Him back into my life. By the way, all the years that have passed to this day was full of God's gifts for the entire family. Does it mean that when the Spirit comes into my life, that we are free of committing sin? Not by a long shot; sin will always be around and must be avoided, something humans may continue to struggle with for the remainder of their lives. And what is *sin*? Sin is, I think, anything not from God, and there is plenty of that to go around.

Should the world and their leaders reach out to God in order to have spiritual direction? Yes, indeed if we are to live in peace, and besides Jesus taught that He was love and to live as He teaches. Besides leaders are placed there by God and intended for them to rule God's people following His footsteps. You ask, why in the heck don't leaders see the proper way to lead? The same reason you may or may not have found the Lord in your heart. Why then can't the world just be themselves and live in peace? The world finds it difficult, since Adam and Eve were thrown out of paradise, to change. It is in our human DNA side that keeps us from living in peace, as written history shows repeated theme of generations and, time after time, destroying one another; and I ask, is man capable of changing the evil spirit in him? The world is deluding itself if they think they can break the evil spirit that has plagued us since the beginning of time without God. We can break the evil spirit by accepting Jesus.[a]

No Other Way

Wanting and wishing is not the same as being capable of doing. I know from the bottom of my existence, man needs extra power offered by Jesus to give us the know-how to achieve self-peace. There is *no* other way but through Jesus to the Father. That reminds me of what I heard as a kid soon after the Second World War ended. Many people thought that the war was going to end all other wars. *"It was the war, to end all wars,"* they would say. That didn't happen, the world continued to have their wars, and of course, we got into the Korean War only six years after the war to end all wars. So much for human know-how. By the way, sin causes war, and if sin causes war, we can stop war inside ourselves first. Jesus has the power to stop war within us.

---

[a] John 6:44–51.

Chapter 5

Our Education and Leaders

Leadership

Man does not live on bread alone but on every word of God.[a] This discourse was lost somewhere between our founding fathers of America and today's educators. We were designed and built by God to adore Him and Him alone in order to be one with Him. Why don't we want to live on every word of God? What I just wrote sounds boring, right? When you experience adoring Him, you'll know what it means to adore Him. We may think it's impractical, after all, we work to get bread and don't need anyone else when we are self-sufficient. Besides we may have to jump out of our person in us into another that may not be familiar.

For instance, our leaders and educators have it in their heads that money talks, and all we have to do is spend it, and everything will be all right. Just leave it to them, they'll take care of spending money. Oh yeah, do you think they've been doing the right thing in the last several decades? I don't think so. It doesn't appear they've jumped out of that person they were; they are still at the university of higher learning, and they continue going on and on, doing what the *man say do*. Like what we say the definition of a mad person is, "doing the same mistake over and over again." And the leader who says do it, do you think he jumped out of himself? I don't because Congress continues kicking the can down the road, relentlessly

---

[a] Matthew 4:4.

spending money that doesn't help the direct effort we need. As an example, what happened to the *trillions* of dollars Obama took out of America's savings? No one knows, and I asked politicians right after it was announced, and they didn't have a clue. Are they representing the people?

Our Aid

> The aid offered by the United States to developing countries has been purely technically and materially based, and not only left God out of the picture, but has driven many men we tried to help away from God. And this aid, proudly claiming to "know better," is itself what first turned the "third world" into what we mean today by that term. It has thrust aside indigenous religious, ethical, and social structures and filled the resulting vacuum with its technocratic mindset. The idea was that we could turn stones into bread;[a] instead, our aid has only given stones in place of bread; the issue is the primacy of God. The issue is acknowledging that He is reality, that He is the reality without which nothing else can be good. History cannot be detached from God and then run smoothly on purely material lines. If a man's heart is not good, then nothing else can turn out good, either. And the goodness of the human heart can ultimately come from the One who is good, whom is God. (Pope Benedict XVI)

I think Pope Benedict summed up one of America's current condition in his above quote. Why do I say that? As you know, I keep repeating—hoping—you should understand the gravity of all

---

[a] *Jesus of Nazareth*, 33; Deuteronomy 8:3–4.

that is around us. I've read and reread Scripture and observed world events when reading since the early 1950s, and one major theme persisted in the Old Testament that we can see over and over again. We see the rising and falling of the Israel's people many times. I searched for comparable nations to compare with Israel, and what I found was all the nations that were once considered superpowers, that indeed declined because of corruption within them, never became a superpower again. Only when Israel asked the Lord for forgiveness did they come back to being a great nation and even a superpower again.[a] Never ever has any other nation in history come back again into its former status, except Israel.

Rich America

What is alarming is that America is rich and seems to be going through a dark phase, similar to what Israel often went through at the top of their game. However, Israel—and only Israel—kept rising and falling throughout their history, beginning when they came into the Promise Land, about 1240 BC until Christ came. The cause of their ups and downs was corruption as with the other powers, but more importantly, a turning away from God caused their own suffering. You see, I found when we search for God, we want to do better. God made us to do good or, better yet, to love Him. When the stymied Israelites reached that superpower mode, they slowly abandoned the God of Israel, similar to the way America is abandoning God in this present day. In 2013, antichrist government and Pentagon officials announced that "Religious proselytization is not permitted within the Military." Note: I saw similar things coming months before I was discharged out of the army in 1966 (proclaiming Jesus is what God wants of us). "Court martials will be decided on a case-by-case basis, the government says."

So back to above. Soon after Israel stopped proclaiming and relying on the Lord, they began another fall and suffering. How

---

[a] Second Chronicles 15:1–7.

could they not realize their elusive predicament? We don't see it either. They would suffer and realize their suffering and begin the cycle over again by calling on God to help them. Hence the ups and downs throughout Israel's history is a historical event. However terrible Israel suffered, it was forgotten until the next time they fell. You'd think America, and at least the world, would learn from Israel's mistakes, but *no*, we seem to be abandoning God for our own selves. What is our own self? I can say it's complicated, but that would be a copout. We are abandoning God for extreme pride, sexual desires, careers, riches, abortion, anger, drugs, material gain, self-induced power, trusting man first and thinking to ourselves we know exactly what to do with our lives, and we don't need God watching or directing us with His footsteps.

What do we do about the law for the military not to convert nonbelievers? We obey the law, as Christ wants peace and not rebels. However, so much of a copout that it sounds like He wants us to pray and rely on Him. So it is out of our hands and into God's hands, and He will judge the merits of the action of the law and make it fit into His plan (that is the crux of informing you, it's in His hands, and this is why I write these things). All we do is admit we are weak and rely on Him. He'll take care of all things as long as we continue to pray, asking for Him to intercede. As Barbara as my witness, every time we threw up our hands in desperation and asked God for help, we got it. However, more times lately, we just ask in evening prayer, and it is granted. Hopefully, I can remember and tell you every incident. If the Spirit wills it, I'll be able to describe it to you.

Sin and evil, especially the Eastern Coast (the whole world) of the Mediterranean area, four thousand to six thousand years ago, was rampant throughout the ancient world, just like today around the world; and America is no exception, except Americans had a relationship with God and were able to thwart themselves from being drawn into national corruption. Please understand, this is where I understand Israel's Old Testament enemies as being the evilest people of the world, and God instructed Israel to physically eliminate the evil, which Israel never accomplished completely because of their diluting of faith and later paid the price when the evil wasn't eliminated. All they had to do was ask God as a nation, and angels would go ahead of them and physically destroy the evil; and when they did ask, it was accomplished. You'd think they would get it and continue asking. Nope, Israel was full of pride and didn't ask. Now I hope you aren't angry because of the evil ancient people dying. Check for yourself, they were a bad bunch, most compared and found to being child molesters. They were at par with Nazi Germany in atrocities, even to each other and their own children, and they were completely void of God in their lives. But more importantly, the history behind all of Israel is intended for you and me. And I think of the Old Testament as physical warfare eliminating sin and the New Testament as spiritual warfare eliminating sin. And what is sin? I know for sure sin causes war in ourselves and others.

As we should know now, Israel's faith wasn't solid and secure in their communities to ask for God's help. Instead they looked at their own physical might and not the might that would come from our Lord. However, now we have the New Testament, and we still have evil enemies as evil as Israel had; but instead of physically eliminating evil, God had something lasting in mind. He sent Jesus to teach a new strength to Israel who had those inner qualities, but like today, many of Israel's leaders failed to recognize Jesus, and it was only in Jesus's name they could *perfect* His commandments' qualities. He taught the most powerful weapon for us to use against our real enemies, and that was prayer, forgiveness of sins, and He left us the Holy Spirit to help us achieve what was in us to achieve. Why should we go to war as a nation when we, as a nation, can prevent war by praying? *What*, why, oh why, and how can praying for our enemies be productive, especially forgiving them? The enemy would certainly come into our communities and wipe us out. A good example was back in Israel's heyday, their enemies knew Israel, without God, was easy to destroy. Today prayer, more than any other force, will achieve seemly impossible tasks. I know, impossible outcomes have happened to Barbara and me, time and time and time again. Amen. But for some, I can make one hundred backflips, and it won't leave an impression. So I ask, why do I get up early each morning writing this book? We hear God's Word better early in the morning, and it is simply because God expects us to relate His Word when we hear it. Besides my insides would explode if I held back communicating what was inside of me.

Will He Be There for Us?

We see from Israel's history that God and only God can save people that ask Him, and He saves us, and a whole nation can be saved when asked. Folks, from what I've seen, by the way Jesus taught us, it is with the utmost importance that we come to understanding and pray to elect good leaders. Hopefully the leaders we have will help organize, inspire, and lead our country and this world into safety. After all, it is God who appoints the leaders of countries. I hope my saying He appoints leaders is not too much for you to grasp. He will be there for us if we only put effort into it ourselves. Maybe this will help; all of us are given additional wisdom when we ask, and an understanding from wisdom that God elects leaders is very basic to understand. Leaders have the same chance as we do to understand what it is that He wants. An example, if God controls every hair from falling out of our head—and He does—He can certainly ensure leaders are placed over a nation that may be a challenge to be sure. If we have what we think of as a tyrant, as the North Korean leader is thought of today, and we live in constant fear, all we are doing is hurting ourselves.

Note: for all of us, it's a *sin to live in fear*. We aren't supposed to fear anything, but if we have to fear, then fear God. So what are we to do with tyrants? We pray for them to receive wisdom and graces and not for us to rebel in violence. Isn't that something? You'd think reading and hearing those ancient Bible stories that it would be okay to kill tyrants. Yep, it was okay back then, ridding sin from the world, but what our Lord wants of us now, since his First Coming, are spiritual life lessons to help us enter the kingdom of God. We learn that the Messiah of Israel, Jesus, the Son of God, teaches us a new and *stronger* lesson, and that is to love. Remember my definition of love is simply to do good and not bad, and most of all, God is love.

An example: When I was in the army, I found it easy to think I could kill the enemy. But now understanding what God wants and doing now what He teaches is more difficult to achieve than my primitive ole self of physically striking back could ever achieve. So you may ask, what about all of the military that have killed the enemy, will they go to heaven? If you depend on God, I truly think everything is possible. After all, do you think you are good enough to go to heaven right now?[a] I don't think a person should think they are good enough, it's God's decision; and I think, we should pray constantly and hope that we'll be there someday too. And by the way, I have a slight thought that just about everyone will go to heaven. Why do I say that? Jesus said that the Father has given Him all mankind, and He doesn't want to lose any of them. So maybe that is what I'm a part of, attempting to not lose any person to Jesus. And also, maybe that is what is expected of you.

Inspired Leader

How can any good leader inspire? He can inspire by communicating good uplifting truth rather than what may be the politically correct view of the day. You know, God put that inspiration into all leaders, but few may achieve, while on earth, what it is that God wants for the good of His children. The world absolutely needs good brave leadership to lead us in positive moral directions. He must have compassion in order to get to the combination to unlock his follower's hearts and be determined to keep it. Our leader and his followers desperately need good insight into what was implanted in each of us since the beginning of time.

King Solomon hit it on the nail when he was a young king of Israel and realized how *delicate and diverse* the people subject to him were and realized himself how he needed something more in him to rule Israel. Solomon severely lacked an understanding how to rule

---

[a] Luke 18:24–27 (so it shows us, God isn't a candy God).

and wanted to find the answer.[a] Solomon knew from simple knowledge that God had put special knowledge in the hearts of men, and he had to find what it was that God wanted him to do to rule or inspire God's people.

Like today, we are all God's people, and there are no leaders to be found to inspire us like King David and King Solomon did a thousand years before Christ. And it's a shame we're wasting our time quibbling about things that aren't closely related to that which is in us. The Catholics in America are falling into its grip too. The church's leaders are highly educated, yet they are failing in the last few decades to bring more believers into the church. Why? I ask, and I find that Catholic leaders may be overeducated. It seems when the rubber hits the road, they project they are all about a finance balance sheet, especially relying on the wealthy in lieu of going to the real richness of the church, and that is the Gospels, poor in Spirit, if we haven't lost them yet. And after all bishops, what is worth more than silver and gold? You know it's wisdom, and who has wisdom, the rich and educated? Not likely, from what I can see, and it isn't most of you or our political leaders that fully understand the depths of the faithful people that built the church in America. You'd be successful by now if you had more wisdom yourselves. The answer is that the lowly of our parishes have been thought of as unfortunates and not taken seriously in their circumstances nor given the responsibility they should carry. No, the naive people of the church and our nation figure they should be cuddled and treated like infants. They—the poor—are the ones with understanding, and we're not tapping into them. Why, maybe because they don't have education. But there is hope, I'm glad, as we see suggested in Vatican II Council.

Catholic Education?

I remember being issued Catholic teacher confirmation manuals in the 1970s, written by nuns, and the impression given of the

---

[a]   First Kings 3:9–15.

manuals was that we are all children of God, and we don't necessarily have to teach our Catholic values. And by the way, one of those values was the Ten Commandments. It got worse as I read into them and decided they didn't know the *Gospels* nor the *Catholic Catechism* nor *Vatican II* and their justifications, I thought, was blowing secular smoke. They claimed to be experts about how theology works but didn't show an appreciation for the church leaders. My impression was maybe they were full of themselves, thinking they know better. I wondered, who the heck initiates and approves such books, and I found that there were four major movements going on in the 1960s decade (see note below).

One was the media began spewing out all kinds of dissension and fake information. The second was college professors and students began spewing out anger and insinuating love statements to us or what they thought was love. They were disguised as the new elites of thoughts. The third were the new politicians emerging full of anger during that period, and now looking back from the 2018 time, it was noticeable. The fourth was a mini-Catholic mid-leadership crisis thinking they knew better, or they revolted, disguised themselves as saviors of the Church as I indicated above in Catholic manuals.

I understood what was going on with America and Catholics of the '60s, when I looked back to the '60s and saw the many attempts of their unknowingly disorder, especially the Catholic University of America[a] rebel educators being cultivated by anger in lieu of understanding and fixing a crises problem. The attempts to fix their problems were from emotions, political correctness, and not from a clear vision of the Gospel or Vatican II (latest church council) as proclaimed by the people of the day wanting to destroy a good system that only needed tender care to change. The 1960s Catholic extremist jumped onto the secular tidal wave as did the Vietnam protestors, National University Affiliations with what appeared as emotional anger as their motivation. Even some young and older priests began repeating the same rhetoric that was heard in the national news media (keep in mind, my observations, since the decade from the 1940s, it clearly

---

[a] See references at the end of the book, especially *The Coup at Catholic University*.

indicated the national news media and what they were doing and continue doing today is disunity of Christianity). And again, why?

Quaker Town

Barbara, I, and our three children were at a Catholic Sunday Mass in a predominantly Quaker town in Wilmington, Ohio, nearing the last few months of my army career. During those last tour of duty days, in the mid-1960s, a young Catholic priest began the homily at the Sunday Mass and immediately began spewing out offensive remarks about the Vietnam War and how immoral it was and people being involved with it were immoral too. I remember, at that instance, standing up in the pew, while both of us looked at each other, while he stood at the pulpit with his fierce descending spirit, and I turned my back on him and walked out of the church.

The next week, he was back again at the pulpit, and he looked at me as if talking to the congregation and said, "I won't apologize for my remarks last week, but if the shoe fits, wear it." However, he didn't say another dissenting word about America's war and stuck with the Gospel homily as he was ordained for. I thought he judged and twisted the Vietnam War subject about the people being involved with it were immoral too. However, he missed a great opportunity when he failed to explain what the church teaches about all wars. If he paraphrased the church's teaching, I think he would have gotten to the root causes at that Mass concerning all wars, and I think he would have given the people there a true reason to contemplate on what causes war. All he had to do was explain that sin causes war, and how do we prevent wars? But I have a different twist on how sin causes war now. I believe sin causes war, and by us not being forgiven of our own sins, we cause internal and external wars within us that spreads.[a]

---

[a]   Psalms 106:13, 14, 21, 25, 43, 44; Proverbs 28:13.

First Education Classroom, 1952

Could comparing expose a trend? It was 1952, and I was a new student in Patchogue, New York, in a class of forty-five Catholic kids. The classroom had drab-color walls, examples of writing skills and some math illustrations shown also. You could hear a pin drop while the teacher taught the entire day. The kids were sitting up straight and not falling asleep from lack of a good breakfast or something like that. As I looked around the room, I noticed a sign on a machine in the corner that looked like today's paint department mixers. The machine had a slight modification in that it had a leather strap attached and a sign that read "Spanking Machine." I wondered each time I came into that classroom if it was used often. To my knowledge, it was never used, but it remained forever a reminder.

A-B Maker

A Second Classroom Years Later

I was in another class room in 1999 with twenty kids, and there were no spanking machines but flowers painted on the nice calm-color walls with types of games to be used as an award system for the kids that received coupons when they behaved themselves. However, inside the room, it was loud and disruptive, caused by a few boys walking around and disrupting other children. They didn't seem to know where they were and continued playing and not learning the lessons for the day. Matter of fact, I was a rotary volunteer instructor as an assistant to the teacher and wasn't able to complete the rotary lesson prior to the end of class. What a shame, the teachers are paid much more than the nuns got paid in the 1950s Catholic schools when I was a student. Are the kids better off today or yesterday?

Liberated Doctor

So I ask you, how did we get from the organized classroom in the '50s to disruptive classes in the '90s? Well, I enjoy looking at small-scaled examples as possible larger trends. As I thought back to the early '50s when a very popular Dr. Benjamin Spock wrote a best-seller book, selling *over forty million copies*, and wrote weekly columns in newspapers, advocating many various messages that parents should not spank or reprimand their children and show more affection to their children. His writings will later be responsible for changing parenting in America. After his death, his own children admitted it never happened in their family as their father wrote it. So is that another do as I say and not as I do? Their father never showed affection. Later Spock recognized the inconsistencies between writing his book and his own life were insurmountable gaps. He was thought of as a big conversational figure in a new era of American homelife, and little did his readers know he was not quite right. I wonder since deterioration of America appears to have begun in the '60s, and I further wonder if his influence wasn't a major cause in home breakups too. When I think about it, he was some sort of a pied piper, don't you think? He reminds me of another pied piper—but not as bad— that attempted to change the world, and his name was Karl Marx, highly educated and one of the founders of Communism.

Marx was born in Germany and left due to the anti-Semitism in those days. He lived in England with his wife and seven children while he developed concepts of Communism. He was away one winter, promoting Communism, when part of his family starved to death in a cold London apartment. The one old saying I always remember, "A man's first responsibility is to his family." So Marx desired to save the world but couldn't save his own family. Sorry for him, his family, and the world; if you can't do little things right, how can you do big things right? But I have to admit, the majority of capitalist in those days were self-serving and left many people in their wake of profits destitute, and Mark recognized it and attempted to do something. But as a lot of great leaders attempting to change the world, I found no evidence he asked for God's help.

So we have two different kinds of extreme entities. One kind of entity taking everything and leaving a wake of helplessly poor but creating work for some, and the other advocating killing capitalists, using armies to make change. And again, we see from the past into modern times the same ole thing—the world struggles to find truths. Truth is in our hearts and not in our brain, and when we find truth, we find God. Am I a sort of pied piper? Yes, I am, but not for myself but for the world to discover what is planted in our hearts. And above all, my struggle to find and communicate truth does not hurt others but strengthens and reinforces them. Truth may hurt at a certain time but heals over time.

As a teenager (twelve) in the '50s, I didn't think Spock was correct in many of his news articles, even though my father was extremely harsh, and Spock seemed more into passivism. I understood there should be a middle ground from extremism, and I view both my father and Spock not focusing correctly. But a great deal of Americans was influenced by how to raise kids the Spock way, and you began to hear rumblings, back in those days, that the old true way of disciplining children works, and Spock's method doesn't but maybe for a few. The rumblings came near the beginning of the undisciplined affectionate kid walking and appearing in parks, shopping centers, and malls. It was real, I saw the beginnings in the '60s through the '90s when several children kicked their mothers and absolutely no correcting of the child was made. Not a word from their mothers. There is something to be said about correcting children when they are unruly, and something deeper and not good if the correction isn't done. So how bad is bad? When bad actions without correction consumes a family, whole nation, or worse, the world it is not healthy. And above all, how bad can it get when people don't consider kicking other people worth reprisals?

Year 1968: Liberated Leaders Not Listening?

An example is the day in 1968 when we voted in the primary polls in Ohio. The vote against abortion with 80–90 percent of other people that voted in that election across the country and voted *no* to abortion. Well, that should have settled that, having a large majority at the polls, even a primary poll shut the abortion issue down. It did for a while. However, our vote, as we will see later in January 1973, didn't mean diddly.

January 21, 1973: War Ends

What do we do about this deception that penetrated our nation? I remember coming home from work in November 1973, sitting down on my favorite chair and reading the front page of the newspaper. It illustrated in large letters, "Vietnam Armistices," or something like that. I was glad for America that we finally had peace, but because we didn't own a television at the time, I naturally read every bit of the newspaper and became stunned to my bones when I was near the back of the paper, and I began reading a small three to four-line article that read, "Law approving Abortion by the United States Supreme Court is passed." I had to read it again and again, thinking it had to be a sadist joke. No, it was no joke; it was true, and I felt, for the first time, in my life that I *was violated*. I had to do something to ease this pain in me, and I went outside and took the flag off its post and would never again fly it until the beginning of Desert Storm when Michael, my youngest, insisted we fly it. But, removing the flag in 1973 didn't satisfy my inner self, and I would continue suffering abandonment and contempt angry moments for years to come concerning our government's betrayal.

What am I to do with this basic intrusion on the US Constitution? I thought it was in the back of the newspaper and how many people read a paper. This bad law is just now being born and will surely grow and slip unnoticed into American society as it is hidden in the back of the paper. This stroke of evil is an insight of political cancer that kills not only bodies but kills America's soul.[a] The American soul I thought could only be killed by going against the grain of what America should be about (life, liberty, and the pursuit of happiness). The first of my reactions was to move my family to Austria and get away from this disease. Barbara was beside herself when I wrote Austria for permission to relocate there. The government turned my request down, and I had to do something—anything—to get this sinking feeling away.

However, as I found out later, that wasn't what God wanted me to do. The second choice was to become a lawmaker, activist, complainer, slanderer, and/or mock the proponents of abortion, to include our congress for not bringing this issue to the forefront as was their duty to do. The third and many years later was to submit myself to our Lord, putting up my hands, knowing full well I can't do a thing myself to stop this madness. The problem I discovered that made me seek God was that most Americans were rich and walking the fence and not in any mood to get outside their comfort zone. Our family, however, was still on the lower economic scale, struggling financially. However, in the 2000s, Americans will begin to see the horrors of what the abortion industry was doing to baby body parts, family breakups, and what appeared to be obscured was the downsizing of the father's authority. The slow downsizing of the missing black father is not a phenomenon but a modern example to see and view the damage evil is causing, and now the same pains are there for the white father. Is it a conspiracy? Yep, it began that

---

[a] We are warned to be careful with people who kill the body but more when they can kill both body and soul.

way when the court elected to make their ruling on the day of the Vietnam armistices take the headlines and intentionally hiding it.

Note: If the government brings home the family bacon and not the father, then who is it that the family naturally looks up to? This alone is enough to discourage any father from exercising his responsibilities. Can you say for certain that this is one of the root causes why the black fathers disappear?

Inspiration Again

Again why can't we elect good leaders to inspire America? Maybe it begins in the attitudes of the classrooms mentioned in the two classrooms above. After all, in our society, what is the main purpose of school children? No other than to learn and prepare them for future adult independence. What caused such a drastic change of values to be discarded and disruption allowed in the classroom, preventing them from becoming independent? Could it be a lack of society understanding the concepts of tough love, or understanding what breeds laziness and attitudes that take away prosperity? So here we are and unable to fix simple basic problems due to our method of leadership understandings.

Yet poorer countries are achieving higher education levels, helping their children to do better and prosper while many of America's kids are not being prepared properly for their own independence. Is the situation today with leaders and teachers that they would rather see the kid fail than to step up and do the right thing? Many disruptive black kids have been thrown under the bus because of political correctness thinking (ignoring the main issues). Will America be inspired again to do the right thing? Inspiration comes from within us, not from others, and is difficult to obtain if it is deep inside and especially if we are unhappy. For your information, the comment tough love above was used years ago as a positive successful booster for the success of many people today.

More About 1963 Korea, a Poor Nation

When I arrived on a troop ship in Incheon, Korea, in 1963, the surrounding area was at low tide and a mess. The low tide stunk, and it was cold to the bone that day in October. Poorly dressed people in rags were all around us, kids were eating snails off the dirt road, and disorder and dirt was everywhere. It was evident being highly educated wasn't in their vocabulary. It was the kids I noticed first after getting off the troop ship; they were in groups saying something and giving us the sign of a finger, but instead of using their finger, they used their leg as the Koreans do. The kids would lift up their leg in our direction and, with both hands, clap their knees. We were in the rear of large open trucks being transferred to a processing area when a couple of Korean kids were lifting their legs up at us and yelling something that sounded like *wonzinggy*, which was translated by a veteran black soldier next to me as meaning "monkey," and the kids were saying *wonzinggy* toward the black soldiers in the truck. The black soldier next to me was on his second tour in South Korea, and he knew some of the negative words that the kids were calling him. I discovered months later that all cultures feared or disdained people darker than their own skin. So there we were, watching and listening to the poorest kids in the world calling the richest black people in the world names. What does that mean, I asked myself; where do they get off calling someone names, did it make them feel better? I don't know, I was twenty-one and still trying to figure out things, but that observation on the dirt road will stick with me for over fifty-some years to figure out.

Back to the kids with tattered colorless clothing and the shoes they were wearing. The shoes were called *edewa* shoes and were made from some type of thin rubber that could not possibly keep them warm out in the cold and snow. The kids came running out of their huts with steam rolling off their backs, and their heads appeared like frozen ghosts. We were certainly frozen riding in the back of a troop truck and were wearing heavy insulated winter coats and thick leather boots, attempting to keep warm. However, I didn't notice the cold until later. I was too absorbed in all the strange scenes coming from all around me and wondered how things could have gotten this bad for a culture of people. I knew that poor existed in the world, but this, this was surreal, and there were hundreds of them and only twenty-six days away from America by troop ship.

The Korean culture was simple, poor, and uneducated. They've been the blunt of invasions from both China and Japan for centuries. And for the most part, to assist foreign invaders, they were kept as rice farmers in the hills and cabbage growers in the lowlands. Their factories, what little they had, were scattered about the countryside and were small and primitive except in the two largest cities, Seoul and Pusan. Both cities had light industrial complexes that helped with some economic balance. The average Korean family were primitive farmers and usually brought their farm produce into market places with oxen pulling a cart, or they pulled a cart themselves to the markets. The average person in 1963 did not own an automobile, and walking was their main mode of transportation. Their average annual income was around $26, and if they didn't produce a good harvest that year, the whole family could starve to death. The other primitive wonder was their method of fertilizing their fields.

The local farmers fertilized their rice fields using their own excretion stored in village cesspools over the winter. When the season of fertilization arrives, they would dip buckets into the cesspools and carry two of the buckets, with a stick balanced on their backs, up to the mountainside to a flooded rice paddy. The excretion is then poured into a selected paddy pool dug out from the mountainside that appeared to be at least eighteen inches deep to contain a certain level of rain water. The rain water helped spread and dilute the human waste and was available as the main source to grow rice in the hot summers. So the farmers would simply go to their home cesspool, fill two buckets of their waste into open jars the GI soldier called honey buckets, and carried it across their backs, up to the dugout mountain, and empty them into the rice paddy until each paddy received enough buckets in order to achieve a good harvest.

Honey Bucket

I didn't feel I was better than these people after learning of their various methods of survival. I felt they did not have the same process chances as we have in America and wondered, if they did have those chances, what type of country Korea would be like. It took about thirty years from the '60s to find what chances the South Koreans would have and how they would capitalize on their good fortune and pass America in some industries. The good fortune was similar to what General Macarthur and American leaders did after World War II to help the Japanese get on their feet. The Japanese, like the Koreans, using their energy and self-determination, soon passed America in many industrial endeavors. So between the Marshall Plan in Europe and the initiatives in Japan, I'd say Americans coming back from a terrible war were able to forgive both Germany and Japan, and America did not cut their noses off to spite their faces as European nations did to Germany soon after World War I. England and France insisted and made Germany pay and pay, more and more, until nothing was left of ragged Germany but a madman named Hitler and became set on wanting to revive and take revenge for Germany (can you see the self-made conspiracy of godless decisions from other nations?). We should look at good or bad situations using the root cause method. I'll give the root cause method later.

Missile Site in South Korea

While stationed on a surface-to-air missile site in the early '60s just south of the demilitarized zone (DMZ), I had fortunately been given an invitation to be a volunteer to become part of South Korea's future. I became a volunteer to represent the US military working with the International Rotary Organization that met with South Korean businessmen in Seoul. Most of the rotary executives were Americans attempting to help war-torn South Korea to advance themselves in industrialization. They met often, and at one of the meetings, I remembered vividly when a rotary member asked the Korean leaders in English, "What does Korea want to do?" he asked.

A Korean leader stood up, beaming with smiles, and, in broken English, said, "We want to build cars." I instantly loved them. These people were the world's poorest, and a few were educated, but most were farmers; and I wondered how they could transform their surroundings, but never did I feel anything but admiration for them and their goal and saying what they said. I admired the Koreans for their audacity, having nothing to lose and all to gain, and I still think of them to this day. The big difference of Korea compared to America was their hope, and America was beginning to show fear and no longer can do.

I left South Korea in 1964, and my army enlistment was up in 1966. I began working as a civilian as a maintenance/construction engineer and, by the mid-1990s, as maintenance, safety, environmental, and construction manager in Grand Rapids, Michigan, and again as a volunteer in Grand Rapids to help teach Rotary International concepts, but this time, to American school children in the area. What I found one day, while studying for a class in the Grand Rapids school system, was the most fantastic news I have ever read. There in the middle of the rotary lesson plan was a caption that said, "South Korea builds their first car."

I was elated just from the headline and continued reading the article several times over. The article explained how South Korea was rated in the 1960s as one of the poorest and the most uneducated nations in the world, and they picked themselves up and are beginning to become a prosperous nation, and they raised their education level from the lowest to one of the highest in the world. And they did it in thirty years. Incredible and good stuff from leaders of both countries. Why was I there? I look back at all of my other past experiences, and I could see God was there all the time. I know God knows the past, present, and future. He knows everything, and how do I know the future? I just wait for the next day to see what the future was. So for some reason, God allowed me to be in Korea to listen to those words of the Korean leader and know the future in the 1990s. I love it mainly because I know God is looking over my shoulder as I type. I asked Him for help, and I wonder how many people will read these inner thoughts that we all have of Him.

Frugal

What Korean leaders did, as I thought back to the mid-1960s, was to begin raising their standard of education up to world standards, and they did it without wasting and pouring money beyond their means into the system. Their frugal working attitude, dedication, and resourcefulness were tremendous prosperity boosters and beyond any other nation in the world at the time. Korea was a model of bringing their education level equal up to an advanced-nation status and later surpassed American average school test levels in certain areas. You know, I ask myself what made Korea surpass American world-class education levels, as poor as they were. Basically they compared and were influenced by America and its wealth, military might, culture, and last but not least, they had access to *Sears Roebuck* catalogs. You know, the catalogs with one thousand color pages of everything in the world to buy. Even their modern rock country western bands portrayed themselves as cowboys, with clothing from Sears and sung western songs in both their language and attempted to have accents like American cowboys. However, they did not throw money at education like the American government did because they just didn't have money to throw away at a problem. Besides they were frugal and looked over across the Pacific at us and saw money being used recklessly in education and not working as America intended. I observed throwing money at the same education failure time after time when I came back from Korea as a waste of money. They understood, watching America throwing all that money at education and not getting results was madness. But later after coming back from Korea, our local Catholic grade school was failing, and we managed to keep it from going bankrupt, made proper changes, and all without throwing large amounts of money at it, as the story goes below.

Wouldn't you say our definition of madness is when you keep doing the same thing over again and again, and it doesn't work? We are *mad*, folks, we haven't learned from mistakes or from what a close friend, and someday it is gonna bite us. The Koreans have worked hard and looked outside the box, hoping to achieve their own higher education standard for their people. This is exactly why I'm writing this story—to let you know about inspired Korean education, industry, and their leaders in hopes we can make adjustments too.

Adjustments in Attitude

Sad as I think of it, but what I heard getting up close and personal from people who support more money for education is their higher educated thoughts from books and why pouring money into the system hasn't worked because of what they *whispered* to me. It is the blacks that are holding us back from achieving higher average education standards. I detested those whispers and excuses of those types of people who said it. And later, I interviewed more highly educated white folks, and across the board, they whispered the same philosophy to me. What a shame; they know the problem, but they are too politically correct to do something about it. I have nothing but contempt for people not seeking the truth and attempting to make their surroundings better. Our education leaders stopped advancing in ingenuity, folks, right in their tracks, when they could have made a difference; they reminded me of dead people walking around. But no, they are politically correct, allowing their fear to overcome themselves and continued throwing the Yankee dollar[a] at the school system, in lieu of getting to the root cause. I know the root cause, and they can find it, if only they would pray and search their hearts.

However, it got worse later, and the educated leaders became secretive and developed yet another system called CORE. Many teachers and parents across the country agree CORE is a bad process. Are these the same type of people that shoved CORE into our laps similar to the same way the health care system was shoved into our laps? But think, why do they have to shove it into our laps? *Because* America isn't their common goal, they think only of their political party and not America as being the focal point. Do you think the Koreans thought of Korea above all? Yes, yes, yes. So we have hands-on teachers not convinced, how much time and money will be wasted again? Will, they convince politicians to be frugal? I know, like other patriots, how to solve the problem, and I know the world would scoff at my credentials, so I guess we'll see CORE go down as other initiatives in the past and throw it in another waste heap.

What Is Holding Up Education?

The people in the know depend on themselves and their education to figure it out, and all they substantially come up with—the blacks are the bad guys. Well, fine, if it is the blacks, then what do we do about it? Some of us know it isn't the blacks, although many blacks do fit into their categories that come from welfare living. It is our culture of pessimistic attitudes and weak families holding back, allowing the invisible man to do it. Money isn't the answer but to have self-conviction is, and the black community must be involved to figure out how they can prosper without being completely dependent on the distant federal government and instead depend on their fam-

---

[a]   In the late 1950s, a song about the glorified American dollar was popular.

ilies. However, will the people in power allow a bunch of inner-city folks to help dictate? By the way, the federal government should be set up to do what we want, not the government making us do what they want. The government should guide and help and not get in the way. Sort of like those Korean businessmen and their dreams. Their government helped their citizens to achieve the dreams from 1963.

I like listening to other constructive opinions just to get a quick heads-up of something that may be brewing now and in the near future, and what I discovered was the highly educated, especially teachers and the news media, in this country are close contemporaries, and they feed off of one another with their own news, sort of like the Grammy Awards. And when real things happen in the world, other than how they perceived the world, they are hindered from communicating the truth. Their news would invariably be taken as gospel and go straight to the newspaper mills to be printed as the real thing. And it often appears as fake. Is that what happens when we lose relationships with the people and for the people?

So the common people with gut feelings, common hands-on sense, and those of you that paid attention to what was actually taking place all these years have seen different scenarios than what was reported in the news media. Example, why isn't the money that is being given to failing school systems not being reported on detail sheets? And why isn't the media indicating who is responsible for the unacceptable results? To this day, many school administrators, like their political leaders, think if they don't get more government money into the broken system, they will be doomed. They are doomed anyway, following the same ole failing unaccountability process is madness.

I think living through examples of being poor in American standards, Barbara and I raising eight kids and learning of what makes kids do well in school and sports without much money, is an eye-opener that we have to tell you the story. However poor we were, all the kids went to college and five got degrees. As a family, we just didn't have spare money in the house to throw around. In fact, I stopped smoking and drinking beer in order to maintain a balanced diet for the kids. And what did I do to satisfy my alcohol craving? I learned to make wine. Anyway Barbara sent a strong message to our family that good basic food helped balance our physical and mental awareness, and attitudes and good morals will keep our spirit level high too. The children were also motivated by certain family disciplines that helped them develop themselves. The disciplines stimulated their thinking and self-awareness. Oh, by the way, I just remembered one of the disciplines that we had was not purchasing a television set in those days. We simply could not spare the money for one, and we resented the quality time it took from our children. We looked back later and could see what a great benefit it was not having a TV. Because of not having a TV, we had to entertain one another, and we felt the kids' biggest purpose in children's life other than knowing God was family life and their abilities to do good in school. We achieved it all without money flowing from our pockets. Much like the Koreans doing it without money, with sheer faith in the right way to do things and similar to what we all did concerning our failing Catholic grade school in Hamilton, Ohio.

Private School with Little Money, 1970s

Here it is, folks, a modern-day school being saved. This is a brief example of a school with little cash flow, large classes, and good high scholastics standards that survived. As mentioned above, when I was out of the service, our school was in bad economic shape. It is Saint Ann Elementary Catholic School in Hamilton, Ohio. Saint Ann School was a grade school that had all eight grades years ago, but slowly it began cutting back from the first to second grades and from the eighth grade to the fifth grade in 1973, and finally the pastor wanted to fully close the remaining classes and the front doors to help keep the church from becoming bankrupted too.

There was no way we, on the board of education, would allow the school to close, and we began thinking of concepts to keep the school from deteriorating further and to create opportunities to rebuild its infrastructure. A time later, we had a strong inkling we could remake the school resurge back to first through eighth grades and to include a kindergarten. The concept would be tuition-free and opened to the public with modified religious training for non-Catholics. I bet you are thinking I'm high smoking something right now? I'm not, but in the '70s, we had a group that was high on the Holy Spirit (the third person of God).

Anyway to give you a quick peek, a year after we had begun the effort to save the school, Saint Ann had a first to eighth grade tuition-free school and was running in the black. All the initiated praying and extra work paid off, not only preventing financial ruin, but the school became better, more advanced in academic and sport activities. Please don't think I haven't a clue and don't know how to advance our national schools because I do, and it came from using a little practical experience like benchmarking, praying, determination, and outside-the-box thinking and initiatives. But most of all, the spark the South Korean business leader gave me. I wasn't particularly trained to tackle the problem, I did not have a bachelor's degree, and I certainly ruffled feathers on the way to helping to solve the Saint Ann problem; but there was something stirring—that God would help get us out of this mess.

It's pathetic to think that as a nation, we've allowed certain school systems to fail, and we did it with highly paid social and educational experts within our system, and they couldn't correct their inner predicament. Maybe, just maybe, the attitudes of passing the buck was an enabling condition, and personal responsibility didn't take hold of the situation. Instead their findings and understandings went through a winding system of red tape into the federal government chambers and diluted. Well, in that case, we can blame the government process, right? Not entirely, but maybe, just maybe, the whole problem we're facing today is with a government too big to fail and lack of Americans accepting their *birthright* responsibilities. I have contempt for educated people and their colleagues not being able to do the job they were trained for. It's like more wasted money being thrown away. And I certainly don't want the government to fail, but it should purge itself like other entities do and be in accordance with the US Constitution. The red tape strangles *and doesn't allow breathing.*

To make another point, I'll give you some of the parent experience and occupations that were on the Saint Ann Board of Education when the school was stopped from going bankrupt. There were housewives, nurses, factory managers, manufacturing finance officer, office personnel, and a young first-year teacher that had the authority to make changes too. You know, I look back in years past and notice my failure to plan adequately was because I did not include prayer. So how do we ensure we don't waste our time at Saint Ann School and plan something that may not be part of God's plan?[a] All I can say, we should truly keep asking God for guidance, and it will materialize. Keep knocking, and since we can't see the future and shouldn't waste our time on it, we certainly see the past with clues as to what may happen when people ask God.

Compare Teacher Pay

The *Kalamazoo Gazette* newspaper from May 14, 2017, published the Michigan 2015–2016 average teacher salary, indicating their salary continues to drop and gives the impression you should think that the children would suffer because of it. I think that is further from truth and the reality of what the news articles are insinuating. First I want to say any college degree difficult to achieve should have good pay ranges, but it doesn't work like that with teacher compensation in various areas of the country. It's location, location, location that dictates their reward to be paid, and when teachers move to higher paying districts, their salaries increase. But why should a teacher be forced to move from familiar surroundings to a place unknown? Unless we go to an all-out unreal socialist government that control such behavior, we may all become low paid as shown presently in socialist nations. So what's the alternative? We can look further behind the lines of the articles and see that the Michigan teachers were getting paid far better than the rest of the world, and our education system continues to be flawed in lower economic communities. But it doesn't *end* there.

---

[a] Proverbs 16:9.

Tough Love

Some American cities are paying big bucks recruiting teachers to come into their low-income areas to teach kids that are not so willing to learn. Most of those highly paid teachers depend on themselves only and still may not be effective for what they're being paid to do. The cultural environmental differences of understanding make it too difficult to overcome for the well-meaning teacher, unless that teacher goes deeper into their heart and finds empathy and not a bleeding-heart type of feelings. So here we are, sending the best teachers to the ghettos for years, and they are only making a scratch. I suggest we come together as a country and ask God to help the social scientist up there to make necessary changes to help in lieu of them kicking yet another can down the road. And what social changes would allow the teachers and students significant advancements in education? The teachers want to do what they can do best, and that is to create classes of highly educated students by helping them learn. They don't want disruptions each day in their classrooms, and somehow, we have to learn as a country to eliminate disruptions. And most of all the teachers nor the students want to feel bad about coming to school. Lastly trained government officials should guide rather than dictate.

How do we do it? We start with a long range, basic, easy conceptual plan involving parents from every town and city wanting good things for their children. The contacts can be made at town hall meeting places or, better, in parent homes. But most of all, like the Korean experience, the people on the front line should be made responsible with some guidance.

No longer should we think the trauma, abuse, drugs, and disruption in family life should be allowed to become limitations of our students. Leaders and teachers should be empathetic, that is to understand your surroundings but not using it as an excuse to not teach; thinking that unfortunate children have an excuse to act the way they do is another way of giving up (an excuse). After all, just look at the millions of poor kids coming out of the 1940s and understand neither teachers nor the students understood their cultural life was an excuse to hold them back. Too many people in the past have gotten past excuses and made something more of themselves. You know Anne Sullivan didn't hold back when attempting to help Helen Keller, right? The most recent is a whole country of South Koreans. The moral of this story is, figure out how not to be a baby for others and learn to practice Tough Love.

There are many valuable tools to use to motivate kids and teachers. Absolutely not wanting to be at class and feeling sorry for each other is not the answer. How do we use our talents to understand the root cause of various situations? First and foremost, be sincere in communicating that kids are important and *listen to what they think is important* and learn from it and be inventive. We should continue asking our Lord for understanding, even after we received that fantastic four years or so degree.[a] Tough love, structure, and positive reinforcement may be what we need in all classrooms. Remember the story of the South Korean people and how a whole nation worse than any ghetto in America became a world leader. And by the way, the Koreans were enslaved by conquering armies as China and Japan held them in slavery. So slavery is not an excuse! Are there any other excuses? Yes, there are. We aren't allowed to go further as individuals because of the stringent red tape caused by highly educated government officials. I know, I've seen it grow in the army, and their procedures were not negotiable. You stayed where you were told and planted and had no imagination room to improve a situation. We are under the same restraints of self-hopefulness of using our sacred imagination.

Love and Structure

I'm bringing this serious problem to light and not complaining but stating a fact of failure. If we complain and do nothing to help correct the problem, then we become part of the problem. I can envision determined black men fixing the problems by finding solutions to improve their community, economic, and education situation by

[a] CCC 158.

figuring it out. Why do I point out black men? Because it takes men and women to progress, and the black community has been too long overdue without equal black men representations. A root cause of the black community failure to become prosperous is a lack of good active black men, and I ask *why*? I know why; many are in jail, and we will all have to change, and I think when it does, all America will prosper. Meanwhile we don't give up or let up, this is for the championship. We ask God to help us ASAP. Amen.

Hold on, the March 12, 2017, *Kalamazoo Gazette* just came, and I was struck immediately by a news article paper that proclaimed the city is backing a coalition to aid recently released jailed prisoners. The plan is to help prevent Kalamazoo residents who got out of prison for breaking the law receive assistance to keep them from going back into jail. The coalition plans to reduce by 50 percent the number of people who return to prison. God will almost certainly bless those people for attempting to do what they hope to do best and more if it is done for Him. I hope it works, and it is not another throwaway scheme to help us rid the reservations we have developed of many other initiatives. The black community can't go on like this forever without adverse effects on themselves and our national community.

Just look across the Atlantic at the money we threw away to undeveloped countries and the countries that used it properly and appreciated it. We sent billions and billions of foreign aid to the Far East, and it wasn't appreciated for what it was intended for, and we should ask why. Why are we giving hard-earned cash away and doing that which turns people off? Much of it got into the hands of greedy leaders and did not help the common folks as intended. After all, I think everything that is good is a gift, and America should respect and be frugal and honest with money and not just throw it around wastefully, as we do with education, stolen Social Security savings, and the welfare systems.

Note: Praying and dreaming developed insights on how to approach and correct the serious situation we were in at Saint Ann grade school above. If you think that Saint Ann school prospered because they were determined and their selected families helped make it that way, *you are correct*, and I hope Saint Ann School becomes a benchmark for inspiration purposes. I hope too that the above Kalamazoo coalition is successful and becomes a benchmark for others.

It Was Fierce Determination

The Korean people in the 1960s was not prepared as advanced nations of the world were to live a higher standard of life. However, their determination, common sense, hidden intelligence, and giving their countrymen responsibilities helped them to dare to emulate others. Do you know what else directly helped influenced the developing Koreans? You'll get a kick out of the following.

I discovered one day that a well-used tattered American book motivated many Korean village people. While walking through the hilly villages of various parts of South Korea, hunting with a bow and arrow, I found Koreans had very old used *Sears Roebuck* giftbooks in many of the villages. The kids were especially excited showing me the pages with guns and weapons in them. It was amazing looking at their eyes and them smiling, realizing that these boys loved the guns and weapons as I did. By the way, the adult Koreans loved the bow and arrow that I was carrying for hunting, and they loved touching it. I found out later that the bow was part of the national heritage of Korea, and soon after the conquest of the Japanese, it was lost.

I was amazed as they looked through the wrinkled pages of the giftbook, and from my perspective, I could see how intent everyone was as they allowed me to turn the pages. I didn't see Korean people at that time, I saw brothers and sisters. I continued to turn the pages to see more and watched, at the same time, how intense and softly they mimicked the swimsuit model pages. Ha ha, everyone was laughing and giggling, and slowly the villagers seemed to identify with the photos, and possibly were thinking they could become and have those same nice things of their own. I know as a kid, I dreamt and thought so too. They did become those people they imagined by working hard toward a better life to include and not limited to a major national initiative to improve the education level in South

Korea. Similarly it'll take similar determination of Americans today to advance their communities to achieve a better self-sufficient life and not rely on total government assistance as we currently do today.

Wasted Our Manufacturing

Talk about recent nonfrugal money matters, just turn the pages of history back a decade or two and see how we gave away too much of our working sweat (manufacturing), but someone filled their pockets from the deals in the 1990s. We gave away actual factory machine procedures that were written by engineers for their companies here at home, but instead the procedures were sent overseas for another country to benefit and use in operating their newly acquired machines. I was there in Kalamazoo, working as a safety and environmental manager in a manufacturing aircraft factory in the late 1990s, as I watched the factory give our secret aircraft information to unknown Asian countries. The documents clearly showed how to make the special aerospace parts and were classified confidential. It appeared to me at that time, we were being fed a bunch of bull and okayed by our government and local Kalamazoo business leaders. I don't have to tell you, big pockets were made full from those deals, and maybe they should have been, but what followed was empty pockets and mass job losses for American workers. I assumed everyone was on the bandwagon to include government leaders who sent much of the manufacturing equipment in those days to China. Well, what followed decades later was massive welfare handouts due to job losses and noted TV excuses from Obama blaming American workers not having the "gumption to get something going again" is why we were failing economically (A saying in the old days was to take responsibilities for your action). He said it was because "America has always created necessary jobs and what was wrong was that America didn't have the initiatives to do it."

The difficulties starting up new businesses was horrendous, if not impossible, because of how the current political party changed the tax code, and made it nearly impossible to start a business. So why was he blowing smoke up America's butt? They are irresponsible elected officials blaming others for their failures. It's no wonder things are getting out of hand in 2020 (in my studies as army installation intelligence, it was noted that Communists got additional worldly power through blaming others for their mistakes). You saw it, folks, right before your eyes a decade ago, and you could have done something, but could we have communicated the infraction properly? This will be mentioned again in chapter 8's time line.

You know, it was the backbone of Americans that built this country, and they don't deserve to be slaves today to a certain political system. But the burning question is, what caused this to happen? Look even further and see how inner-city poor were given more welfare in lieu of jobs. But the downside of welfare is that when people don't work, they are more inclined to get themselves into mischief.[a] The cities are becoming dependent on social political parties for their handouts, but worse, the politicians help make people less independent and slaves to the new process without any strong movements out there to get them off of welfare or employment. They will be happier and more content if they belonged to the workforce. But then again, the big money pockets sent thousands of jobs to China in lieu of striking a balance at home but instead sent our lifeblood abroad (research the dates and coordinate who was in charge of those initiatives. It won't make changes but you making determined outcries will). There is no excuse for weakening and exposing a whole country to bad times anytime in history. So instead of having bad deal after bad deal, we need to pray, beginning now, to help our leaders make good decisions. I'm serious, folks, that is the reason I wrote about comparing Israel's greatness and lowest so many times. I wanted, more than anything, for you to see history is repeating itself in America, and we'll be responsible if we lose touch with God and lose our land.

It's no wonder we see more discontent, killings, and rioting, making the average American look in dismay. Many of them think how lucky the poor are with at least a welfare system and not having to work, yet the people receiving the welfare don't appreciate their

---

[a] Tobit 4:14.

gift. Of course not. People who appreciate their surroundings work for it to come about. But it goes beyond that; Americans see expensive cell phones being used by the poor individuals and ask themselves, how can they be poor and afford cell phones? Yeah, how did they get the money to spend on cell phones?

Politicians might even think throwing money into a welfare state system will keep things calm; however, we see from current media articles and captions that a welfare state cannot guarantee calm when people don't work but may cause further disruption. However, now a new kind of leader looks beyond sending free machines overseas, which promotes foreigners to take jobs away from the present American unemployed and welfare citizens. It begins to help people come across our borders to fill American jobs. What is wrong with this picture? For one thing, the welfare person should work and not sit around collecting money. It is only for their good. America, we will have our heads handed to us if we cannot find good moral solutions for both American and foreign labor.

We hear "We need more people to do farm labor." Yet our government behind the scenes in the 2010s imported illegal laborers. That is true, and we have people—millions of people—not working, and nothing is being done to get them into a job. But our leaders have a separate agenda bringing people into America to do work and vote them in another term. Sounds a little like throwing money at the education problem, but now it's throwing money at welfare and our congress doesn't seem to get it or know how not to throw money at it. They are kicking the can down the road by not solving problems that will cause future extreme national hardships. But worse, half of American voters seem to have no heart in electing strong moral-driven politicians. Careful, no-heart people, we always get what we ask for.

Talk about the people across the border. We should continue helping our neighbors, even allowing them to come here if necessary, but it shouldn't be at the expense of the unfortunate. We got ourselves into a mess and can't seem to get out of it, but to enslave our own people, little by little, is not the future. To get out of this mess, I hear it is complicated. Why, oh why did we allow ourselves to become complicated? I know why; I followed the money trail, and it went along corruption paths, and naturally, unwittingly, it became complicated as a snare does to a trapped animal.

Work WPA Work

The poor, like the Koreans of the 1960s, want to feel good about themselves, their work, and their accomplishments, and we aren't helping them to become self-sufficient in order to feel good about themselves; we continue enslaving them, pushing them under the bus, and handing out welfare allotments like it was candy. They are currently getting madder and madder, and most of the time, they don't know the real reason. Figure it out, leaders of America, we had thousands of men during the 1930s working in various parts of America to get a piece of the pie during the Great Depression. But what is happening today that our factories and work is shut down and being sent overseas, leaving the lower and middle class in a heck of a situation? Is it a form of slavery to depend solely on a master government, wouldn't you say?

The middle class began losing their homes, going deeper into debt, attempting to send their children to college, and not getting out of a financial hole. You know, look around, and you can see a trend for the last thirty or so years, no matter what good the middle class did for the last three decades, the badness in this country will ensure that opportunities will be taken from them. I could see the beginning of that evil happening when I was in military service in the 1960s, looking out into the civilian world I wanted to be in. I was alarmed at how smooth a corrupt system, dedicated to their own material gain, would work simultaneously without knowing one another and without an organized forced human conspiracy. It was a simple process of greedy people not too motivated by morals but concerned only for themselves. Some conspiracy, huh? But wait, that was one of many trend observations I made that continues today. I recognized that a movement was taking place but wasn't able to prove it until it came to pass in our recent history. But wait again, are you beginning to think I am angry or bitter? No, I'm a tough love guy and want you aware so we can ask God together. I somehow think that through these writings, we will somehow counter the storm that is appearing. See the time line in chapter 8 (you can tell the future by the past).

Speaking Truth

Note: You can tell when a prophet speaks and if he speaks the truth or not of God. So as years have suggested, that if that person said something from God and it doesn't come true, he is considered a false prophet; and if it comes true, he is a real prophet speaking the truth. In the 1960s, I suspected that not too long in the future, the average American having large families were going to find themselves in a below-average predicament because of the zero population trend sponsored by background zero population social science government organizations. I knew they were organized because they were attempting to make the military in 1966 stop giving free medical benefits for more than the third child being born of military dependents.

I saw my dollars shrink as our family grew, even though I managed to get good promotions and raises. We managed to stay ahead of the ever-pressing financial curve situation. And as a constant reminder, I heard from neighbors and family ask the same question, "How will you ever be able to send your kids to college?" My take on those remarks was that they were the ones scared as hell but wouldn't admit it. I took those comments to heart and began praying and figured out how to get all my kids through college. I was blessed in having all eight of my children have the opportunity to go to college if they so desired, and it was without acquiring financial debt. I'm telling you, I am nothing without God, He was always there for me, even when I didn't deserve it; and the kids found ways of getting their own education, all eight of them.

I've got to watch myself on this one because I gained contempt for zero population, and now global warming is so much like the others with the same MO as I track them with root cause systems. Have you had enough? I told you abortion was just the first big disruption, and can you see it now? The second is relocating factories overseas, and if you look closely, the third is Obamacare. I think of it as deceptive leadership. For the removal of unwanted babies, it's abortion; and for the removal of unwanted adults, it's the beginning of the care programs. You don't believe me? Follow the money trail. As you investigate, you'll see what types of persons spawned the movements. Above all, don't allow yourself to go into anger but ask God to help us. Now back up to the beginning of this paragraph—are there prophets today? Yep, we are all prophets when speaking God's Word. The Word is inside us already, some more than others; not like the prophets of Israel's time when God spoke directly to them. The Word began coming to all men when Jesus left the Holy Spirit in the world just prior to Him going back to the Father. It was given to us in order to help in the salvation of mankind.

And in case you are wondering, I'm not in great anger anymore. I turn it over to the Father and no longer have bad feelings toward self-guided people. I shake my head and wonder, what will it take to rid evil from our nation? It is us, together with our Lord.

Divorce Information, 1950

Again I was about sixteen in the late 1950s when I read an article in the *Phoenix Gazette* about the divorce rate in America being at about 15 percent, and it was projected that divorce would rise in years to come. They cited factors like people wanted to be free, happier, less children, and more independent. What did I make of that? I thought about it and felt having less children did not make people happy. How did I know the news wasn't truthful? I was already looking around at my age and observed large and small families, and the smaller families weren't any happier than the larger families.

My grandmother, whom I stayed with on many occasions, had thirteen children, and in New York, there were plenty of small families around to observe. There were interesting observations that I enjoyed doing, unwittingly viewing social behaviors. You may think that I'm only opinionated, and you may be correct. I did develop visual and listening senses early at a pretty good clip as a youngster.

I remembered watching for family incidents in my life that became painful as my father would almost certainly beat the crap out of both me and my mother. My defense at an early age was to watch and listen for abnormal behaviors from him which I think gave me a jump-start in other life situations to help prevent pain. I forgave my father later but didn't forget his craziness, and you are now getting a look at those youngsters in a dysfunctional family. After all, I can give you my observations backed up with written history and facts, and it may not amount to a hill of beans in convincing you of mountains of problems heading our way and how we can solve them.

It is coming, folks; it is a matter of time. I truly observe things coming our way by comparing similar happenings and abilities to scale it up from family problems to present-day happenings. Some incidents happened during some phases of nations in the past. The proof, I know, will be if we don't ask God to help us, we'll know my warnings were true. For sure if we fall. So you can get a glimpse of the future by looking at the past of the world, especially Israel's history. And from the past, we can see how to help prevent miseries. And if you can see what is coming, you will also understand some solutions too.

Another recent thought is that America is at another crossroad, and it concerns the next leaders that are elected. You have now seen and can compare two very different and less-than perfect presidents in the last couple of decades who may set the stage for the next president. So if the next one is your person, let us hope that person is good and not bad. Either way, God elects the leaders and that may be the person you voted for. For you to be sure, the next person, their past will be a testament from God to you as to a direction we are going to go. Having a not-so-good leader doesn't necessarily mean we're domed; it means we need to depend on our Lord to change things for the better.

Divorce Judging, 1960

I have to stop for a few seconds to explain something about judging others. I hope you don't judge me when I write the following, and I certainly don't judge you if you feel offended. I almost took the following "Divorce Information, 1960" out of this book to help forget about it forever but couldn't. I have to say what is deep inside of me; I think it is truth and can help our nation and the world. Because of the love I share for my country, it is you whom I want to share it with. And I observed certain episodes since the '50s that I have to inform you about as evidence in hopes of helping to save my nation. Now for starters, the following information is by no means unforgivable, it is another indication of our weakness but a major weakness for the good of a nation and is exploited today.

New Zealand

Now let's fast track back to the late 1960s when I obtained a copied excerpt from a New Zealand newspaper about a study made with two thousand New Zealand married couples. One thousand couples agreed to use contraceptives, and the other one thousand agreed not to use contraceptives. The couples that used contraceptives had a divorce rate of 55 percent, and the couples that did not use contraceptives had a 15 percent divorce rate. What did I make of that? Well, it's kind of proved my thoughts, right from about ten years earlier, that less children don't necessary make marriages happier.

But there was something else happening here about procreation, and it seemed like there was a conspiracy to cover up informing Americans about what could happen to our marriages. It wasn't a conspiracy as we know of people purposely banning together to push their agenda, it was plain ole evil that was showing up again. It was not mentioned in the news media. We began to see again, it was a weakness of selfish thoughts that didn't need any organization to direct it, another quick and easy direction. But the most sinister thing that is going on today in America, following the footsteps of divorce, is that 75 percent of parents are single parents. I see a direct correlation of loss of fathers to what I see is happening with the phenomenon of disrupted classrooms as mentioned above in CORE under education.

Do Broken Homes Hurt?

It is a rejection of children, and years later, it seemed similar to the same evil that got the supreme court to allow abortion and the same that pushed to help get prayer out of schools. However, about 1960, I was getting back into the Catholic Church, and the issue of using contraceptives was a sin and forbidden. Many people asked if the church was behind the times and old-fashioned. I wondered and I decided to wait this one out and see what the future brings. What I found was that the church was 100 percent correct in calling contraceptives a sin. However, did they yell out, write warnings, and screamed at Catholics not to use contraception? I know during this time of my spiritual life, I wanted to shout caution to everyone about using contraceptives. More importantly, the seemly inaction from the church was the correct response to a growing number of people already submitting themselves to birth control. The church knows, from Vatican II held during the 1960s, that it is not for the church to judge and knowing, almost every sin is forgivable makes the church stronger. However, there is a danger on ourselves when we do not follow what the church has to offer.

One evening, as Barbara and I went to a meeting in the 1970s concerning the use of contraceptives, the people at that parish meeting got a pleasant surprise. I remember a group of Marianist Brothers were heading the meeting agenda, and the first announcement out of their mouths was that it was okay to use contraceptives. After all, they said God only wanted large families from the Israelites to help on the farm. You could hear a pin drop, and my friend next to me felt me jerk in reaction to that statement, just prior to standing up without any recognition. I said, *"Nothing could be further from the truth that God only wanted the Jews to procreate in order to help on the farm. God wants us to simply multiply and be fruitful."* And in my best ex-military voice, I asked, "Do you know what that means?" They were stopped in their tracks, attempting to make excuses, and it got worse for them when most of the assembly applauded what I had to say. *Where did that come from?* I asked myself. Was it in me wanting truth and justice, especially from the Marianist Brothers who should know better? But then again, we had many people on the side of social change in lieu of the truth in the '60s. In 2016, I found why I think the Marianist had those ideas and spoke the way they did without church authority. Those beautiful men didn't want their audience to suffer, but I hope they found out later what Vatican II was attempting to communicate. So millions suffered due to loss of their marriages, and they had one or two children. So I ask, what does that mean?

As above in 2016, I read a book called *The Coup* at Catholic University and could see what was happening to Catholics rebelling from Scripture and church authority. Catholics in America were facing daily secular understanding in lieu of the church's wisdom. However, there still remained in many Catholic institutions the Vatican II findings about the possible harm of contraceptives.

I understood better what Pope Benedict XVI wrote about in *Jesus of Nazareth* concerning modern theologians. They were watering down their writings and the faith by recopying other theologians from the past in lieu of going back to the original foundation of the church and contemplating the Bible for their initial thoughts. So, my Protestant and Jewish friends, especially Protestant friends, we can see how the church messed up Scripture understanding for the last few centuries, except now of course, I think there is a glimpse they're getting back on track. Amen.

The question remains, why do I support the church's stand on not using contraceptives? Answer: Not using contraceptives can make us stronger. Ask yourself, why do the majority of people use contraceptives? Go ahead, ask. Go deeper. Hint, Barbara and I used an approved church rhythm method to help us have our eight children and to space them out in what we felt was a managed way to grow our family.

There are blessings in Scripture, especially the Beatitudes that tell us of gifts from God for certain people. As an example, the first was for the poor in spirit, the gentle, the mourning, thirsting for what is right, the merciful, and pure of heart, peacemakers, and the persecuted.

How in the world can we get to be like the Beatitudes' expressions? Answer: difficult, if not impossible, but possible when asking God.

My take on above is that the sooner we find God, the better, and the people above may have found our Lord sooner because they found what God planted inside of them. And to find it isn't easy, however, a rich man, an adulteress, or crook, etc. may not have ready strength to find it. The poor find it quicker because of being helplessly stuck, and the only thing left in their life is God. They prayed, they got closer, and they were transformed and became strong individuals. Hence blessed are the poor. The same strength and values that makes a nation of people great. So as a modern example, do you think the world would be better off right now if people seeing the suffering that came out of WWII stopped and did nothing to help develop Europe and/or Japan out of their despair and allowed them to suffer? I don't think so. Those Americans living through the war most certainly suffered and became lovers. And love wants to do good, not harm.

But the dark side came when newer generations didn't experience that suffering. Citizens had begun to become rich, and they didn't need God and found other areas of joy that weakened them. What contraception does is takes away another need to find God. By the way, Catholic families were the lowest major religion to go past the 15 percent divorce rate until contraception began its destructive effects on families, beginning sometime in the '70s. Please, whatever you may think of me writing about divorce, I beg you not to harbor in you that I judge divorced individuals. I'm the last of many that can judge, or I may be judged myself, and that would be an awful situation for me. I want you to know the harm that may come to us.

Faith or What?

Remember back before Barbara and I got married that she insisted we marry in the Catholic Church, and I later spoke to God concerning her comment? I didn't kneel or go into church to pray, all that occurred was to be alone, by myself, and have a one-way conservation with God; while relenting with both arms up, I communicated to God, "Okay, if you want me to marry in the Catholic Church, then you have to help with the kids that we may have." Plus all the rules and regulations that Catholics seem to have. Now I ask you, was that faith or wishing? It was faith, folks, of knowing where the buck stops, and if I was to put a grade on it, I would say it is the same kind of faith I have now but now stronger and refined. I always knew in a matter-of-fact way that God was among us, but what I didn't know was how to love Him. And by the way, when our family needed something and Barbara and I prayed, it was given to us.

After listening to some good faith-filled people and various comments from them concerning faith and understanding Scripture, the more I came to realize we are given faith to start our lives, and the rest within us remains to grow. And if that is where we think we should go, then we must be determined to begin asking God to grow in faith, or what we presently have, we may lose.

So as mentioned in the Bible, if we have the faith of a mustard seed, we could say to the tree, "Be uprooted and planted in the sea,"[a] and it would obey. Huh, sounds like I'm going out of my mind paraphrasing seemly impossible feats humans can do, doesn't it? Well, yes, in a way, I am out of my mind, but let me explain more. Some of the comments I hear from suffering people that have loved ones with illness is that they ask God to heal them, but in the next breath, they say, "But if it be your will, let it be." They are right in saying that, but an important smidge of additional faith is missing that could cure their loved one. They certainly aren't at fault nor are they saying something not true. They just haven't gotten further with their faith that could actually have the person cured.

As an example, go into the book of Luke[b] and find where a leper appeared to Jesus, and he said, "If you want to, you can cure me." And Jesus responded by saying, **"Of course I want to."** What in the world did Jesus just say here? I've read that passage for the last forty-five years, and I thought maybe it was just a causal figure of speech, just saying something to fill in His sentence. However, as I am now convinced, every single word read in the Gospels shouldn't be taken lightly. Those words are meant for us to get closer to our

---

[a]   Luke 17:6.
[b]   Luke 5:12–14.

eternity of salvation. Every single word from Jesus's mouth is the Word of God, as I discovered again and again; but this time, it hit home when Jesus said, **"Of course I want to."** What He means, of course, is that God wants us whole and wants to confer prosperity and happiness among us. Do we have the tools to find happiness? Yes, we do, we received it through Jesus.

We depend on ourselves entirely too much at times as shown in Israel's history and the beginnings of Christianity in the Gospels. And I know this has shown in my own life. At times, in the Gospels when Jesus was teaching His apostles and curing hundreds of people in view of an assembly of witnesses, there were yet a few who would not believe what was happening in front of their very eyes, so much that some had animosity to kill Him after miracles were performed.

So what do I think of those men wanting to kill Jesus? Their crime, their hearts were closed and hardened and could not be opened until God allowed His Spirit to go into them. They were rejecting something right in front of their eyes and refused to believe. They thought, I guess, they knew better than the multitude of Jewish common folks witnessing and shouting with joy, "The Savior of the world has come." Or maybe worse yet, their comfort zone was not to change for the better but to stay with trusting their old self. Jesus and His followers showed the whole world and continues showing the world how we can achieve happiness when we allow God to live in us.

Here is one beginning of proof for you to know you are reaching God. When you pray with complete dependence on Him, when you have nothing left, you'll know He is there. It isn't just a feeling but an assurance that your heart knows He hears you. And like myself, the Spirit assisted me directly thousands of times. You may even cry tears of happiness when you find Him. To get to that point of dependence, there are trillions of connecting ways for man to be, but for me, it was learning to love God first. And how do I love Him? I sincerely began striving to follow the commandments and/or Beatitudes and remember each and every morning as I wake up. The early mornings were the best to be near Him, when the day was still without distractions. Amen, God is good.

I wondered at this time if I should copy the commandments and Beatitudes below for your viewing but later thought differently and decided it would be better for you to read all the details in a Bible. Deuteronomy 5 has a good detailed description of the commandments, and Matthew 5 has a good description of the Beatitudes. However, you may include Luke 6 in your search too. By the way, as you study Matthew and Luke, you'll come to the conclusion, as I have, that the Jews had the first opportunity to become the renewed instruments of God, but many of their leaders rejected and were responsible for demanding the Romans to kill Him. And before Jesus gave up His last breath, He called on the Father and said, "Forgive them Father, they do not know what they are doing."[a] Now get rid of that notion that you have to be full of mind-boggling rules and laws to get close to God. I did not need those rules when I experienced God's forgiveness, but for now at this stage of my life, for various reasons, I'm slowly driven to completely understand them. But for you to begin getting closer, all you do with your heart is ask our Father, in the name of His Son, Jesus Christ, to be in you.[b]

Jesus's Brothers, 1970

But in the meantime, if you're old enough, you've heard spotted stories of less-than desirable teachers and teachings of the faith for the last fifty years. I know this to be a fact; I've taught part-time high school Catholic religion to teenagers since the 1970s and rejected most of the books of the time, written by the supposed new modern religious that did not seem to follow concepts of the faith but their own human understanding. So what happened, how'd they get so far out from basic teachings? I know from being around Amish religion, up here in Michigan, most of them stick to their simple principles but still not without challenges because of the way of living the same from year to year with modern society surrounding them. We, on

---

[a] Luke 23:34.
[b] CCC 2664.

the other hand, have more complex changing social structural lives that have to be sorted out, hopefully before too much damage is done. However, if it is because of not having a solid faith community around us to help, we sometimes take a different route.

However, I got into trouble one day, in the 1970s, acting similar to the above nuns and priests while teaching Catholic high school to public school kids. I unwittingly got into a jam and was exposed for not knowing Catholic teachings better. I learned quickly that some high school students actually knew more than I did about their Catholic faith, as I admit experiencing. To this day, I forgot what the subject was that evening at Saint Ann's School confirmation class, but during class, a girl student asked out of the blue if Jesus had brothers. That was an easy question, and I told her yes, Jesus had brothers.

Well, the next day, I was invited to go into Pastor Father Baker's office, he wanted to talk to me about what the girl's mother told him from the night before. When I arrived, he kindly looked and asked if I told the class that Jesus had brothers. I answered yes, and he went on to say that we don't believe Jesus had blood brothers and that Mary was a virgin all her life. Well, my less-than-good Catholic upbringing was exposed and showed my Catholic teaching wasn't up to par, and I momentarily felt inadequate but not completely unqualified to teach. Why did I answer as I did? I answered the way I did because of my love of literal interpretations I have with the Bible. I'd study the Bible to understand the verse as it first comes to me, and later if I am proven in error, I naturally change my thinking. What happened was a few days before the class, I read a passage that said Jesus had brothers. I didn't question the verse because it was simply a fact and happened to be plainly written.

Nevertheless, I respected Father Baker immensely, and I know what I may have read was probably my literal interpretation of Jesus having brothers. From that moment, I made it a practice not to discuss or teach any Catholic doctrine that was different than what the church determined until I fully understood the doctrine in question. It wasn't until I was teaching a Bible class at Saint Catherine's Church in 2016, some fifty years later that I discovered, without any question, that Jesus did not have blood brothers. For all those years, I kept the brother subject inside me, waiting for understanding. I wondered if being called a hard-headed Irishman back in New York, in the 1950s, wasn't too far off the mark. Anyway as a kid, I appreciated having the Irish identity that seemed to be me, but I would slowly rid myself of what I began to see as a pride of a hindrance, preventing my spirit getting closer to our Lord.

Second Zero Population in 1966

Here is where I pick up a sort of private agenda by people not of my faith hired by the government. My first impression, while in the military, was a not good one. The social scientist hired by the government slowly grew into projecting their own private agendas using taxpayer's money. I found out later they were bona fide and hired to help congress make decisions. They were, for all practical purposes, highly educated men and women. The same type of people that will later influence abortions, relocate American manufacturing, and last but not least, the disguised health care law.

Since religious differences is strictly avoided in military regulations, I would like to tell you how in 1966, while stationed in Wilmington, Ohio, a military directive was issued with the help of the social scientist that prevented servicemen from receiving additional medical benefits after their third child was born. That didn't sit well with Barbara and me, having committed ourselves to wanting more children. Needless to say, I felt violated that the military would come to such an intrusion on my religious preferences. You can say, they pay the bills. And you can say it is a benefit of the job. So what is a person to do? It was the last and final nail in my military career. I was going to get out the army when my enlistment was up in a few months, without fail.

The government's zero population social scientist made it clear that the world would be better off with fewer kids. Nothing I knew and thought could be further from the truth. A bias and incomplete study at that, but then again, they had math and educated political experts on their side, and they didn't seem to be guided by morals or to ensure holistic rights were included. Instead they only went partway to obtain their narrow self-interest facts of life. They seemed, to me, to be little men with big government sticks; but today, I am bigger and have a bigger stick, it's called an oxgoad (see pages 7–9), to help me in my spiritual endeavors as mentioned in the beginning of the book.

Zero population didn't make sense anyway because China and other European countries obtained zero population, and those countries have many and continue to have social, moral, and economic problems we won't take time to discuss in this book. And the once-stabilized American family continues to dissolve with alarming rates, reaching an all-time high of 55 percent divorce rate yet having fewer children. Okay, so if you want proof, answer this question. If we're happier with fewer children, have more money, why then are American marriages failing at an alarming rate? Why aren't they happy? Is it a lack of material happiness? Don't forget, when I was a kid, I listened intensely to many adult conversations and watched and listened intensely to my father's every mood when he came home from work. My main purpose was to watch for any sign of abnormal behavior when comparing him to other men. If he showed just a slight catlike intention to work himself up into a frizzy, I would leave, go to my room, and usually hear him and Mom argue or duke it out physically. Well, anyway that continued until I reached sixteen, when I became bigger and stronger than him. And now, history is repeating itself for me. I've become bigger, wiser, and stronger than my surroundings, and I can see those family feuds developing in a small worldwide scale, and money is being thrown everywhere and the receivers are not happy. Hence a major reason for me to write this book is that I'm bigger and stronger than ever with God next to me. And above all, powerful people do not frighten me because I know God is here next to me. Well, guardian angels to be exact.

Now we see the Europeans opened their doors to questionable refugees that are sponsored by the European Common Market, only to find England leaving the common market, and what was their first action after announcing their departure? They stopped refugees from flowing into their country, and why?

It appears Europe's zero population concept isn't working so well and in order to maintain their economy. They need more people to replace the people they prevented from having families themselves. Their only economic choice is to relocate people into Europe from the Far East. But there is a problem with a few of them. A few are outcast themselves and unable to cope with modern society; and to get down to the nitty-gritty, they can't cope with their own society either. And most important, if the administration we've had for those years understood the US Constitution, they would understand the government has the responsibility to *ensure our safety*. But are they disregarding and divorcing the constitution, and I wonder when they will reach 55 percent too?

So what is the solution? First, are Americans ready to permit any person into the country without screening? The answer is, we hope not in these times. But if you look at the political wants of 2010 through 2016 as an indicator, it clearly shows we're going to have internal challenges from unscrupulous people who may be coming into our communities. And are Americans ready for foreign people coming into the country without a desire to live and build their lives here? I don't think so, and they should stay and waddle in the home of their origin if they too aren't willing to accept the US Constitution of the United States. It is easy to relate or check history to the time when ships were full of people coming here from Europe and Asia. However, I don't know of any group of individuals coming here, wanting to kill American citizens and not willing to adhere to the rules and laws of this land. But these modern educated and non-educated groups are weird-thinking. The one issue of not willing to adhere to our constitution should be the deal breaker, but is big money and government getting in the way again? Or is it the social scientist pushing? There is money to be made in farming, industry, and manufacturing, and they need bodies to make money. Well, it appears zero population isn't working here either. What a waste of professional social scientist tax money.

How'd we get into this mess? Think back, what political rhetoric was hot and heavy to take the attention away? Think back to another example in January 1973, when the abortion issue news was put on the back burner. I'm telling you, from what I've learned in the US Army Installation Intelligence about our enemies deceiving us, they don't hold a candle to our present politicians and the news media. They shipped our factories overseas and left America ripe for low-paying socialist jobs. Do you remember? I do; we were told Americans will buy cheaper goods from the deals. But it *never* materialized, instead prices skyrocketed beginning in the '80s. We no longer have a ruling middle class since a multitude of well-paying jobs disappeared, and I ask, why? Why? We can ask why from now until doomsday. Instead, let's ensure our government doesn't get any flakier by disregarding its people and the law of the land any further and ensure we support good morals and common sense in the government. I went into the military to help prevent enslaving governments from interfering in American free way of life, yet our very own political system today approves of slave-type rules and laws that continue to gain each decade, allowing the subtleness of it all to continue. I do think we're being dictated by a few political agendas with the news media and not by the total conscience of Americans. We better watch our step, or we'll be put on the outside looking in, like other nations.

I'll just reflect a little. Can you see how we are leaning toward a dictatorship, socialism, or progressivism by extreme politicians throwing crumbs at us? I can see it. That is what we're becoming, someone to throw crumbs at. We should be throwing crumbs at them, but that should never happen either. I hope you don't like being told what to do by a government with your life. If you do, the new and upcoming world order may fit your needs. If you don't like it, now is the time to start praying for a better life. God can stop this inner most exhaustible direction we seem to be on if we'd only ask Him. However, if we, as a people, continue abortions, sex crimes, drug crimes, lewd fashions, corruption, and adoring everything but God of what little of us that are left may not be enough to make a difference. This happens, folks, to those that succumbed to corruption for at least the last six thousand years of written history that I can see.[a]

---

[a] Genesis 19.

Social Scientist

Three major changes in America have occurred since I was a kid. The first was the slow diminish of the independent farmer to 1 percent of the population, and with them, a certain spirit of self-assured national independence; the other is the current like welfare population of 50 percent, and a certain dependence on government process rather than their self-advancing determination, and the third is the killing of millions of our babies. And now the glimpse of getting rid of undesirables in the new health care program. Do you see what I can see? I see Americans willing to be pushed around by social science politicians. You know these social engineers are in it to advance their own self-indulgences and not the Lord's. Something similar to this disruption happened to major religion denominations by depending on social scientist to rid their religious officials from sexual corruption. It failed, as we know it today, and I wonder if those leaders asked God before discussing such an important issue.

I remember, in 1983, I was listening to a political documentary and was flabbergasted of what I heard a government employee say, that "America will be a service country in the future and other countries will manufacture and grow food for the United States." That was alarming how that spokesman looked into the future and could say America will be a service country and be confident about it. You know, there is supposed to be a transfer of power with new presidential elections to help prevent control over the people. Yet there was the proof in the pudding and is coming to pass this very century. So I ask again, does proof guide us or does God do it?

Hold on, I say to myself. I remember being in architectural class at the University of Cincinnati and having privy to study the future growth of the city of Cincinnati and, at the time, an existing study from 1949 with five-year projections.[a] The study plan was flawed badly by the time we studied it in the 1960s. Needless to say, Cincinnati spent a lot of time and paid plenty of dollars for the future study that began with years of hoorays from the city, and

---

[a] Metropolitan Master Plan 1947, Cincinnati, Ohio (out of print).

as quick as the social engineers cashed their paychecks, the study began to crumble. And years later, I asked myself if those experts ever prayed for its success. Which of us can detect the future of our lives with accuracy and be right on the mark? However, we get glimpses of the future in the book of Job[a] and in the very beginning of our own chapter 1. So if the world order plan doesn't work when we're halfway into it, what will happen to the surrounding order? I bet they have a plan B, but it may not be relevant. No matter, I like changes to make life better but cautious of experts who do their thing for money only and not love of community and God.

Intrusion

During the period of the late 1960s, Cincinnati had flood problems along the Ohio River, and it was our job as the architectural students to go into those neighborhoods and convince the mostly black population to move into nicely proposed apartment buildings, far away from the flood zones. The first meeting was set and should have been one of many. We presented a well-designed high-rise apartment building complex for the local neighborhood association to view and comment. After each person got out of their seat and viewed the plans, you could hear the start of a buzz saw starting to rip the architectural drawings apart verbally as the community leaders couldn't hold their emotions back.

The mostly black women that were the leaders of their communities came at us before we could even show them the remaining nice-looking aesthetic pleasing apartments we could design for them. The meeting got loud and wasn't pretty, and I loved it. However, I wished there was an equal amount of black men present to give another view of what was needed. You know men and women together make life stronger, even though they may have different views. I thought back to that South Korean meeting in Seoul

---

[a] Job 1–42; warning, I've read Job forty times so far, and each time, I find more of what is in us.

and wondered if these people in this meeting have the same energy and determination as the Koreans did and would certainly succeed too. Anyway my fellow young students at the meeting were stunned, scared, and disappointed of the community's negative reaction, and I only had to wonder how powerful and spirited they were, even though they didn't have the same requirements as the average white person at that particular meeting had.

This is cool, I thought someone was going to call the cops because of the shouting, accusing us of creating a sneaky way of relocating them out of their current neighborhoods. They mentioned several times that they've lived there for all their lives with friends and families and weren't about to be moved out. They further stated angrily, they didn't mind relocating to higher ground each year when the floods came, and they looked forward to it. I fully agreed with their determination and independence to stay the way they were accustomed to living, and felt uncomfortable that we were pushing a preliminary agenda onto them. But as I discovered years later, our plan for the flood zone area was probably already in the works, and we were just students *used as decoys.* I got a bird's-eye view years later when I visited Cincinnati and was crossing a bridge over the Ohio River near the flood zone. The entire area that we students wanted to redesign and was rejected by the local leaders, years earlier, was now replaced with large buildings and stadiums. River Front Stadium was the first to go into the flood zone, and I knew progress was another way of saying, "Get out of my way." Sort of like the 1953 world flood scare of Manhattan, New York, that is in the next paragraph.

Here is another for your cap that appears to be the work of social scientist. Barbara and I lived in New York City when the populace heard many scary stories, in the early 1950s, about how Long Island and Manhattan was going to be underwater in one hundred years. It would be caused by the ice melting in the North Pole. What followed after many New York City news releases concerning the oncoming disaster was a rush of all small Manhattan landowners and merchants to begin selling their properties before it was made useless being underwater. And you should know the rest of the story; soon after the biggest selling and buying spree, we began to see new major high-risers, stadiums, police stations, apartments, museums, and bigger businesses, like the Twin Towers replaced the old smaller structures that was supposed to be submerging into the Atlantic Ocean in a hundred years. However, we see the new landowners made out better economically then anyone could imagine.

N.Y.C. 2153

Note: I was reminded of Chicago mayor Emmanuel stating one day, "Don't let a good disaster go to waste." I thought he must have been familiar with the 1950s New York City underwater perversion message and with Al Gore's doomsday global warming message. However dumb the message is, I'm always reminded of the elementary story as a kid, when a coconut fell on a sleeping monkey's head, and he began shouting that the sky was falling.

Now we see in the 2000s an even scarier story that global warming is about to consume us if we don't change. Even the former vice president of the United States makes a big deal of it and made a few extra bucks in his investments. Easy money, and that is how you follow big bucks in this book—by their money trails. We were once told that we're in trouble, and especially when it is learned that bad science proves it. I think money is to be made in most new endeavors, especially creating new energy; however, lying about it makes it cheap talk. Besides, in lieu of yelling Manhattan will be underwater, we can now yell, "We're going to melt."

Review of Chapter 6

Hate and Fear

I was stopped in my tracks one day in 2016, preparing for a church speech as I read, "Our Father gave all mankind to Jesus and Jesus doesn't want to lose any of them." What is this, what did this just say? Does it mean Jesus won't lose anyone, and all humans go back to Him, and no one is to be lost? I've read those words a multitude of times for the last fifty years or so, and never, never saw them until now. This message would send me back to that way-out lady in the beginning of this book when she said, standing alone by herself, "There is no hell." *How could she say such a thing?* I thought at the time. But years later, when I remembered her, I could understand her joy of being forgiven. She seemed so completely full of happiness that I think she could not imagine there was a hell. You know, we have indications of the Spirit in us for short periods, but for her, the Spirit seemed to have consumed her completely for that time.

I wondered what sin could cause absolute turmoil in a person that when they were free of it, they would praise God, minute after minute after minute. The lady seemed to be in complete peace and ecstasy. Then I thought of the one of the worst destructive sins there is and wondered if it was anger that slowly turned into *hate* that was the couplet. Whatever it was, she remained with me for many years, knowing she was able to let go of her sin and experience God's love in a special way. I think hatred is a damaging murderous state of obsession and causes extreme emotions of sins. No matter, though, she was back to life, and our Savior was in her heart. Amen.

That reminds me, in a small way, of my son Michael, and what he wrote about a couple hours before passing. He wrote, as I said in chapter 1, the morning of May 2014, while sitting with a blanket around himself outside, observing and feeding his chickens, "This must be what heaven is like."

I have seen hints in Scripture that heaven will be familiar.

Chapter 6

Hate and Fear: The Cancer of Life

Nikita Khrushchev, the Russian premier, shouted to America while visiting America in the 1960s, that "We will bury you!" And another quote, he said, "America will be destroyed from within." Were his words of hate or fear?[a] Surely they weren't good, and if it wasn't good, they must be bad. I think the Communist Party recognized that America was alerted by those words and preferred instead words that can't be recognized as a threat. Khrushchev let the Russian leaders down by exposing their bag of tricks! Soon Khrushchev was retired and never again allowed to wake America up, even if it was only for a short time. Oh, why bring up Khrushchev? I bring it up to show you the same evil threat is still around, similar to Kim Jong Un, the North Korean dictator.

Just log it in the back of your mind, we'll always have the negative around, but you should begin finding a way to offset their power. Keep in mind, for the good that is done, there is evil around to discredit it. It is a natural thing like negative and positive; one force replaces another, and so on and so on. And I ask, what wins at the time evil and good duke it out? I think it is the way God created the world to have opposites, which can be seen anywhere and be challenging. Not to say dictators only have evil; there is plenty to go around in our own land, and we should be mindful that it is evil that

---

[a]   CCC 2302–2303.

causes problems, and it does come in all walks of life. I guess for most of the populace, it boils down to if the bad is capable of causing great harm to us or not. We as believers need not have our lives threatened to the point we fear or hate. We should, as believers, call on our Lord to intervene when it happens. Do you think this New World Order appearing on the scene will create everlasting peace? I sincerely doubt it, just look at world history. It just doesn't change—we do the same things over and over again. The conflicts of murderous killing of one another began early in history, and it remains today. Look around at American and world events, even today murderous hate,[a] fear, and angry people continue destroying themselves and others. I don't think the world order has a handle on justice.

Hate/Anger

Anger can harden into resentment, and hate falls under the fifth commandment that could become a desire for revenge.[b] To desire anger in order to do evil is a cancer of life, and in order for a person to live without becoming a slave to themselves, they should check anger immediately prior to it reaching out and hurting themselves and others. If we hold onto it, it will certainly eventually hurt us. I wonder if Kim Jong is nearing that state of emotion by demonstrating missile launching over the sea of Japan, or is he merely a cool guy setting the stage to negotiate? Certainly ISIS hates to the point of murderous proportions, and I ask, how in the world did they get into such a life condition?[c] If you see what I see by all means, you and I, by seeing it, should plead with our Lord for more understanding and strength to counter it. Our Lord didn't come to us allowing us to be passive. Or like every other hate movement in history, whether it is a nation or ourselves, it begins to destroy from within. Hate does that to the individual and grows if not checked.

---

[a] CCC 2262.
[b] Matthew 5:38–48.
[c] CCC 1765.

Should We Fear ?

We cannot go to heaven with hate or worldly fear disproportionate in our hearts. And both are involuntary situations of not believing totally on the love of God but a condition of believing more in our own abilities. And like early Israelites that could not call on God when facing violence, they were left to their own demise and suffered from their own very own making. We are free to do whatever we want, but be sure we will suffer the consequences of sin. And what is sin, I ask?[a] It is anything not of God.

Cancer eats away at our bodies, and hate eats away at our soul. Both afflictions affect our health, relationships, and death.

Accepting the World Order

You know, American leaders seem to accept the New World Order that is beginning to take shape, and it appears it may bring the world together economically. I know that bringing the world together is similar to other good periods of world developments, and

---

[a] CCC 1472, 1473.

169

I think it closely resembles God's plan. All we should do is follow His footsteps in order to succeed. The New World Order concept should succeed, and if not, it will fail like all other endeavors developed by man, for man. And if it begins to fail with the whole world being involved, how disruptive will it be? The progressive leaders of our land promote world order concepts and demote organized religion to the point of even accusing ISIS as being a religion. Today we can see how the world is coming together in a New World Order, and in order to come together and succeed, it will require good moral people to help direct its endeavors. Without good input, only bad will develop into the voids, pushing this world order concept into yet another obliteration.

Is it hard to see? Scale down a little and watch certain couples starting out together happy and carefree, but in time and without seeing it, their marriage is in trouble, and both aren't asking for God's help. Thus they wind up just like many marriages that are on a journey of destruction of what was once so beautiful; you wonder, how could that have happened? I wonder all the time, why. Now scale up a new exciting marriage as the newly developed world order. Will it go flop as the couple above did? Yes, indeed it is in our present DNA; they will go the same as all other world orders and nations have in the past, gone without good morals. And then again, they will fail because that is the way of nature or the way the world concludes. Why, I ask, is this the way the world works? *It is the history of man.* How do we break out of that negative course of nature? We break out of the negative snares of evil by following the steps of God.[a]

The people will pay the piper again, but this time, it appears it could be the big bang if we don't direct the course of this world order properly. After all, the whole world is getting involved, isn't it? You know a computer analogy that says, "Junk in, junk out." Nature can't stand anything sitting back and doing nothing. The one who made nature built us to work together toward the good of our neighbors, helping to improve our surroundings, that is if we are up to it. If we're not up to it, we'll go the same way the world has always gone.

---

[a]   Luke 18:1–8; keep knocking.

Little Things Can Indicate a Problem

My eldest son, Guy, went to Israel on a business trip in the 1980s, and when he got there, the Israeli government directed all visitors getting off the passenger planes into an auditorium. The objective of the government was to indoctrinate all visitors to be familiarized with Israel's travel laws and customs. It was a certain section of the indoctrination that dealt with Israel preventing violence from their Palestine neighbors that didn't sit well with Guy.

The host nation, Israel, went on to explain that they kicked out all the Palestinian children from their schools. Israel took that action to impress upon the adult Palestinians that Israel won't stand by and allow disruption from them or their children. Guy raised his hand and asked, "Did you stop to think that all of the kids missing school may cause future turmoil?" He further asked, "Wouldn't it be better to have the children in class, in a safe and calm environment, rather than have them at home listening to their angry parents." Needless to say, the host staff wasn't in a mood to answer contradictions and immediately called the assembly to a halt. This reminded me of what my grandmother Meegan used to say. "Don't cut off your nose to spite your face." Israel did a lot of that during the 1970s.

I often thought in the late '60s and '70s, when Israel and the Palestinians were duking it out and were giving each other bloody noses, that Israel was really too smart for doing that, but I was wrong and it continued. Did they really have so much hate that they couldn't see how their backlashers made things around them worse? Or was it just the hate on the Palestinian side that Israel was trying to project? In any case, I held Israel in higher regard, and Israel should be able to overcome what was currently happening. Why, why couldn't they act differently and properly? What was clouding their eyes from the truth? After reading more of their history, it was becoming apparent, they were stuck in their old ways and not what the Messiah[a] wanted them to do. But then again, we're similar to Israel and seem to cling onto old ways and habits too. So I ask, what is the root cause of

---

[a] Luke 18–27.

hate and fear? There it is again, that *root cause* word. My root cause process is a simple quick gotcha way of seeing where trouble is originating from. I used it as a tool to find the root cause of safety and environmental problems in industry as follows. So as an experiment, check out the root cause of trouble below.

Root Cause Method

A basic example of how to perform a root cause analysis is similar to following a money trail. First let's imagine a critical industrial machine broke down from what appears that water was getting onto an electric switch, causing it to shut down. You are responsible to investigate what happened in order to correct the problem and to become operational again. And in that process, you will ask as many times as needed: Why? Why? Why?

You approach the machine and ask the first why. Why did the water burn out the covered switch? You determined that water got inside the protective covering of the box and damaged the switch inside. And decide to change the damaged switch. Hold on, you aren't finished with that analysis, and you should continue with another why.

Why or how did the water get into the cover in the first place, and you find that a small hole in the cover allowed the liquid to seep in. You aren't finished yet because the liquid is coming from somewhere, and you ask the next why. Why or how or where did the liquid come from? Upon checking further, you discover the liquid is coming from a dark hidden area above the ceiling, and you continue searching for the cause, and you ask again why or where it may be hidden to find the couplet, and you notice a water pipe needlelike leak, allowing liquid to gravitate down to the switch area below.

Well, that's it, you may say. However, you shouldn't stop until you find the reason why the newly found water pipe leaked, and you go to the next why and notice a slight liquid drip in the shadows of the pipes above. You notice liquid coming from a different pipe near the roof, dripping onto the water pipe below. You discover the pipe near the roof leak is an acid delivery pipe joint that has deteriorated slightly allowing its corrosive acid to damage the water pipe below. And what damaged the acid pipe is the next why. The acid pipe that was recently installed did not have the proper amount of sealant between the pipe and the fitting. There you go, folks, a quick analysis of a problem that could have been missed by just accepting the small leak on a switch box which wasn't good enough and not a big deal, thereby unwittingly allowing the acid pipe leak to spread into other areas as the leak worsened.

By the way, I use the same (why, why, why) often in my investigations, especially why social behaviors infest further than what they should. The analyses may be worth the time but not always accurate, and a different approach is always needed to continue pursuing a quest to find the truth. It is all too easy to just change the machine switch, thinking the problem is solved when we haven't solved the root cause. And so, as a summary, I found after reading Scripture for fifty years or more, I discovered the human why, whys are all around us for exposing the truth and healing. And a truth I want to explore is why we've had wars since the beginning of time, and why haven't we eliminated them all these years? We do the same thing over and over again, attempting to rid the evil from among us and it returns. Why can't we go to the root cause and stop it? How can we stop war? I know how, and I hope you see what I see in this book. If you see a hint what I see causes war, it is sin. And sin is anything that doesn't come from God.

Hitler, Feared and Hated

Did fear and hate prevent Hitler from following God? He had a messed up family life that may have left a permanent scar and was extremely fearful and paranoid. He feared cancer more than we first knew, after he watched his mother die of breast cancer, and then later in life, he had a polyp on his vocal cord that was removed. I wondered if his worries consumed him and was blocked with fear from hoping for better things to happen. Was he driven to be angry and afraid to hope for a better life? Could his pain prevent him from hoping, was pain and worry his only Comfort Zone? (To be discussed on page 179) Was he constantly feeding on negative thoughts, lashing out at the rest of the world in frustration and revenge? Did he sense he was a prisoner in himself? Could he get away from the wrongs he saw from other European countries continually *punishing* Germany for World War I activities?

I wonder how much he hated Jews, or did he fear cancer more than having certain Jews around. He had a certain Jew around, a Jewish physician with cancer knowledge, and was the doctor allowed special protection and privileges? The doctor was Jewish, and Hitler made sure that the SS knew his doctor was not to be hindered in any way. The doctor had free access to anything necessary they had to find a cure for cancer. I wish Hitler could have understood that cancer comes in two forms, one physical and the other fearing. The physical one destroys our body, and the mental one destroys our soul; and eventually it destroys the body too. Hitler presumably was able to see how his hate spread and killed more people than cancer did. How do we communicate to the world that hate is more destructive than cancer, and it grows faster than cancer affecting communities? We do it by teaching the Word until we are exhausted, and then pray for more strength to help change the hearts of would-be frustrated people.

Sin and hate are related and, in a destructive way, become fierce partners. Both eat away at us, preventing us from fully being all we can be. However, sin, fear, and hate will most certainly lead to a cancer of life and can be healed before it is too late. How can we help cure the world? The Ten Commandments were given to Israel to rid themselves of being weighed down by sin, thereby creating a people of *strength* beyond any people on earth at the time. The above truth is my take on why the Ten Commandments came into being, and then later why Jesus, the Word, clarified the commandments with emphasis on the Beatitudes that most certainly Israel should have grown into by the time Jesus came but rejected God's only Son.

We can see a therapist or take temporary medicine to calm us, or we can rid hate from ourselves forever by simply asking the Father in the name of His Son, Jesus Christ, to help us remove this stigma of life from within us. I think a practical way we can remove the stigma of life is to confess our sins, stop sinning, forgive others, and turn all our ill feelings, hurts, pain, and anger over to the Lord. You know the New Testament has a passage that plainly says we will never be made to suffer beyond our strength. If that's the case—and it is—keep being determined. I would most certainly bet you are now being tested, and to find out, just ask Him if you are. Keep knocking, He will answer you.

Hitler Would Admire Our Law

What two American laws do you think Hitler would have admired and have less anxiety toward Americans during his spree of terroristic crimes in the 1930s and 1940s?

Hitler was from the same wired mind as other unfortunates from the past and the current world, wanting people shaped for their own desires, avoiding God's way. Have you ever noticed highly educated university socialists think they know what is best and their scientist attempt to shape us into their way? We had seen it in Russia and China between 1900 and 2020, between the 1930s and mid-1940s with Hitler, and now we're seeing it in America. But now it appears China is changing their political landscape a little and got a little of capitalism going for them. However, the Old Guard is still there, excising power.

American leaders are becoming less intolerant toward today's fundamental Christian America, and those leaders believe they are the only ones in the know. Matter of fact, now it is easily seen as the two leading parties fiercely fighting each other for their survival in lieu of fighting for America's survival. The party's welfare actually takes preference. So we elect Americans to represent us, but instead they represent their party. Step back further and see how our nation was designed during trials at the hands of European tyrants. But could this new attitude we see be the start of a divorce from a legal 250-year constitutional marriage? But first, I better answer the above question on what law is it that Hitler would admire? The answer is abortion and the health care law. Hitler's abortion and health care initiatives helped rid Germany of undesirables. As a matter of fact, that is similar to what is happening today with unmistakable undesirable babies and adults by words being whisked away by the health care system in the shadows of the law. This time, it didn't take a supreme court ruling to create the health care law but an American Congress that didn't read the details of the death law. Easier said than done, folks, they did it under our noses.

The one-sided political party did it under a cloud of rush-it and that it was for the poor. So abortion was too to announce the ruling on the best day of the decade, the end of the war to get less attention. But I see it, and I'm not losing my determination to announce that the ruling is another step in gaining social control. And it is done under our noses and appeals mostly to the rich white folks. I walk the sidewalks of abortion clinics, and I observe who comes in and out of the place and what appears are rich above-average white people driving expensive cars and trucks. I drive a dented 2002 truck and a 2005 car to get around, so the understanding who has money and who doesn't is noted. And I wonder, why does congress give money to the abortion industry when there are plenty of rich money pockets to pay their own way?

So the past reasons for killing undesirables are not as different from America's reasons for killing. Reasons to kill undesirables change from century to century and from leaders to leaders, but each nation seems to have the same common theme—get rid of their undesirables. Whereas God's law has always been the same—to love each other; and we find love builds relationships, and we prosper. This coronavirus that is gripping the whole world is going to be another fly in the ointment. I don't think, from my viewpoint, we will ever again prosper. If I'm wrong, I'm an old fool; if I'm correct with the above observations, what are you going to do about it? I'm asking God to stop this madness. I know He will stop it when enough of us ask.

Our Lord Jesus, God's only Son, came into the world to help us find God's way of living. The way we should live is in every man's heart, but evil wants no part of the Truth and creates diversions attempting to keep us from finding it. The disruption caused may appear, at first, reasonable or not concerning, but in time, you can look back and understand what kind of destruction the diversions may have caused or are presently causing. Now that you know the fundamental exercise of a root cause analysis, try a small experiment at home, just to get started.

I remember reading a comment made by Karl Marx, one of the founders of Communism, who said in the early 1900s that America could not become a great nation due to a *disorganized* fragmented section of capitalism running rampant in America. What Karl didn't see at the time was that all Americans were struggling to make a better life for themselves and worked harder than their socialist neighbors and soon aspired to become the greatest nation in the world. And from my analyses, majority of Americans believed in God. Most Americans understood the good fortunes were from God, and it clearly is visible in the US Constitution.

There would be nothing to stop the unplanned American movement, but it has stopped. The modern-day politician, news media, political correctness, and the leaders in our universities are blinded to self-determination because it was not politically correct to find what made America strong. Individual faith and determination made America strong. But no, they, the university-smart people, continue to make halfhearted attempts to find the truth. It was their way or the highway, their plans or no plan on paper, and they looked from their narrow perception of the world and cancelled all other thoughts, especially truth. I found, if you get in a debate with a social professor about conservative values, their self-made trademark of open-mindedness doesn't fly anymore. My experience is that they laugh at your comments and try to change the subject. I felt like a parent in college classes instructing naive professors when invariably, they should switch their self-made political views and continue with their class subjects. Again what many politically active professors surely missed, and it appeared to me, was what made American strong. Most of them did not want to consider a strong Judean/Christian belief period. That was too easy and not complicated enough for them or highly educated for them. It was faith they couldn't understand because it couldn't be proven on paper, and they had no idea what it was.

So why the change of attitudes in American values all of a sudden? It was not all of a sudden; I watched slow changes from the 1940s until now, and they weren't necessarily good changes. It's like the more obstinate a solution was, the more enticing it was for modern educators. It seemed in class, many college professors were high on themselves and not the basic truth. They—and I'm not being nasty—remind me of blockheads or stubborn to find the truth inside all of us. Is it pride that causes a mental block seemly like they are made of wood?

Family Violence

When I was growing up, I never knew other families weren't yelling, making accusations, threatening, fighting, and damaging their homes and furniture as what was happening in my home growing up. I'm not sure if my father had PSTD after he came home from World War II or not, but it doesn't matter; he projected pure fear nearly each night when he came home from work and/or the tavern, and the fear continued. I was alert at all times, watching for signs if he was drunk or angry or mad enough to start pounding away on us.

My alertness stayed with me forever and figuring out other people too, especially in the military, and always finding a calming respect for others that portrayed integrity. I became a good reader of body language and facial expressions as a kid, and while hanging around on the New York streets, I learned how to diffuse bad situations by beating up the other kid before he did it to me or protect myself from fearing that would become a body-shaking experience.

My everlasting encounter with violence wasn't the awful beatings I had gotten, but the day my dad tried to hurt my mother with a large butcher knife. My sister and I were at the kitchen table, eating supper, and my uncle and mother were standing by the kitchen sink when my father came into the kitchen, angry and yelling at Mom. He hit a high note, and he reached over and got a butcher knife from the counter, holding it above his head, going toward Mom, and thrusting his arm forward with the knife. My uncle, a recent veteran himself, was between both of them and grabbed my dad's arm and made him drop the knife. That was it, except for cursing and swearing between Mom and Dad. Things settled down that evening, but I kept a close eye and ear opened the rest of the evening.

It was fear almost each evening he came home for years. I quickly learned to avoid him and get away from the madness by spending my free time drawing illustrations of objects when I was a kid. I noticed very quickly how art gave a calming effect and was an enabler to escape and feel calm again. And years later, after leaving the army, it was Scripture that took the place of art. Art was not needed any longer for relaxation or calming effects. Having a job and working to keep the family going was satisfaction, but later, I began to see satisfaction in spiritual reading, and that seeing was a magnet getting closer to calmness and our Lord. By the way, I never had any desire to beat Barbara. She was a gift that I recognized while she gave birth to my children. And speaking of children, I maintained what Barbara and I thought was good discipline that was surely a benefit for them and us. I learned even more how to raise a family by reading the stories of Scripture and applying the teachings of Jesus too. And besides, I learned a fantastic thing. Oh, another interesting family happening was occasionally, after disciplining my child, they would come up to me later to be held. I certainly held them and held them tight, reassuring myself and the child of forgiveness.

Comfort Zone Phenomenon

I found later that what we become accustomed to and familiar with goes deep into our makeup and often difficult to change. For instance, as mentioned before and as an example, if you spent many years of raising your family and only had $100 in the bank and suddenly you spent it, you would work very hard to get that $100 back. And if you had $5,000 in the bank and you suddenly got an extra $10,000, you would work getting that money back to $5,000 savings. When people do such things, it's called comfort zone, and just like the people in the chapter above concerning the flood area, their comfort zone was experiencing annual moving from the flooded neighborhoods to higher ground, and they should not be made to change for another's profit; but then again, that is progress living in the fast lane.

However, my comfort zone never lost abilities watching and listening for adverse conditions around me and watching or reading the news and the patterns of newsmakers and their purpose. I would become quick in guessing an outcome from the negative or positive incidences that the news was attempting to project. It was, I'm sure, my dad's irregularities that influenced my inners to see what comes next. The news media, it seemed, would scale up episodes of various activities at will, drawing attention to their views of how it should be in lieu of how it should be. Once I assumed that small things could be like big things, I found it easy to compare various activities at will, drawing attention to their views only of how it should be done and not how it should be done from the reader's input. It was easy to see Israel's world history as what was going on in the '70s and '80s and today. We're all presently in an instigated negative system controlled or processed by social scientists, and we can break out of it, hopefully, by demanding the truth. Also before Trump said fake news, I was saying it in the 1960s until present day.

His Plan

I find it tantalizing and exciting that God knows everything to include our personal future. I always believed God is all-knowing, and I remain always inquisitive about the subject[a] until one day, I was reading about newly anointed King David in the Old Testament, and God said that David is a man *after His own heart*. Well, how far can I go with that? How did God know David was a man after His own heart, did He know how David would conduct himself in the future? Yep, He knew, and the question was, what was it that made God say that because David wasn't a saint-kind of a guy in some parts of his

---

[a]   CCC 280; 1 Chronicles 28:9; Acts 13:22–23.

life. The only way I could find out was to ask for more understanding when studying David's life.

The clincher finally came when I discovered how deep David loved Israel and served God's people. His serving was similar to Moses, Joshua, Elijah, Daniel, and the apostles, and hopefully us. So God knew what these men would do eons before they did it and did not interfere with their free choices. Well, David sinned and was later punished.[a] You'd think God would interfere beforehand and not allow Israel's king to make mistakes in the eyes of the world, especially David symbolizing the temple. Had God interfered, it wouldn't be his free will; and besides, I think God wanted us to see good and evil for our benefit, in order to compare, so hopefully we would sincerely choose the Word. Sometimes I think it is already in us to do good, and when we choose the right path, we become stronger and do not go into despair and lose everything as King Saul, the first king of Israel, did in 1 Samuel, going against God. Our heart is programmed, and once we find the codes or His footsteps, we shouldn't take it for granted. I think that is how it works; men are programmed to have free will, but we will lose each time if we elect not to follow in His steps.

Well, you might ask, if God can see ahead, why did He have Saul anointed king and lead Israel, when God could have picked a perfect person to lead His people and not embarrass Israel or maybe Himself? God does not and cannot be embarrassed. Well, Jesus was the perfect person, and look how many people listened to the Word. Look around, do you see any perfect people or leaders? Were Adam and Eve perfect? They were even thrown out of the heavenly garden. We have to learn about God's love, and I don't know of a better way to do that then by picking ourselves back up again for another try and learning what others have done to correct their lives too. I don't know of a better way to avoid sin than by asking God for help and continue banging on His door and continue knocking until He answers us. I do that a lot. So I ask myself, do I want free will? And I say yes, but I need help to improve my life, and when I notice that I improved my soul, it begins to swell into sweetness and calmness.

---

[a] First Chronicles 21:1–30.

I think salvation is possible, even for me. So most of us know God loves us, but the question is, *do we love God* and how can we tell when we love Him? We know we love Him when we obey Him and follow His commandments.[a]

The *salvation* word came up, and I have to say something about it. It would be nice to think all we have to do is believe in Jesus, and we'll go to heaven. I don't think it is that easy *to maintain* that belief; we are warned that we could lose salvation. In that case, what I do think is that the biggest surprise of all is when we are saved. Or we find ourselves in heaven.[b] That is the day of my salvation. There have been too many times in my life I messed up, even after knowing that we have problems that must be solved. I'll tell you a story of this girl in Cincinnati that asked me if I have been saved, and I asked her, what does saved mean? She went on to tell me that if I believe in Jesus Christ, I'm saved, and I will go to heaven. I asked her if we committed adultery right here and now and died immediately after the adultery, would we still go to heaven? She thought a minute and said she didn't know, and I responded back that *she better know.*

If it is as easy as saying Jesus, why do we need to go further? However, people on their deathbeds have the opportunity right there and then. They ask for forgiveness, and they will get it. Some people may not need to go further, but I need to go further in order to become steadfast and win constant spiritual battles. We need to become stronger spiritually to keep our faith from being ripped to pieces on earth in order to maintain our focus on Jesus by ejecting the evil one. Besides I don't think many of us go straight to heaven when we die. I believe we need to be purified, and that purification is an intermediate place known as purgatory.[c] Sometimes I think of it as another level of heaven. The Israelites think there may be three heavens. I wonder and continue to look.

By the way, let's back up a little. Just like God knows what we need before we know it, remember, one of the ways of determining a

---

[a] John 15:10–11.
[b] Romans 8:18–27.
[c] CCC 1030–32; 1 Chronicles 16:27, 30–33.

false prophet is if his prophecy doesn't come to pass. When we hear true prophecies, we see them come to pass; and if they don't come to pass, they are not from God. I believe this means that God's plan is eternal and in us, especially when we follow our hearts, that must be pure. And how can a prophet know the future? He didn't know the future until God gave him the words to speak. The Lord sometimes stepped into Israel's lives when they were highly screwed up, but just prior to the catastrophe, He would speak to His prophets, warning the people to wise up or suffer the consequences. From who? From man, that's who. Just like the modern prophets filled with the spirit are doing today, they are telling the world to wise up. So do we need to see the world coming to an end before believing the truth of world corruption? By the way, from what I see in the book of Revelation—it's the last book in the Bible—we'll still have a chance to believe the truth when the destruction begins. After all, Jesus said, "The Father has given Him all of mankind and I want them all."

His Plan

Remember back a couple of chapters when I was spared twice from harm, after hearing the buzzing in my right ear? I can truthfully say since it came to pass, I can tell it was God's plan. Think of it, can anyone change the course of his life the way God sees it? Not really, God already knows what course we take since the beginning of time, when we were created. Now was my life spared after hearing the buzzing sound? It seemed like it was spared, God's plan is forever; and in that particular case, it was a warning of some sort to understand. We have free will, but God already knows how we will conduct our lives. Well, then we can say, the heck with it, be irresponsible and stop trying and enjoy a loose life. He sees that too. However, as I age and concerns truly come my way, I find God when getting closer to God, my fears are less and less, and life becomes more enjoyable than when I was younger. I now appreciate knowing God is in charge of me, and by following His footsteps, I'll be with Him completely.

Come to Pass

Whatever you see that comes to pass is what was supposed to happen, and we can look back and make adequate changes to our lives. Nothing, absolutely nothing, can change God's plan. He already knows what is to come. If you question my reasoning, just don't sit on your hands; get up and find the truth yourself. There is plenty of reason for all of us to ask God for wisdom. Then you'll be, I hope, like others, hopelessly in love with God, Trusting Him and willing to give whatever it takes to be near Him.

When I think about the two buzzing incidences mentioned above from my right ear, I think it wasn't to save my life but to communicate to you and me how awesome our God is. Why then did He not let me die? I guessed at the time, being a sinner, I should have died. I don't know why, but I do know I'm supposed to be here, right now, with you, writing about the incident. So after all these years, my final thought after hearing the buzzing in my ear was a warning for you and me to find Him. You'll see in the Old Testament many warnings to Israel to strengthen up or suffer the consequences, and when they wouldn't listen, they self-suffered because of their own failures to communicate with their Maker. They, like us, for a lack of a better word, have God's DNA in our hearts and cannot go against it without adverse consequences. Oh, by the way, I've had many other incidences that kept me from death besides the ear sounds. I could probably write a book on those other incidences.

Warnings

When I think of prophets like Elijah in Kings and how he was warned to tell the various kings to change their bad habits or die, I think the message is personal and continues to be for us today. Sort of like the buzzing in my ear? God knew what kings would do with having free will. They would do whatever they wanted and continued showing the world their intentions. The kings weren't stopped but allowed to pursue their own self-indulgences until hopefully they heard the words of life which they were supposed to, like us. Just look at King David, a man after God's own heart, and see how he lapsed into sin. Sort of like the blind man being born for Jesus to cure him of blindness.[a] Elijah was one of the persons *born* in ancient times to communicate warnings. And part of God's plan, I suspect, was for the benefit of the world, not just Israel. And as I look around, I wonder how much of those warnings are meant for us?

Political Correctness

Do we see trouble in communicating our views to others? You know, like kind of a political correctness, and maybe we shouldn't do it. Well, if we don't correct our children when they need it, how can we correct others? We have to be reminded the world prosperity is in danger around us when we follow a dangerous path of sin. However, we have an advantage in correcting the world from destruction in that it is God's wishes, not our wishes, that keep the world turning. So if you think live and let live is the politically correct thing to do, think again before not becoming involved in a kind way. We are commissioned to speak the truth and help save the world in truth, and we do not do it by being timid but by being determined. So look into your already programmed heart of good and find what it is that you're supposed to do in life. First you are breathing, right? Guaranteed, you breathe because God is allowing it. Our first response when we know our *breath* is from God should be humbleness or happiness, *thanking Him.*

Plan Continued

What I think, first and foremost, is that "God has the whole world in His hands," and no matter what happens, He wanted you and me here today because this is what was supposed to happen. His plan is happening all around us, and we can usually see it when the

---

[a] John 9:1–3.

day progresses. I look at yesterday and see what happened. It was supposed to happen because God knew and allowed it to happen. Maybe I can look at yesterday and see tomorrow? I think if you look at repeating history, you'll get a glimpse of today and maybe tomorrow. Wait a minute, isn't that a fatalist way of thinking? Yes, it is, except we have the power to change our course in life, and our Lord already knows if we changed it or not. We have the power of asking God to change our lives, and again, He knows what we want even before we ask it.

So as an example, Hitler didn't win WWII because we can look back and see that he didn't, it came to pass, he wasn't supposed to. Could it have happened any other way? No, it ended the way it did because that was the way of God allowing it to happen; however, our input and prayers helped end the war that man started and God stopped. How could that be? The Father already knew the faithful would ask for it to end by millions of our prayers to Him. Make no mistake about it, churches were full near the end of the second war (if you didn't get to church early in those days, you would have to stand), and people were visually concerned how terrible things were in the world. The Father did not make us pray; it was our free will. He knew we would pray on our own, asking Him for an end to the horrors.

Can we change future human history? Yes, we can, and our asking is already known to Him. However, again God knows the future we ourselves helped change by asking, and it is part of the ultimate plan. World War II ended because people asked to end it. We can say it ended because we prayed; it ended because God wanted it to end after we understood it was our responsibility to initiate the asking. I ask God all the time, thinking I am a nothing, a no account of a person, and day after day, I ask for forgiveness. Every day it's a reoccurring theme that I wonder—and really wonder—why He puts up with me, but He does. But what comes from knowing I'm nothing is that I'm something belonging to God who has ultimate control over the whole world. That gives me strength, happiness, and confidence that He is my Master, and it continues getting stronger. It is already in us to come to that conclusion in order to be saved on the last day. My ambition is to find more grace that I may forgive others and my physical and spiritual life improves. I just close my eyes, sit, stand or walk, and ask for forgiveness, and my physical and spiritual self improves, every single time.

Getting Closer

My faith is such that God knows everything. His plan is without errors and knows exactly how each individual, creature, and the world will progress. I'm not a fatalist, we have our free will as mentioned above; however, our Lord already knows what the outcome of each individual, animal, tree, and everything on earth is. And there are times when He sends angels as messengers, helping to ensure we know we have help around us. I liken this to the soldier in Korea that told me that I will have eight children and one will pass. I often wonder if he wasn't an angel since the Lord already knows what is in the future.

God blesses us even if we don't pray for it. Why would God bless us without us praying? The whole world is blessed, and they may or may not know it. Think about it, look at all the rich and poor people in the world, but they may or may not think they are experiencing God's love, which is given to all, and it seems only a few find who it is that gives us graces. The Beatitudes give us insights into what can bring us closer to God.[a] It's us that need to get closer, and it's already in us to do so.

Old Testament King Saul (Hate and Fear)

Why did King Saul trick the soothsayer into conjuring up Samuel?[b] First God allowed it to happen, allowing us understanding of what Saul had allowed himself to turn into.

Now the soothsayer, and especially Saul, were sinners for doing what they did without asking God. Why is it a sin—and a terrible

---

[a] Matthew 5:1–10.
[b] First Samuel 28.

sin at that—to ask a soothsayer or to be a soothsayer? They purposely bypassed the Maker of the universe by looking for another god in themselves; they defiled the first commandment, and as we saw, Saul got deeper and deeper into *despair* and did not have the strength to get out of it. Saul got further and further away, and all he found were dark empty promises.

The world today seems to do the same as Saul did. Man avoids God for more attractive idols that come faster and easier to them and rather enjoy their worldly pleasures instead (maybe this is the message why it is hard for a rich man to enter heaven[a]). It takes effort to find our Lord, but it's worth the pain and struggle getting closer. What happens when man stops knocking without putting more effort into finding the truth? Things go badly, sooner or later, for man until man repents. Remember, God made us to find Him, and when we don't, we do ourselves harm. What was the very first indication for things going badly for man? It was the basic story of Adam and Eve, being in the middle of the garden and eating of its forbidden fruits. And later God attempts to show man how to achieve happiness by forming the tribes of Israel and giving them the Ten Commandments to find Him, but Israel couldn't hang on to God's love consistently and instead found love in all the wrong places. Israel was the earthly example from God to bring mankind closer to Him by praying together, giving one another strength and prosperity. The story is for us.

What Happened to God's People?

Well, if Israel was the earthly example, what happened to God's people? Just as Adam and Eve succumbed to temptation and followed evil ways in lieu of the path laid right out in front of them and were casted out of paradise. In spite of all the drama expounded against God, He never divorced them, they were watched over. He thinks the same of us and will never divorce us either. Why else would God

---

[a]   Matthew 19:23–26.

have Israel's history written if it was not to prepare Israel and the rest of the world for the truth to come to save us. And what about the truth? Israel's prophets wrote about the Messiah (Jesus) coming, but Israel's leaders rejected Him when He came. They predetermined He would be a fierce fighter for Israel, instead a man that talked of forgiveness of sins and died to only be resurrected and to be seated next to the Father. The hardened leading Jews could not see beyond their noses and missed the Messiah. They just couldn't see that Israel's world changed from *physical wiping out of their enemies to a spiritual converting of their enemies* and would, at the same time, make them closer to God. All that Israel and the world had to learn was to pray for their enemies as the new teaching suggested. That is a tall order—to pray for your enemies—but Israel had the tools to trust; and today, a slight window is being opened in Tel Aviv, indicating such actions. They are God's people; Christians are remnants of Israel, and it will never change, and the key is for the Israelis to ask God, in one voice, for help.

My guess is it will be difficult because of Israel's fear having to overcome. As an observation, I see tidbits of Christ's influence presently in Israel and modern Jewish understanding of what it takes for lasting peace. If Christians can stand next to Israel as spiritual support for peace, both beliefs will become an overpowering force calling on God. Something common to Jews, Muslims, and Christians is that our Lord taught us to come together in prayer. Why do you suppose that is? When we have two or more believers alongside of each other, we create a strong voice to God. Can you imagine Jews, Muslims, and Christians praying together for what the outcome would be? Ask yourself first, why did Jesus, a Jewish rabbi, teach in the synagogues? It was time, God wanted His people, the Jews, to come to a fuller understanding of Him, similar to creating the Ten Commandments, first for Israel and now advancing forward, sending His Son, the face of God, to give Israel the Word for their salvation. Remember, there was no salvation for the world until Christ died and rose from the dead. It appears prior to Jesus, when Jews died, they went to a place similar to what I call is a form of purgatory. Soon after Christ was crucified, He went there to gather the dead, to bring those who were to be saved with Him to heaven. It isn't a simple task, achieving strong faith togetherness, especially in this world; but among Israel, Islam, and Christianity, we have the tools to ask God to grant us favors.

Islam, the Brother of Israel

So that brings me to Muhammad's Islamic teaching. Modern history indicates Muhammad was born in AD 570, and lived in the Arabian Peninsula, a descendant of Ishmael, son of Abraham.[a] Muhammad lost his father before he was born and lost his mother at about the age of six, and a guardian grandfather at the age of eight. As an adult, he became a merchant with his uncle, involved in trade between the Indian Ocean and the Mediterranean Sea. He later married at twenty-five, a woman much older, and around AD 613, began public preaching and converting his followers to Islam. Muhammad had a knowledge of who Christ was as slowly seen when Islam was developed.

Summary

In summary, any measure of hate and fear prevents natural healthy growth in some fashion or another.

---

[a] Genesis 16:1–16, 17:1–27.

Review of Chapter 7

Why Am I Catholic

My friend Ann Nesbitt, a non-Catholic and an independent Bible reader and lover of God, said to me one day, several months ago, that she thought that I do not act like other Catholics. To me, what she said was shocking and could be a sad testimony of Catholics. I wondered if others see it her way too. I pondered what she said and began searching for answers. What is so different about me and Catholics today? And why did she claim I do not act like other Catholics? I questioned myself, and at the same time, I wondered if I acted like a normal American too? And this is where I found the difference. I wasn't like a normal American anymore and neither was Ann Nesbitt. Our normal America began flaunting in material wealth years ago, which both Ann and I both lacked because of the different course we took, but what does that mean? I think it means America has become dependent and adopted itself to wealth matters. And it has. However, I hope at the same time, the modern materialistic American man learns to love. But the modern appearance of high divorce contradicts that thought.

Note: I half-believe America will learn to love again, if I may be so bold as to say, I think we learn love by giving and suffering, and it may take tremendous hardships to achieve in America with the new wealthy class and the ever-growing intrusion by the state. We are becoming more reliant on government to take care of our basic needs and, in many cases, not work for it. But looking around now, as I'm editing this book during the coronavirus, I wonder if we will have the same wealth standard. Presently I see other American leaders countering America's prosperity.

Well, why am I Catholic? Sometimes I wonder why, and most certainly, if I found something better, would I take it? But there is nothing—absolutely nothing—better for me. There may be something out there better for you in the many different ways of expressing God, but it isn't me; and believe me, I tried finding something else but to no avail. So what is the priority here? It's a person's relationship to the spoken Word, and what is the spoken Word? It is Jesus Christ, the only Son of God, a bridge made visible for all mankind to see. He should not be rejected, but each individual should ask Him for repentance in their own deep down way. Maybe the reason Ann thinks I'm different is because of my searching and conclusions. I searched my heart out for truth, and maybe she sees that.

I found the passage in the book of Numbers 28:4–8; it relates to the Catholic Church's daily offerings, and the church continues offering up the Lamb today as did Israel while they were wandering through the desert. To me, as a Catholic, I have opportunities as did Israel to celebrate daily sacrifices.

Chapter 7

Why Am I Catholic and a Remnant of Israel?

Statue worshiping, the pope telling us what to do, confession, Eucharist, purgatory, Mary interceding for us as a mediator to the Father were the most negative comments I heard from non-Catholics since I was a kid, and their comments made me search for truth; and I found it—in the Catholic Church.

Childhood

I went back into my childhood, daydreaming of what I remember Catholics and Americans said and what they did and how they worshiped. The first thing I remembered from the '50s was women wearing hats or babushkas inside various Christian churches.[a] I don't recall seeing people praying to statues or at them, but when I came to the Midwest, I heard and saw practices similar to that at Catholic Churches, and it disturbed me. Again I can't be sure they were praying to the statue, and I wondered if it could had been a cultural thing. In any case, since my kids all went to school in the Midwest, they were instructed that they know the correct way to pray to the Lord. I also went and researched the standard *Baltimore*

---

[a] First Corinthians 11:1–16; the1950s *Baltimore Catholic Catechism* is out of print.

Catholic Catechism, Edition 2 to find what was officially taught by the church in the 1950s. I thought maybe praying to Mary might be documented in church rulings; and I searched, it wasn't in the 1950s *Baltimore Catechism*, and it being absent from the catechism meant the church officially wasn't pushing it.

Prayer and Mediator

First, praying or worshiping—Catholics believe prayer is the raising of one's mind and heart to God.[a] And secondly, *Jesus is the only Mediator* to the Father.[b] So we'll begin with what the Catholic Church teaches, and what it teaches should come from the catechism of the Catholic Church as indicated in the references at the end of certain sentences. But first to answer Ann Nesbitt's comment, what is so different from me and Catholics today? I think the middle and above-income class families in mainstream Protestant and Catholic Churches were improving their financial situation, and at the same time, they were all depending less on God. However, my family and Ann's family had to depend on God for everyday food, clothes, and material items. We certainly were at the bottom half of the economic recovery of most Americans. At times, Barbara and I were classified as poor, but unlike some of the poor we see of today with stored up anger, Barbara and I didn't see shame in being poor and kept up our hope and strived that someday, we could be financially better off too. That was my main drive when I attended evening college—to help make a better economic life for my family. Barbara and I understood the need to work a little harder, smarter, and pray for our rapidly growing family. That working harder included the priorities of the family too. I did a lot of juggling of time for work and time for family, and quite often, when I couldn't get the balance that we liked, Barbara would make it up in my absence. She was, as we planned, a stay-at-home mom and was always there for the family.

---

[a] CCC 2559.
[b] CCC 771, 426.

Confession

Many non-Catholics are skirmish about confessing their sins to a priest, and they are in good company with some Catholics too. The last thing I wanted to do is to confess my sins to anyone, but the other option would be to confess to a friend. However, it only takes one friend to blab your confession, and the secret is no more a secret. I found most friends couldn't keep secrets and realized a Catholic priest is mandated and bound to keep your confession between him and God. Remember, I take the Bible literally or until I find my translation may not have been on the mark; and in the case of confessing our sins to each other, I agreed.[a] However, we do make a general confession in the beginning of every Mass to each other, and it has been a practice since the seventh century when confession took an additional step and began being performed in private. I like that.

Statue Worship

First, I have to say, I've never worshiped statues nor had any person or thing had to intercede to the Father for me, except through His Son. However, I would look at visuals, photos, or statues as a reminder of one thing or another when I was a youngster and still do at times; as an example, looking at all the visuals and objects in our modern commercial society. Like a statue of Saint Christopher holding a baby, crossing a river to safety. I think there is something good about that. The figure is indicating a man with a child on his shoulders that is now a saint but lived centuries ago. Matter of fact, now that I'm thinking of it, that may be the reason I go very deep in protecting unborn babies from being killed. It may be the graphic of that image of a man saving a baby is why I'm repulsed by abortion, or we may look at the fifth commandment, "You shall not kill" (I've heard of other translations of kill that says it could be murder).

---

[a] James 5:16; CCC 1446–1447.

Visuals

Talk about visuals that affected us, take another look at Germany on TV today. You can see nicely dressed men and women strolling through the parks, walking past shops and businesses, and who would think they were grandchildren of past German generations that were once destitute and shown in movie theaters? I once saw a different Germany, right after WWII, in movies and on black-and-white television. Newly created television was finding its way into homes, and I remember some of the early news episodes. One episode depicted women and children wearing dirty rags, bending over and shifting through garbage containers looking for a meal. They were Germans of the mid-1940s, starving and with only the clothes on their backs to keep them warm.

Today you wouldn't think a great nation like Germany experienced that just seventy years ago, but they, did and the sufferings from their nondepending-on-God leaders brought them to that terrible condition during and after the war. Similarly there may not be a thing we can do to stop the same faith coming into our country with bad leaders and unaware population, as what happened to Germany. It can be stopped when all Christians, Jews, and Muslims cling together as one, asking God for mercy and direction. The German post-war leaders never thought to ask God. If they had, maybe they would have corrected their ways and would have been able to thwart WWII from igniting. But as you'll see in chapter 7, under "Planning," I don't think it could have been any other way. The Germans or the world didn't ask God for help. And the leaders of the world saw it coming.

Adore Mary No, Devotion Yes

Well, I looked up the word *adore* to see if Catholics were taught to adore statues or Mary[a] in my childhood catechism from the 1950s.

---

[a]   CCC 971.

I searched, and I can't find anything related to adoring Mary. However, you'll see in the modern catechism of the Catholic Church, number CCC 971, what most Catholics believe (it is devotion, not adore). I'm not going to put my old 1950 *Baltimore Catholic Catechism* book as a reference because it has been out of print for years. However, the new Catholic Catechism is referenced and recommended in the back of this book as a source of information. At this time, I'll paraphrase the statement and page from the official Catholic Catechism of the 1950s as follows:

My old catechism of the 1950s:
Adore:

1. We adore Christ and venerate the saints, 222.
2. The purpose of the Mass is to adore God, 361.
3. We are to adore Our Lord after Communion in prayer, 374.
4. We pray first to adore God, 476.[a]

(By the way, I just realized number 4 above, and why I don't pray to my deceased son, even as my heart was breaking and splitting. I do, however, ask my guardian angel to tell him I love him). I know, had I not learned from the church's teachings and the Bible, I would be determined to contact and talk to my son. And I ask, how many people pray to their deceased loved ones? I bet a lot. And how do you communicate the right thing to do to a deep aching person because of the loss of a loved one that we shouldn't pray to the dead? How can you say to a person, be careful, you shouldn't pray to a deceased loved one. You say it before the tragedy. However, praying for the dead to be with our Lord is high on the Catholic list of prayers to help console our breaking hearts; but most of all, we pray for all the dead to go to heaven.[b] I like to think of it, similar as asking for your prayers, to pray to God for all of us too.

---

[a] CCC 2680.
[b] CCC 1032.

Modern Catechism

I just looked up the new catechism of the Catholic Church, and it gives a better more concise explanation of adoring God. To adore God is to acknowledge Him as God, as the Creator and Savior, the Lord and Master of everything that exists, as infinite and merciful love.[a] And to Mary, "All generations will call her blessed."[b] The church rightly honors the Blessed Virgin with special devotion and veneration of the saints.[c]

What About Images?

How easy is it to look at an image and see something? I think it is easy, and so does modern industrial man in their surroundings and commercial settings. We are bombarded with images on TV, billboards, posters, food stuff, business cards, you name it, but is it good? It seems to be good for business but doesn't seem to help our souls, when you think we are the image of God. What does that mean? It means we don't worship images of man-made gods that neither breathe nor move for sure.

As a youngster, I had, and still do have, a flare for art and projecting architectural images and not so much a flare for verbal or literary communications. Well, that was true until about seven years ago. And later, I learned to project various architectural visual images from college training and experiences in architectural work places. How easy it was for me to communicate through images and not be bothered by thoughts of my English instructors shaking their hands in grief, listening to me fumble in verbal and written communications other than the proper way. I learned quickly to use visual images in art and architecture to communicate a message to the point. If I was speaking to anyone about any subject, I would find myself taking

---

[a] CCC 2096–2097.
[b] Luke 1:26–49.
[c] CCC 971–972.

a pencil and drawing some kind of an image to communicate the image thought in lieu of words, be it architectural, travel directions, or almost any kind of descriptive conversation. I would simply draw a rough visual sketch of what I was thinking, and the recipient would just about always get it; but I was a handicapped communicator if a pencil wasn't available.

I think the same is true for statues, although I've advanced much further than to look at a statue in order to gain a visual thought. I can now close my eyes and think of God and His creatures, sort of like reading the book of Revelation and its many images that purposely come into you. However, I take that a little further, and in some of my deepest, most private, most satisfying moments, especially in the mornings, I think of God; but honestly, I didn't always have visuals. I do now. I often kissed my children on their heads, showing my love for them. Now I find myself kissing Jesus and the Father on their heads in a love gesture image, and I love doing it. I have a love episode that consumes me. I love those moments when He seems so near, and my son Michael is with God and near me too. I love God. Similar to the story in 1 Kings and a prophet being told to go outside the cave and look for God. The prophet went out and heard a strong wind that tore the mountain, and God wasn't there. Next an earthquake came, but God was not in the earthquake. Next a fire came, but God was not in the fire. And after the fire came a gentle breeze, and then the prophet Elijah covered his face and spoke to God.[a]

Women

That should take care of Catholic teaching of adoring. However, Catholics are made up of thousands of cultures and in various stages of believing. Some may not even understand the word *adore*, and because Mary is a woman figure, a person may find it easy loving the human type of gesture in her womanhood. However, for sure, Catholics come together united with Christ at Mass, eating and

---

[a] First Kings 19:1–18.

drinking together as He wanted us to, as it was a memorial of Him at the Last Supper, the new covenant.[a]

During a Discipleship Course

An example of loving a woman like Mary, I think of various religious cultures, like when I attended the Diocese of Kalamazoo Discipleship course, a fellow student told me he just could not go to Jesus because Jesus is a man. He tried many times but could only go to Mary. I guessed he may have had a serious problem with his father, and his mother was more of a loving figure as God intended a woman to be. After all, God is love, and we're always searching for love; and besides we can only obtain salvation from God's Son, Jesus. I reassured him that Mary intercedes for us to Jesus, and Jesus is the only Mediator to the Father. However, before the end of the two-year discipleship course, he said with a sincere gesture that he now goes to Jesus directly. I wondered how many other Catholics and non-Catholics had similar problems, not being able to go to a man figure or not advancing from the woman figure? You remember my bio father wasn't a saint, and I never thought of him as a kind of heavenly person, and I didn't think of my mother as a divine person either. So maybe I was blessed, but I had other problems that were exceptionally more difficult to overcome.

The good part for my friend in the discipleship class was when he figured out, it was okay for Mary to intercede for us to go to Jesus, but Jesus was the only person to intercede for us to go to the Father. I'll paraphrase what the recent Catholic Catechism says about intercession to the Father below.

Intercession is a prayer of petition which leads us to pray as Jesus did. He is the one intercessor *with* the Father on behalf of all men, especially sinners.[b]

---

[a] Luke 22:19–20; Matthew 26:26–29; Mark 14:22–25.
[b] CCC 2634, *Catholic Catechism*.

So, my friends, the correct teaching is there, but how much of the teachings do the billions of people absorb at certain times can be complicated? It makes me wonder why there are over thirty thousand non-Catholic denominations in America. Maybe because of the many ways to believe, I guess. That is why I think our own salvation from God should be the number 1 priority. He wants each of us to teach and witness, communicating to the world about Christ. But then again, how do you get the attention of the multitude of people in the world? And remember what Jesus told Saint Peter when He handed the church keys to him? "What you gain on earth you gain in Heaven and what you lose on earth you lose in Heaven."[a] That statement has lots of real practical implications. And to me, the implication is that we're not perfect, and God, not man, has the last to say of what is lost or saved.[b]

As an example, if I say something stupid or the church sends people running away because of a doctrine, then we lost something on earth, but our Lord has the last say, and everything was given to Jesus by the Father, and Jesus doesn't want to lose anyone.[c]

Another example of misunderstandings of teachings come about from the multitude of various cultures. A good example was when a Protestant missionary helped me to better understand the different concepts of religious cultures.

A Protestant missionary informed me that many Protestant missionaries changed their tone in demanding that certain natives that were converted be spoon-fed, and they not immediately demand they change 100 percent from their pagan ways of life. They allowed certain indigenous natives to hold onto certain customs for the time being, even though it plainly disregarded some Scripture verses. What caused such a change was a few overzealous fundamentalists were attempting to change these natives to Christianity overnight, and they just couldn't do it. The natives, in frustration, gave up (sort of like modern man giving up too) and revolted, thereby disrupting and killing mis-

---

[a]   Revelation.
[b]   John 5:44.
[c]   John 6:39.

sionaries. Little by little, the Protestants, like Catholic missionaries, learned to accept a few of the pagan ways and practices until hopefully, they would become strong enough to remove the evil themselves.

I remember as a kid, Catholic missionaries allowed certain people to hold onto some of their different customs. I can see, in some past centuries, the church learned valuable lessons with bringing people closer to God, and now Protestant missionaries are doing similar things too. I know for sure, without a doubt, I had to have more patience raising our children, especially the girls, during their teenage years, let alone the church caring for billions in two thousand or so years.

Hold up a second, I want to tell you something I invented when the girls reached sixteen years of age. And you are free to borrow it. I invented a machine to put the sixteen-year-old girls into hibernation until they reached twenty-one and took them out. Ha ha, sorry about that, I just had to tell you a joke because many people shake their heads when I tell them I have six girls. That's how I got my girls out of the terrible teenage years. Ha ha!

So getting back to the above culture difference, I wanted to tell you about that old saying, "Rome wasn't built in a day," and is a real statement for the church yesterday and today. Just how is it possible that we, the church, can convert all people at once? When the various different cultures have been around for centuries? I found the study of the Old Testament revealing when it came to Israel coming to power and losing that power many times, and it was only through the graces that God overlooked their faults, and they were able to get back onto their feet.

Of course, the American missionaries stationed overseas could see the evil customs Americans were developing, preventing people from becoming closer to our Lord. That was disheartening for all missionaries to look over their shoulders and see a country, that has the most materials of all nations, turning away from Christ. What I think is regrettable: people coming from the Middle Eastern countries see Americans as the great evil. Especially the visiting Islamic people seeing the sins of America while here and or what Hollywood has to offer as entertainment all over the world.

Women and Old Testament

I've heard comments, especially from women who are concerned by some Old Testament descriptions of how awful women are treated. Just remember, ladies, the culture of most men in those days seemed to treat women as inferior, and you can still see that in today's cultures. Jesus made it apparent that women and men both were high on His thoughts. I could not find much on what went on with women's personal lives other than what I read about in the Old Testament. I know even before political correctness made a bigger deal out of this subject a few years back, if I ever tried to treat Barbara anything but as a woman and wife, I think I would face serious problems. However, she is comfortable that I lead the family, and I'm comfortable with the nurturing strengths she provides for the family and her being confident in her natural abilities and strengths.

Although I find many men in the Old Testament were treated harsher than most women. It seemed our Lord was stricter on men by keeping them focused and from constantly straying. Often you see men that strayed and were disciplined severely for their infractions. However, many courageous women like Ruth, Hannah, Judith, Esther, Naomi, Athaliah, and others in the books were held in high esteem. Why is that, I ask? You wouldn't think it by certain phases or just glancing at the Hebrew Bible, certain women were held higher in admiration when you dig deep into Scripture. I found women to be stronger and closer to God. I think they have more natural love characteristics, whereas men have to dig deeper for it. I think King David had it and was called out by God to "being a man after His own heart." Even though David sinned, he loved Israel. I think there is a message here of loving His people.

When we look at the New Testament, we see Mary being shown favor by an angel as the Virgin Mother of our Lord or, as some people like to think, the carrier of the Word, and she was. She is so blessed that her baby doesn't have an earthly blood father or blood brothers. God kept her from being touched by any man, before and after. Not even Joseph, her husband, was allowed to touch her. Sort of like the protection in the Old Testament of the ark of the covenant which also carried the Word of God and was carefully protected by Israel and God.[a] And like the early Israelites protecting the Word in the ark of the covenant, the Catholic Church protects Mary's image, the carrier of the Word.

Modern Women

For centuries, the various Catholic Churches throughout the world held Mary in high esteem, even the Islamic and some Lutheran religions do too. But now in this century, I wonder how the image of Mary will fare? Women are being projected, especially in Hollywood, as not being so kind, tender, or forgiving but as possible sex symbols, war symbols, police, and unfortunately not projecting a nurturing nature, which the nurturing state, without a doubt, is as close to God humans usually get. Isn't that strange that women have it and men have to do extraordinary things to reach that level? We are challenged to find love and to love.

Just recently, US Marine women posed lewd photos on social media, exposing their bodies, and some of those leaders pretend, without admitting, they were responsible for demanding that the military put women in military soldier positions based on their political association. They demanded we forget about gender identification, that everyone is the same. That is a great naive misconception and another lie by social science thoughts. Why do they think such harmful things? You know, it can be considered borderline hate, attempting to push their agenda down our throats to a corrupt way of thinking. I think it goes against the good of a nation, but then again, look back a little further and see other hateful acts. It's bad enough we have young men going in combat, and now the great minds say it should be women too. Can you see why it is damaging? Can you see why lewd fashions, photos, and movies coming out of Hollywood, rousing our sexual desires is bad for sustainable marriages? Could we say lewdness helps leads to hate and does hate lead to war? We, who

---

[a]   Second Samuel 6:1–8; 2 Maccabees 2:1–9 (not found in Protestant Bibles).

are trying to have good marriages and build up our communities, are being bombarded from all directions by others who attempt to destroy a good pillar of a community. Why? Why? Why? Root cause analysis can get the why answer.

So I ask, is it good that modern man look at women as sex objects to be used to satisfy their desires only? Or is there more to women than meets the eye. And when lewd men are found looking at filthy nude photographs, who is at fault? Of course, the lewd person is, but it goes deeper, and maybe you can experiment with using the root course process to get to the basic problem—who is at fault from the start. A good research project to study using the root cause method is the gymnastic doctor in Michigan who is currently in jail for sexually abusing over one hundred girls. My biggest concern is, how did he get away with it for so long? The other question is why those girls weren't strong enough to say something convincing and get their parents involved immediately?

Childbirth Saves

Then we see something else in the New Testament that seems to put women on a higher level than men. We see something special, "women are saved through childbirth."[a] What makes childbirth so special? Why do you suppose that statement is in the Bible? Well, I think a good guess is in order here. Every time I looked at my wife, holding each of our eight infants and nursing them, it seemed to me, she was in ecstasy. I could never forget many of those images of her holding our babies out of my thoughts. I think women experience more of a natural love of God having children than most men do in a lifetime. Men have to work harder to find God's love, and I think many women have that natural ability and understanding given to them right after childbirth, and hopefully they understand and hold onto it. So my conclusion, deep loving is ecstasy, and women

---

[a]   First Timothy 2:15.

experience high love of overwhelming emotion through childbirth. However, if they are not vigilant, they could lose it.

What About Men

But what about men, can they find God in such a beautiful ecstasy setting as women can at childbirth? I think so, especially those men that can speak to God in tongues. After Jesus resurrected, He sent the Holy Spirit to us to help better our community. Right now, looking at what we do as a nation, I wonder if we have a chance of opening the hearts of all men to experience God's love. It'll take all of us with all our strength in prayer, kindness, tenderness, and forgiveness to win over evil. So to win the spiritual battle, we must seek God first and find what He wants and how He made us to succeed. All the strength we need is depending on God the Father as people have done for centuries. When Israel did what was written or programmed in their hearts, the Israelites prospered and remained safe. Since Christ, we have the Word programmed in our hearts, and it is exciting or maybe even ecstasy to find it and pass it on. All we have to do is ask and continue asking if need be.[a]

Eucharist

What I heard, every now and then, was that Catholics were cannibals because they ate the body and drank the blood of Christ, and/or the Eucharist was only a symbol or memorial of what Christ said. Eating and drinking the body and blood of Jesus Christ is what we do at Mass, and it is at the heart of the church's life and mind.[b] It is a memorial we should do in remembrance of Christ, but also it is truly the body and blood of Christ after being transformed at the

---

[a]   First Corinthians 15:58.
[b]   CCC 1322–1419, 2177.

altar, similar to the Last Supper.[a] The understanding used to designate the unique change of the Eucharistic bread and wine into the body and blood of Christ is called *transubstantiation*. Through the consecration of the bread and wine, there occurs the change of the entire substance of the body of Christ and of the entire substance of the wine into the blood of Christ, even though the appearances of bread and wine remain[b] (Jesus says so).

Ran Away

We see in all Gospels the references of bread and wine becoming the body and blood of Christ. Matter of fact, there were some disciples that when they heard Christ say, "This is my body and this is my blood," they too, like a few modern people, took off in disgust from hearing what was said.[c] Jesus didn't turn around and say, "Hey, come back, come back, I was just using a metaphor." No, Jesus stated a fact of what the new covenant had in store for us. And the church today doesn't say, it is only a metaphor. They repeat what Jesus said, "This is my body and this is my blood."

Purgatory

I've heard there is only one chance in this life, and you go either to hell or heaven. That couldn't be further from the truth from what I understand God does for us. I can only speak for myself, whether or not I'm going to heaven or hell when we die. I can't say for sure if I'm going to heaven, but I'll be ever so happy to find myself there. I step back a little when I look inside of me, and I know there is still a long way to go. Know for sure it is Jesus that has the last say, and it is not what I can do or not do. All I can do is hope, and the biggest surprise

---

[a] CCC 1376.
[b] John 6:1–15, 6:51–58.
[c] John 6:35–66.

for us ever is when we find ourselves in heaven.[a] I do have a chance, even if my heart isn't pure as I think it should be at the time of my death, I'll go into a state of final purification before my entrance into heaven. I believe when all men die, they are imperfect, and a final cleansing of final state is purgatory.[b] My first hint of a purgatory was when God told Moses to take off his shoes, for the place for which he stood was holy ground.[c] The second is in the book of 2 Maccabees.[d] There are, I see, many other hints in Scripture.

Bible Misunderstandings

Bible misunderstanding brings to mind an incident that happened in Ohio one Sunday when we were getting the younger kids ready for Mass in the mid-1970s.

We heard a knock at the door, and I answered it while my three oldest children were only about twelve feet away, sitting on the couch, facing the door. At that time, Barbara and I were rushing, getting the younger kids ready for church. At the door was a person from some place outside the neighborhood and asked me if he could come in and talk about the Word of God to us. I politely replied that we were getting ready for church, and we didn't have the time right now to discuss anything.

His reply wasn't as polite as mine when he asked what church I belonged, to and I answered the Catholic Church. And before I could get *church* out of my mouth, he spurted out, "Catholics can't be saved by making the sign of the cross because it isn't in the Bible, and it is blasphemy."

I immediately asked him very calmly what I have to do to be saved? I knew what to do, but I wanted to show my children that he was talking trash accusing us of blasphemy. So I brought him into the living room, sat him down across from my kids, and went on to

---

[a] Romans 8:18–27; 1 Peter 1:3–9.
[b] CCC 1031.
[c] Exodus 3:5–6.
[d] Second Maccabees 12:1–38; Matthew 5:25–26.

question him and repeated his words. "So you say if it isn't in the Bible, it's blasphemy?"

"Yes, that's right, that's right," verifying his previous remark, and I continued asking him what do I have to do to be saved, and he said I must speak in tongues. I got him already without a struggle, and I didn't care about being late for church. I wasn't going to let this guy spew out damaging false truths about the Bible nor about our Catholic beliefs, especially when my kids were in hearing distance. I further asked him to find where it says in his Bible, we must speak in tongues to be saved. And further asked him, that if it isn't in the Bible, then he must be speaking blasphemy, is that right? With a quick "that's right, that's right," he opened his Bible and began looking for where it says you must speak in tongues to be saved. His first try that he pointed out wasn't anything close to what his argument was, and I called him out on it, and he sort of agreed, moving around in his chair. Then he started flipping his pages and came to a verse that he claimed was the verse, and I asked him to read it; and again it wasn't anywhere near his proclamation of saving by speaking in tongues. By this time, he was perspiring and began to stink when he suddenly jumped up from the chair and went out the door.

I made sure my kids understood what just happened, and later we heard he made further accusations by telling our neighbors that the devil knows Scripture more than believers do. You can't win for losing with that kind of lying spirit. The moral of my story is, the world has a long way to go to fully understand God, and we need to constantly search for it and proclaim the faith. However, I think if we Christians proclaim Jesus as the Savior of the world—and most Christians do—we can be saved. It is up to Him. We should be exceedingly happy that we believe and quickly unite in Jesus and settle our differences. Or get people like me pushing back a lying face.

Good Guesser or Sensitivity

I remember when I was in Catholic school in either the second or third grade during the early 1950s when our teacher decided to have us play a game during recess in the classroom. She would have a student come up to the front of the class with their back toward the class, and she would give an eraser to one of the students to hide the eraser inside their desk. Each student took a turn standing up and turning around to try to guess where the eraser was. None of the students standing up lasted more than one turn because of not being able to guess. Then it was my turn to guess, and I began guessing. I guessed who the first student was with an eraser, and then the second and third and another until I reached maybe twenty kids, and the teacher called the game off. Later she asked if I would tell my mother to come in to see her. Mom came in to school and talked to the nun that seemed like an hour, and Mom never told me what the conversation was about. Later I figured my abilities to guess wasn't a paranormal thing but pure observational talent sensitivities, making eye contact and seeing something as eye movements and/or a different facial expression. Remember, I constantly watched my father when he came home from work for signs he would explode from watching expressions and listen to his outbursts.

Good Guesser or Talent

Later when I was in the army, and I just got out of installation intelligence school, I soon had my first assignment while stationed at a Nike Missile Base in Wilmington, Ohio. My first sergeant got a call of a new recruit, waiting at the bus station about eight miles away from base, to be picked up for duty. It was my job to ensure authorized soldiers were admitted into our site.

I jumped into my jeep and went into town and picked up the recruit and checked his papers while we were in the jeep before we went back to the missile site. They seemed to be in good order, and we began driving back. Something wasn't right with our conversations, and I kept up the small talk to settle him down and organize my thoughts. Finally he told me that he was from New York, and his family owned a large apple fruit farm upstate with many employees. I asked him what he was doing in the army if his parents had a large farm. He slurred just a slight bit, and I heard it, and I detected something, but I didn't know what. He was doing a good job hiding being nervous, and I tried to look him in the eye to no avail. He wouldn't allow me to look at him.

We got to the base, and I handed my first sergeant the recruit's official papers and told him something was wrong; I didn't know what it was, but something wasn't right. I guided the recruit into a room next to our office while we continued checking his papers. We called the last unit listed on his official papers he was at, and they verified it was him, and he was stationed there. Normally verifying his last unit from official orders would be as far as these types of inquiries would go. However, I still had bad feelings from our initial contact, and we continued checking for a couple of more hours, going back even further into his previous units he was stationed at. Upon further checking, we discovered the second and third company had no knowledge of him and claimed he was never stationed there. Huh, both companies never heard of him, and it appeared like the person in our holding room was bogus or an intruder.

He was an intruder, I was sure of, and I instructed the day armed guard to go into the room with me where the recruit was and stand in front of him. Standing in front of him, I had the guard lock and load a .308 bullet into his M14 rifle chamber and watched the recruit's expressions, falling to his knees. His expression was pure panic, and as soon as I saw his expression, I asked who he was. He quickly added that he was a US Army Central Intelligence Agent and, at the same moment, showed his badge to me. He stated he was instructed to penetrate our missile site as a military training exercise.

Looking back, I can see where several soldiers later made remarks about the outcome of the attempted penetration, that I had some sort of a psychic intuition. That couldn't be further from the truth. I wasn't psychic; I figured it out later, and it was pure alert sensitivities brought on by my family situation.

What do you think, folks, could it be sensitivity, psychic, or a guardian angel? I'd like to think it was from my years of avoiding misfits from my father and his mood swings. I once fantasized it could be some type of psychic ESP thing, but that thought lasted only a short time, and it was kind of a bummer not to be.

Israel Protected by Angels

Do you remember the Arab-Israel Six-Day War of 1967? An estimated 456,000 Arab troops, with 2,880 tanks and 900 aircraft were about to invade a smaller army of Israelis with 264,000 troops, 800 tanks, and 900 aircraft. The Arabs were backed up by Egypt, Jordan, Syria, and Lebanon, and more Arabs in reserves from Iraq, Algeria, Kuwait, and Sudan. America and Great Britain declared not to get involved in the war.

As it happened, the Arabs vowed to make the blue Mediterranean Sea run red with the blood of the Jews. As they were about to invade and wipe out Jerusalem, they were stopped in their tracks. There in front of the Arab line were angels protecting the Israelite Army. The Arabs were awestruck and would not advance or fight. I'm a remnant of Israel and a Catholic. (See Chapter 8 for suspected angel visit in Time Line 2010 to 2020.)

Evil Sees Lack of Faith

Evil can see lack of faith immediately; even the Russians are able to see that as they prod our thoughts and nerves; they can sense weakness. They have it in them to know right from wrong. Just watch the news and see how we are depicted in the news concerning what evil is going in America. Evil men are watching, and it could definitely be a hint of weakness that Russia and others are watching. Certainly North Korean Kim Jong can see, maybe not understand, but he can see America is weakening. They know when God is not completely with us. They can imagine watching Hollywood trash; it is easy to understand we're not completely protected, something they see is favorable for them. How can we not be afraid of evil people? Asking God to protect His people is deep stuff, and our enemies can see it strengthens us. They can see and understand when evil is in control. History shows Israel's enemies watched for signs of when Israel would abandon their faith and attack. Yes, sir, evil knows God but doesn't submit to Him. We have free will, and God will allow us do what we want and may even allow pagan nations to conquer us in spite of our wealth, pride, and preparedness. The Catholic Church can only do so much to prevent war, and in the '70s, the Catholic Church attempted to keep America from decaying. I watched their efforts, and only a few Catholics answered.

Complainers

I hope to dispel any assumptions on your part that I strictly act out every word in the Bible. When I first began reading Scripture, I found basic Catholic understandings to help us raise our children. Scripture was simple, orderly, and to the point. It showed me how to improve, encourage, and console with many others. Especially the New Testament that had lots of common sense life stories, and what was amazing was that we related our own lives to biblical concepts and survived as a family. The main theme was that our Lord wants us to adore Him and follow His way and not our way. We learned fast from the Spirit what to say and motivate our kids, not nagging them was an example I found. Sometimes I wasn't consistent and lost those examples in a scramble of life and went on my own and did not ask our Lord for directions. Example, in one of my class studies of the Old Testament, we see Israel people complaining about everything around them and it got loud enough that God punished them.[a] Why in the world would God punish a bunch of complainers? It is similar to not relying on Him.

Nothing satisfied the complainers; they weren't happy, and the Lord wasn't fully in their lives. Unwittingly when the Lord was out of their lives, they were hurting themselves not asking for help and or being satisfied with what they had. However, God allows us to do

---

[a]   Numbers 11:1–3.

our thing until we ask for help or maybe discipline or nudge us to get them back on track. I asked a class group once if complaining was a sin, and if so, why? The class seemed glassy eyed, probably wondering what kind of complaining can cause sin. I asked again, do we commit sin when we complain? Yes, by not asking God to help with whatever annoys us. Small as complaining is, it will become larger into bigger sins. All I care about is you and making it a paved road to our Lord.

Think about it, are we depending on the Lord if we have to complain? No, it is a sin when we leave God out of our lives. All He wants is for us to ask Him to help solve problems. Complaining distracts us from relying on Him which can cause us to become weaker, thinking we can do it by ourselves or just complain and nothing gets done to correct whatever is wrong. I know, I was the biggest complainer of all. Well, getting back to class. A lady in our study group made a remark, and everyone was listening intently when she said, "Oh dear, I never knew I was sinning when I complained so often."

Her husband rolled up his eyes in approval of her remark. You'd think breaking only the Ten Commandments was the only sin, right? Well, I think looking outside the box, we can see that griping may break contact with God, and it could be classified as being part of the first commandment. What do you think? A little detail, but it can grow larger in our family, community, and nation, and it could become devastating. Even now, I hear complainers during the coronavirus breakout concerning our state political decisions, and I know exactly what they are communicating; and before I know it, I'm agreeing with them with contempt for the leaders. I truly have to stop and know I cannot do a thing about it, except Barbara and I should ask the Lord for justice and removal from the coronavirus. Is it a Catholic teaching to pray for help? Yep, and many other Christians as well.

How Do Catholics Find God?

In the 1980s, when I was teaching high school kids concerning the Ten Commandments and then tried to relate the commandments to Jesus and the Beatitudes in Matthew, I realized that anything we do without God is a sin. It was easier to explain to them that everything not of God is sin, God is without sin, and the daily struggle to get closer to Him is when we feel our best, and it is always when we're not sinning. I remember being asked by a teenager, "How do we find God?"

It was a fantastic question but difficult for many of us to achieve, especially me, until I figured it out. We simply ask Him to know Him. What I found was that God created us in His image. And what is God's image?[a] If He created us in His image, we must look like Him, but there is more than looks to this. God has other special qualities, and we can see many are spiritual and invisible qualities. However, it appears, according to the verses we read in Genesis, that we are the image of God, and it kind of looks like the verse is image only, but later written in Scriptures, we soon see spiritual gifts were given to people as part of God's image. An example are the prophets Elijah and Elisha in the Old Testament writings.[b]

Since Christ came, His teachings have made it easier to obtain spiritual gifts through the Holy Spirit left with us.[c] Obtaining these spiritual gifts through faith, you should be in a state of being humbled, asking our Lord for additional gifts. I don't know how a person can praise God without first having faith to do so, but it happens.

This is what I know about receiving spiritual gifts—we are more than likely in a humbled state of being when we ask God for various gifts. Be careful, remember my story about all we have to do is ask God, and we shall receive? Remember as an example, I asked for a million dollars, and I didn't get it? Why, if I had the faith and asked God for it, why didn't He give it to me? Deep down inside, I only *wished* for a million, I really didn't need it, and deep down inside us, the difference is known by Him for now in our lives. I didn't get a million bucks, so do I say my faith is shallow? Yep, I think the request is shallow. I merely wished and wanted a million to be self-sufficient,

---

[a] Genesis 1:26–3.
[b] First Kings 17–22; 2 Kings 1–13.
[c] CCC 1830, 1831, 183.

independent, and not rely on our Father all the time. What is wrong with me, I'd say. I believe, but why isn't He responding? So what is the big deal? I think everyone knows at least there is a God, including trees and animals know Him. So where does that put me and the rest of man? Man's heart is never satisfied, whether he knows it or not, until he seeks what it is in his heart and continues his quest. We were made that way to continue our quest, and that should be easy enough to gain. However, sin has the ability to prevent us from achieving it. All we have to do each day is to find Him, to seek Him first, and all other things we need will come later. If that is the case—and it is the case—then it makes sense to ask for wisdom while we keep knocking for higher spiritual gifts. And ladies, gentleman, girls, and boys, that is how I obtained spiritual gifts. We ask the Father through Jesus Christ, our Savior.

However, from my perspective, animals and trees were not made to search for Him. He made animals and trees from what I can tell as creatures, and it appears some type of creatures will be with us when we are hopefully in heaven. He gave us the free will to either search for Him or not, but animals or trees, I cannot say they have that free will. They seem to do what God intended them to do and other species to do what they do, and nothing more or nothing less. All animals and plants know God in a special way. He made them to know Him, similar to putting into us the ability to know and love Him.

How Do We Love God?

I know God loves me, but do I love Him? One day, I heard it. The answer was being read from the ambo (podium) at Mass. The lecturer went on to say—and I'll paraphrase it here—"We will know we love God when we obey His commandments." Sounds hopeful but difficult to obtain. It wasn't difficult for me to know I really didn't fully love God. I had to ask God for help, even to learn to love Him. However, once we begin to love Him, the struggle is worth all the gold and silver in our pockets. Gold and silver actually begins to become meaningless compared to knowing God is here inside of us. And it is the struggles we go through that make it worth searching for our Lord. The struggles give us strength, energy, and internal gladness.

As you peek back after attempting to get closer by searching, you'll see it makes for a stronger and brighter you. In my case, I became physically stronger, with it appears a little more arthritic in my older years, but more importantly, I became spiritually more alert and freer. As I got older, I had serious concerns that I shared with God, but because of Him being there for me, I ask for help from the emotion that can paralyze me at my age, and that is fear. Fear is now way back in the shadows. Our Father, without a doubt, does not want us to fear. This coronavirus pandemic has all the qualities of fear. We should be concerned, but fear is presently making life miserable for others now and in the future from what I can see.

Why Am I Catholic?

In summary, I am Catholic because I am a remnant of Israel because Jesus instituted the Eucharist and handed the Apostle Peter the keys to the church. But most of all, my inner faith tells me so.

Review of Chapter 8

Time Line (1942–2020) and Health

How could our nation have gotten this far in prosperity from the 1940s and turn around and head toward a seemly beginning of a storm in recent 2010s? You'll see in this time line my journey from the day I was born in 1942, the comparisons of today, some of the songs of the decade, and how I scaled up and interpreted the changes from personal family and world observations to present-day events.

Chapter 8

Time Line—1942 through 2020, Grass Man or Angel?

It was noisy in New York City on that day in March 1942. Sirens and horns were blasting away, even though the hospital windows were closed. It's no wonder I was screaming at the top of my lungs, being taken out of a warm serene environment. Did you ever try to think back to the time you came out of your mother, and the doctor held you upside down and spanked you? I have many times, and sometimes. I honestly think I remembered that episode of that very moment—being spanked, crying, and seemly seeing everything spinning around me. What a change that had to be for a newborn.

Economic times in the 1940s, during the war years, were financially difficult for many families to purchase food, sugar, and basic living items such as cribs, couches, chairs, heating oils, gasoline, and more without ration stamps. However, most people improvised, like when my mother needed a baby crib for me soon after being born, and the Red Cross told her to use a dresser drawer. It worked all right, and I guess I didn't know the difference of a crib and a dresser drawer, but my mother did; and I heard what the Red Cross did to her all through the rest of her life.

That's what Mom did. She complained all the time, especially to Dad when she had his ear, and I could see the can't-do frustration in him. I never got the impression Mom seemed satisfied with anything in life, but her own annoyance, she seemed satisfied with, like it was her comfort zone. Maybe, just maybe, you get enough people annoyed together, and war becomes a reality. What about complaining? Could complaining start wars? Yep, I think the right conditions and with little hope, various-size wars can begin and grow. Well, what is so wrong with complaining? We want to make things better in our lives, and that isn't a sin, is it? Yes, I think it is a sin of man, not relying on the Father to help make things better.[a]

Early 1940s: Nazi Germany Killed Their Own

Well, Hitler legally began killing six million Jews and five million others with the stroke of a pen. The Nazis were highly intelligent people and wanted to rid the population of certain people, and so they passed laws to kill the less desirable in Germany and eventually brought them in from other countries. Later in the late 1940s, American black-and-white movie newsreels viewed the German soldiers going into Jewish homes and taking them out with long thin bayonets attached to their rifles on their backs, or maybe it was rifle barrels; it was similar to what I could imagine in 2018 during anti-abortion demonstrations I attended at abortion clinics. As I walked on the sidewalk, carrying my placard in front of the Kalamazoo abortion clinic, I could see young women in expensive shiny vehicles with long white skinny middle fingers pointed at me. They would give me the finger going up and down vigorously. Their finger reflections truly reminded me of the long thin bayonets the German soldiers had on their rifles while trotting toward the houses and taking the Jews out of their homes in those historic newsreels.

Oh, by the way, my placard that I carried was printed by the Knights of Columbus for those demonstrations which read "LOVE LIFE—CHOOSE LIFE." Also I don't have any ill feelings toward those women and men that flip me off. I truly feel sad that they are missing an important part of their heart. Amen.

I asked myself recently if the 1940s were the worst or the best of times Americans may go through, and I find that those days in

---

[a] Numbers 11:1–3.

the late 1940s were compared to the beginning of prosperity for America. I wonder today as to what may be happening to our country that seems to be losing its bearings now. Can you see as I do, that something is awry, and we are on a collision course?[a]

Moved West Sometime in Early 1940s

It didn't take too many hard days in New York City during the war of the early 1940s for my father to pack up the family and move to Yakama, Washington. Dad needed a fresh start to find better opportunities than what was happening in the city. When we arrived in Yakama, the economic times were no better than New York. Dad could only find menial part-time jobs on surrounding dairy farms, and when that didn't work, he found work in restaurants; and when that didn't materialize favorably, we returned to New York City in hopes that the economic times improved. Dad was a basket case, and there was no let up on shouting, arguing, and physical abuse to my mom and myself. Matter of fact, Dad continued his mental and physical abuse even after things settled down a little. I often wondered later, after the Vietnam War years, when it became known about the mentally wounded experiences that veterans suffered, and Dad may have been a PSTD casualty from the Second World War and/or was he an unsettled man, given up by his mother and made to live in an orphanage as he did.

Dad was given up by his mother at an early age and put into an orphanage where Irish Christian Brothers took care of homeless boys. The brothers were tough and religiously strict on wayward boys. The boys had to learn to do it the Irish Brother way. Dad would tell me stories of what the orphanage was like, being ruled by determined young men dressed in brown robes that wouldn't allow any deviation from the rules, and if there were, there would be heck to pay for it. The brothers would get an unruly boy and either spank him or put

[a] Second Samuel 23:1–7. Hopefully more people around us are in God's house than what may appear.

him in the boxing ring. My father loved the part of boxing stories. The strong-arm stuff may have worked for most of the boys, but not my father. My father was different, as I later saw his personality surface with my sister and myself.

As I look back at Dad's other relationships, it appeared he was rebellious all throughout his working life and would step up immediately and resist any obstruction of injustice. Dad wanted truth and fairness, and he was too quick to actually push back or fight if he didn't instantly see it. The quick trait for sure rubbed off on me, and as I mentioned, my daughter too. However, both my daughter Myla and I seem to suffer from his DNA and clung onto God's mercy as though we were twins. It is frustrating to watch your own go through similar situations as your parent went through. But the good side of it was that we had to figure out how to forgive in order to withstand the onslaught of unnerving situations in our own lives. The disruptions in my spirit seemed like it would take over my life, and it could have if someone somewhere was not praying for me to persevere through the same hellish inner emotions that my father in the '40s possessed. Dad, so it appeared, could not achieve relief until he was on his deathbed in 1978 and after confessing his sins.[a]

Was I to meet the same fate, inheriting the same negative DNA or PTSD as he had? I spent and I continue spending time especially in prayer[b] to thwart off what seemed like his DNA effects. What could it be? Is this what God gives me as my challenge? He knows my heart better than I, so maybe He is showing His kindness all these years that I have strived to find Him. And in spite of my rebelliousness, God certainly didn't cripple me when I sinned but always gave me a stern nudge.

The war was taking its toll on American citizens, and I actually looked at a poster with a man wearing a large blue-and-white hat that looked grim, pointing his finger toward me. Later the posters were everywhere, supporting the war effort. It said, "I WANT YOU." And later I found out it was Uncle Sam, the government representative.

---

[a] Psalms 116:1–6.

[b] Matthew 21:22

Lower Middle 1940s

The beginning lower '40s economy was about the same, but jobs were slowly becoming available to men and women, only because many men were away at war, and the war effort to support the troops was in high demand. Dad was able to find a job during that time washing skyscraper windows, only to fall from a scaffold a week later and was unable to work for some time. Not willing to go back to washing windows again, he would try any kind of work, but climbing skyscrapers was not an option for him. During the healing time from the window-washing accident, he milled around in our high-rise city apartment in Bronx, New York, until he could not stand the inactivity any longer and borrowed a newspaper to read the "Want Ads." It didn't take long, and he found a sit-down type of job driving a bus. Oh yeah, he could drive, and it seemed like it could be a cushy job too. He applied and was hired during his interview to operate a New York City transit bus, but there was a downside to that cushy job. It was during a union bus strike, he had to drive the bus and his association of being on the bus driving would soon take its toll on him in a violent way.

I remember he showed me a newspaper article photo of himself in the *New York Times* he kept for years. He was smiling and showing his face with the bus window open that day while attempting to break a union transit line. I remember the men in the photo around the bus had clubs and looked angry and appeared to be focused, looking at Dad. Mom felt uneasy looking at the article, but Dad smiled and assured her it was okay. His smile and a rare hug were short-lived, however. Dad had a serious problem; he broke a strong union bus line during hard economic times in order to collect a nice paycheck for himself. He desperately needed the money; the work was great, and he felt he would continue driving and bring home a paycheck forever if need be. But it wasn't that easy, or would it be?

One evening, a loud knock was heard at the door, and when Mom opened it, several angry union thugs rushed and pushed her backward. The thugs forced their way into our apartment, and as we watched, they beat Dad senseless. I knew even at a young age, from the beatings I got from him, that this was different—serious, frightful, and violent. They had my dad down on the floor, kicking, swearing, and yelling at him until, I guess, they were satisfied and left as quickly as they came. He recovered later and found another job, but not before we had more difficult family and economic times. I often looked back at that incident and wondered if I became resolved and too hardened at an early age. Maybe that's why I always dreamed of becoming a soldier to defend the helpless, and when America turned their backs on its military men in the 1960s, I was devastated and gave up my military service after my enlistment of seven years was served.

Disastrous War Ended

The Second World War was responsible for over thirty-five million lives lost with millions more displaced, homeless, and suffering from broken families and hunger everywhere. It was the war to end all wars, huh, so the popular phrase was repeated and rang in my ears many times until other wars came about. I remembered the exact day, and I was three and a half when the war ended in 1945, while living in Jackson Heights, New York, and all the sirens, car horns, and people were coming out of their cars, duplex apartments during the day, dancing, shouting, and hugging one another for joy.

So you might ask, how could I, a three-and-a-half-year-old kid, remember that? I have no clue, but I remembered many things that were abnormal, at least what I thought was abnormal. By the way, for me to remember the war ended was an isolated incident. I clearly remember an earlier time when we were living in the same apartment complex that Dad was beaten in, we had the first New York City air raid drill in the evening. That was scary, mostly because Mom and everyone else didn't know what was going on. She was a basket case without Dad, trying to protect me and my sister, but there was no safe place around. All you could do was just stay in the apartment until the sirens stopped and later find out it was a practice air raid drill.

Atomic Bomb, 1945

The world war ended shortly after having dropped the atomic bombs on Japan of which the majority of Americans had no idea what an atomic bomb was. After Japan surrendered, General MacArthur helped Japan's badly damaged economy into what would someday help compete in world economic trading. It began to appear, as I found out later, the Marshall Plan in Germany, and with MacArthur's leadership, Japan would soon begin to prosper. And indeed, America would benefit with factories beginning to operate at full capacity in America, Japan, Europe, and Germany having economic progress, digging out of their ruins.

Soon After the War: Russian and Chinese

But the negative side was the Russian and the Chinese Communist wasn't part of that growth and instead stepped up their world conquest activities and terrorist propaganda as spoiled children. You'd think the people that suffered the most in the war would be thankful for peace, but not them. By their voices, they shouted peace, but their actions were marching and killing and used politically correct excuses to do their thing. The Russians and Chinese seemed to be impervious to more suffering and began their own terror in their own countries and continued their quest into the rest of the world. It seemed to me, at the time, they were crazy mad, sort of like ISIS sympathizers, cutting off their noses to spite their own faces. The newsreels of the day showed the Communist mustering social unrest everywhere they went and used violent combat to achieve their goals. They appeared untruthful, angry, determined, and couldn't be stopped without another stronger force stopping them.

I surmised that most of the world, at that time, wanted only peace, and most of the other nations coming out of the world war, including the new United Nations, didn't seem capable nor interested in getting involved. But they would eventuality get involved, their concept was peace and forming working relationships with one another. Why couldn't the Chinese and Russians see they could have a better life other than what they were doing? It's been that way since our original parents were kicked out of paradise. I don't think the free world having a piece of the pie seemed attainable to the Communists; they wanted something else. I think they wanted war, and misery was their comfort zone, and they knew nothing else and didn't seem to have hope. They could not bring themselves to rid of the suffering they had seen nor have hope of it improving without more suffering. Both nations were in potholes, and I wondered, what about us now, are we in a present perplexed pothole?

Was It Helping Others That Drove Us?

Why were we such patriots? Maybe the air life that occurred in Berlin during 1948 struck American hearts? We knew how bad the economy was for Germany; we watched from movie reels in theaters and the horror of the killing of defenseless Jews and Christians that resisted German authority. But something began in Germany that was to become sobering. It was the Berlin airlift after the war ended, attempting to bring emergency aid to the German people. The airlift was about forgiveness of the immediate past and the beginning of something far better. A young American took photographs of various military planes coming and going, dropping off needed emergency supplies. The American pilots were in it to help destitute Germans to survive after the war. It was those same types of Americans, seeing the results of the war, that were responsible for opening up hearts and discovering a new concept to further improve the world economic system. They initiated a new revolutionary process called the Marshall Plan, to benefit not only Germany but others on that side of the Atlantic. And grow they did with Europe and America benefitting from the plan too. And the Germans later took a lead in helping others in the world to become prosperous too. I truly loved that American success; it made a deep and lasting impression on us all and especially a kid from New York City. I was internally happy to be an American.

Doctors Made House Calls, 1948

Those were the days in the late '40s when doctors traveled long distances from their office to make house calls. We lived in areas of less densely populated sections of Long Island, New York. It was during the period that the population was just beginning to shift from New York City to spacious Long Island plots. The house calls tapered off as the population grew, and more families owned automobiles. Hence in 1950, we were becoming rich or at least well-off.

Well-off compared to today was sheer exaggeration. But what I did see was a lack of respect for our surroundings. The area we lived in was called Shirley, and it was hardly populated, except for a few summer homes owned by well-off city people. It was an annoyance when the summer came, and the visitors weren't used to not having trash service, and they would throw trash bags full of garbage out of their car windows onto the dirt roads. I thought it was only disrespectful people from the city that did that, but moving to the Midwest, in the countryside of Lawton, it was being done by welfare-recipient hill people. However, the disrespect didn't stop there. During the coronavirus pandemic, those same type of people would throw their used protective mask and gloves in grocery carts, shopping parking lot surfaces, and out their car windows on the clean country roads. My teenage grandson Ethan works at a Walmart store and gives us the lowdown. So I ask, am I a complainer as mentioned above? Yes, yes, yes. That is another annoying thing I have to turn over to God.

Music, 1940–1950

"She's Too Fat for Me," "Standing on the Corner Watching All the Girls Go By," "Peg o' My Heart," "Pistol Packin' Mama," "Anytime," "Walking the floor over You," "Lovesick Blues," and "Chattanooga Choo Choo" were hit songs I remembered.

Sayings

"World War II was a war to end all wars." "Children are to be seen and not heard." "A bird in the hand is worth two in the air." "A cast-iron pot calling a cast-iron kettle black." "You make your bed, and you sleep in it."

Time Line—1950 through to 1960

Korea and New York City

It was about five years after Germany and Japan surrendered in 1945 when in 1951, America began sending large military forces to Korea, intending to stop the Communist Chinese from marching onto the rest of the Korean Peninsula and possibly the Japanese mainland. I remembered when I was ten years old, and troops were being sent to Korea, my dad said, "Well, here we go again." And the past slogans echo in my ears about the big World War that was going to end all wars. It was just a hopeful thought which, to me, meant adults didn't have a clue.

Little did I know when I was ten years old in 1951 that I would be in South Korea as a soldier myself in the 1960s. But when I was ten years old, black-and-white television was just being introduced into American homes when the Korean War began to be broadcasted on TV and shocked Americans. I remember seeing large dirt holes being dug by US Army bulldozers during the Korean fall season. The army was making preparations to bury dead soldiers in the upcoming winter in lieu of attempting to dig in the cold frozen Korean winter. Later television actually showed the soldiers being pushed into the graves with bulldozers and covered with the loose dirt that could have been frozen, had the Army not predug the holes in the fall. From what I could see from the reaction of adults watching TV, it was frightful but for me not being able to compare, I understood this was normal, and I resolved myself someday to help defeat the Communist.

Not Declared a War

The Korean War was not declared a war, and our leaders of the day acted devious by not ensuring the representatives of the people made those decisions. Truman, it seemed, knew what was best and began sending troops to the peninsular country to protect Japan, and later, the young United Nations sent other military aid to join forces with the American military. I think it was sad that few Americans questioned the not-so-legal war, and most accepted that which the government was doing. I surmised our leaders thought it best of what had to be done without asking Americans, probably they were weary just the same, having to go to war again.

It wasn't until after the war and fifty-five thousand casualties that people began to question the wisdom of the war and especially why congress wasn't involved since the US Constitution allows only congress to declare war. But this wasn't a declared war; the leaders declared it to be a police action. So a major beginning of the modern *political correctness lie* comes about, and we could see the same loud and clear political correctness emerging during 2008 through 2018. What a shame, the same type of people probably justified killing babies with political correctness too. So I say to myself again, *Who do these people think they are?* We, the people, are slowly becoming void of responsible masters of America by the professional politicians we're electing.

You'll see during the 1950s, Japan was in danger, and Japan was not permitted by the 1945 rules of surrender to have a military force of their own. Consequently a Japanese Army or Navy to protect themselves from invaders was out of the question and for good reason. However, since the end of WWII, American forces were there to insure their homeland safety. So it appeared to me, a panic took over our leaders, and all they understood was they had to stop the onslaught of Communism from reaching the shores of Japan. But the damn if I do and damn if I don't doesn't come into effect here, and if our people won't pray before making such a decision, I could see why many lives were blundered away. I think our leaders, by not following the US Constitution again, were getting better at their game and put another nail—even bigger this time—by sealing America's coffin. Congress continued being more obstinate, disregarding who we, the people, are.

It's bad, and I don't like saying this, but *we make our bed, and we sleep in it*, and it appears we're all going to sleep in it someday again. I realize the dependence and immediate danger Japan was in, but it was no excuse for not correcting it later. They will disregard us again and again by taking away the best society decision process and eventually making America weaker. The Communist couldn't do as much damage to us as our own leaders have done and are currently doing in the last sixty years. So as we go along each decade, we'll see how more brazen the professional politician and his friends disregard the law of the land.

Late 1950s Radio Broadcast of Being Underwater

The scare and high concerns for most New Yorkers living in the city was that all of Manhattan was going to be underwater in one hundred years. The reason given by scientists was that the North Pole ice was melting, and there was no escape. However, billions of dollars were to be made after the announcements soon after existing property owners unwittingly sold their Manhattan properties to the new breed of skyscraper developers. Manhattan became an even greater city in the world, and it all began with fear news announcing Manhattan was going underwater in one hundred years.

Late '50s Polio

Talk about a scare, each day that it would rain in our community, it brought fears to kids and parents alike. People were plagued with a terrible world crippling disease called Polio, and most people thought we contracted it from going out into the rain or swimming. A vaccine was discovered sometime in the 1950s and given to the world for years until we watched the decline of the world's fearful Polio pandemic.

Dr. Benjamin Spock

Dr. Benjamin Spock, a pediatrician, began his conversational writings with five ideas that changed American parenting. His new liberal attitude toward raising children was a bit too much thinking outside the box, and I thought, as a teenager, it was to a fault. It seemed to me, Spock was raised in a strict and conservative family and was liberated after overthinking in his writings. However, Spock was a good and productive person in spite of what I think of him, even abandoning his time-proven family values. He screwed up completely and left an everlasting revolt in America.

The '50s Divorce Rate

American divorce rate was at 15 percent and indicating a slight climb.

French Leaders Abandoned Their Troops

The majority of the French government were Communists and abandoned and allowed the North Vietnamese Communist to destroy the remaining (three thousand) entrenched French foreign legion soldiers in Vietnam. Hordes of North Vietnamese surrounded the French garrison, and the end came for the Frenchman with no help from France. French leaders refused to send any aid or evacuate their military personnel from the war zone.

Late '50s Phoenix, Arizona

Our family moved again and relocated from New York to Phoenix on a day that was 118 degrees, and the education level in the Phoenix public schools was like stepping back three grades compared to New York schools. Besides the heat being similar to sticking your head in an oven, I enjoyed, for the very first time, being a student with above-average grades. However, I enjoyed the success and never picked up a pencil until the high grades began to disappear, and in the course of a couple of years, I was back to average or below average in class achievements. It had to be my comfort zone. Ha ha, I would break that low-grade comfort zone after taking studying seriously at the University of Cincinnati after military service using the GI Bill.

The wildest incident in a Phoenix elementary classroom I had was in the seventh grade, and it involved my English teacher who loved to hunt mountain lions in Northern Arizona. She would often tell us stories of the hunts in the northern mountain's cold and snowy weather. One day, after she told another story of the hunts, she invited the class to go on a mountain lion hunting trip with her. That was great, I already owned an 8 mm rifle and knew how to use it. Arizona had only a few gun laws in the '50s, and Arizonans were respectful concerning guns. The only big incident I heard about when it came to gun problems was when a few ranches protecting their water rights along the Colorado River. The armed ranchers had a show of force with California and Arizona authorities concerning rancher water rights.

Back to Mountain Lion Hunting

Anyway four boys, including myself, got permission from our parents to go with our English teacher on a Arizona lion hunting expedition, and part of the preparation for the hunt was to bring our gear, ammo, and rifles into class on a Friday morning and secure them into unlocked lockers in the back of our classroom. We'll leave for a Northern Arizona destination that afternoon. Yes, I said the rifles and ammo was put into the back of the room in unlocked lockers. Would you say, this story is a good indication of people respecting guns and one another? Well, the excitement on that Friday morning to go hunting didn't last long. School authorities heard what was going on, and they disapproved of the hunt and the teacher. We had to call home and have our parents pick us up, along with the guns and gear. Our teacher was an Arizonan, and the rest of the staff were from back east cities like New York and Chicago. What a bummer, I could have upped my grade point average. Ha ha!

Army

I had to get away from home, and to do it, I joined the army at seventeen, on May 14, 1959, and never looked back until I began writing this book. You know we cannot tell the future, and we shouldn't attempt to, but you can look in the past and present and understand that it could be the future. So, my brother and sister, look into the past and see tomorrow.

Music, 1950s

"Great Balls of Fire," "Your Cheating Heart," Hang Down Your Head Tom Dully," "Don't Tell Me I've Nothing to Do," "Little Jimmy Brown," "Sh-Boom," "Hearts Made of Stone," "Standing on the Corner," "Sincerely," and my favorite that would continue to echo in my thoughts sixty years later, "He Has the Whole World in His Hands" discussed in the first chapter.

Sayings

"Birds of a feather fly together." "You make your bed, you sleep in it." "Money talks." "Mad dogs bite themselves." "If it works, don't fix it." "Don't wait until doomsday." "And the beat goes on."

Teenage Attitude

Most teenagers struggled and were not rich and rejected drugs. It was almost impossible to find a girl willing to satisfy boys' sexual desires. Most girls learned to say *no*.

Teachers/Parents Attitude

Teachers were strict, and parents were stricter.

Time Line (1960 through 1970)

Something was happening to pop music. The reflection of pop songs and hippie demonstrations exposing America was being shown in bad light. What caused the hippie street demonstrations, unrest, and disregard for authority? Did the Vietnam War cause their dissension, or was it their family situations from a few years earlier? An issue I will look at further later in the 2000s using a root cause analysis.

I remember the music lyrics prior to the 1960s and comparing to the actual 1960s, the lyrics slowly changed from natural positive messages to real-life negative expressions, and later even stronger telltales were in predominate country songs about divorce, going to jail, and bad life situations. I wondered if my life had been sheltered as a young person from the life problems the musicians expressed in their music. Now looking back into the '60s, I did see something. I heard a fantastic beat but was taken aback significantly when listening to the lyrics. Many adults of that period were verbally warning teenagers and anyone who would listen that the songs of the day were countersocial and disruptive. I noticed at that particular time, America indeed was changing from soft values to angry worldly awareness expressed in song from some of the young musicians of the day. And from my observations, many above-average economic kids could afford buying the new music records and accounted for most of the drinking and sex parties. The norm of the day was that most girls learned and knew how to say no to boys that had overactive hormones. But that was changing, and the songs and drinks helped them with lessening of the *no* to *maybe* to their undisciplined sex hormones. Look back and see when pregnancies began changing as the divorce rate already began. And, my friends, kids did not carry condom prevention packs in their pockets until sometime in the '70s and '80s.

Korean Favorites

The one song I heard the South Koreans sing and hum during the year I was there and it was constantly on their lips was "Que Sera Sera" by Doris Day. We had little indication at the time that South Korea would obtain a great future as the lyrics mentioned not seeing the future as Doris's lyrics suggested. The Koreans were wishfully thinking, as I observed back then.

America Justifying through Money

The stakes were higher, and money was becoming overpowering, not that money didn't run the world, but we'll see in this decade that money was countering our better understanding of spiritual values and will continue becoming stronger as years pass. There are stronger justifications to use world trade as a deterrent of war, and it should be. But to leave world spiritual values dormant is foolishness and makes the future questionable. I think it is only a matter of time before we see repercussions from a lack of faith values. I see it today as I write this book. As examples, the blowing up of an oil well in the Gulf of Mexico and contaminating the whole Gulf region, just to make a point and never finding out who did it. That is foolishness, to think it wasn't known who did it. The second example was helping GMC to obtain a loan, the third was Toyota automobiles had electronic brake problems, and it was never solved what caused the problem.

In Desert Storm, we learned how to stand on sidewalks and point electronics at a vehicle and stop it dead in its tracks. And now the worst, to help a party with sympatry win the midterm elections by fake bombs being delivered to prominent Democrat leaders. I'll say this with tongue in cheek, that the bombs will remain a mystery like the other incidents that have happened since the early 1970s and remain unknown to the public. So if you believe that modern-day incidents are not solvable, I have a bridge in Brooklyn, New York, I could maybe sell to you. Just study the Old Testament and see the future for us. It showed time and time again how corrupt Israel was knocked out and came back after asking the Lord for forgiveness. And remember, I matured quickly in the military during my installation intelligence tenure, after learning what corrupt men and governments are capable of doing to control us for their gain. And as I write this, I wonder if they, the corrupt and those with faith problems, will attempt to shut these writings down from reaching you.

Not Declared

The Vietnam War, like the Korean War, wasn't declared by congress. So who has the interest and audacity to go to war? Certainly not the American people, but the politicians that worry about their jobs or don't care about the US Constitution and its precepts. During the early stages of the Vietnam War, I was in the army and in uniform and fortunate to sit next to a Barry Goldwater's political agent on a plane trip from Arizona to California. He was disappointed after questioning me in depth about the war in Vietnam brewing up. And after, he asked by insinuating that I and millions of soldiers like me would go to war and fight for my country without question. I said to him, "Not so fast." I told him, "I will fight for my country, but I'm not willing to fight for the heck of it."

He was uncomfortable, and I guess he thought because I was wearing an army uniform, I just couldn't wait to fight a battle, giving up my life for his ideas. Anyway I was about eighteen, and he was about in the midthirties, and I just figured he was another adult that didn't think real-life situations. Besides I was still annoyed that the Korean War wasn't worthy enough to declare a declaration of war. So my attitude toward America beginning to send troops to Vietnam wasn't disconcerting to me, one way or another. I knew we were holding the North Vietnamese back from taking over all of the country and the South wanted their own independence. I just wanted America, according to the constitution, to declare war not because of a bunch of self-motivated people that wanted it.

So you may ask, how did an eighteen-year-old know anything about the US Constitution? I loved every minute when my teachers in Long Island, New York, discussed the US Constitution with us in the lower elementary classes. Sort of like that nun in Catholic school when she began speaking from her heart about Jesus curing the blind man. I never forgot her nor the love of that Bible verse. The nun knew how to communicate from her heart and so did my US Constitution teachers back in Long Island. I look back now to the fourth grade, and no matter what the circumstances were, as I got older, I hoped that the law of the nation would prevail. So I guess, good positive instruction is good for the soul. However, what a disappointment it was when the law of the land was abused ever so slightly by our leaders.

Missile Accident, 1961

My first tour of duty after basic training at Fort Ord, California, was at Fort Slocum, New York, across from City Island and New Rochelle, New York, on a base called Hart Island, surrounded by the Long Island Sound. The base was an army artillery missile launching base to help protect the immediate New York City area from enemy aircraft. My primary duty was repairing Nike Ajax missiles when I happened to witness my first military screwup and lack of military justice. I was on a weekend pass, visiting Barbara on her home island called City Island, across from the military base, when news got around that a missile was lying on a hill across the bay on the army base. We could see from our vantage point that the missile was lying on its side, facing down at about a forty-five-degree angle.

Wonder How

What we discovered later was that the missile fell off of its mobile carrier and settled on the side of a hill in full view of the public. The army staff sergeant who alone was responsible for the mishap wasn't brought up on military neglect charges. The staff sergeant responsible for the mishap could barely speak English, often commanded lesser projects to do, and that weekend, he demonstrated inconsistencies with his behavior again. He decided to relocate a missile from our maintenance shop to the missile launch area of the island. He began by asking in broken English for volunteers to help him relocate a missile from the shop to the launch pad about six hundred feet up a narrow road. No one volunteered, and the staff sergeant, who was not a physically strong person, decided to move the missile up the narrow road himself without help. He was halfway up the hill when a gust of wind from the Long Island Sound blew the missile and cart out of his hands onto the steep grass embankment where you could see it from the east shoreside of City Island.

I had a pass that weekend visiting Barbara and her parents when we got the news that a missile fell over onto a hill at the Hart Island missile base. We walked from her family apartment to where we could see across the bay, about a half-mile away, and the missile was there in plain view, pointing down the hill with a wheeled push carrier cart on its side. *What a sight*, I thought, this was something, and we began watching a mobile crane lift the missile up and reset it onto the carrier, which was then moved back to maintenance building by other soldiers and crane driver. The missile was immediately relocated to a military transportation center, away from our base for further disposition. You may ask, why didn't I go back to my base to help? We could only use a civilian prison ferry to cross the bay, and their schedule wasn't such for me to go back at that time.

As a sidenote, just several years before this incident at the Hart Island facility in 1959, the army experienced a deadly missile mishap in New Jersey when a missile exploded on its launch pad. The explosion sent bodies of soldiers screened through the chain-link security fence surrounding the site. I don't have any knowledge of what caused the incident, but I know absolutely nothing was done to the staff sergeant that was responsible for our Hart Island incident. Maybe he got a chewing out. Disappointing to me that the army didn't demand military justice be initiated. But then again, as I look back during those times, the press in New York was not neutral.

Prayer Taken Out of Public Schools, 1962

It happened on June 1962, that the supreme court declared school-sponsored prayer and Bible readings were unconstitutional. A woman by the name of Madalyn Murray O'Hair seemed to be the leader heading the whole movement, but years later, when looking back, you can see behind the scenes; it was the national news media promoting O'Hair and a lawyer named Engel working diligently with the supreme court (by the way, one of the founding father of the

Communist Party was named Engel, and Communists were committed to overthrow America and still are). Many Americans became outspoken, fearful, and angry of what the court did by taking God out of the public schools and declared the school system would deteriorate. Well, they were right, and we are able to see the disruption in all societies as discussed near the end of this "Time Line" chapter. However, let me remind you that the court's ruling prevents the school government from pressuring students into prayer and not completely removing prayer from schools. It'll be well into the 2000s for school officials to comprehend that students can hold their own separate prayer groups in schools. So a lot of unnecessary poof by the news media.

Germany Bound, 1962

Soon after the missile incident, I received orders to be transferred to Kaiserslautern, Germany, where I worked in supply and experienced another incident when our military driver and I went to an ammo supply bunker to obtain TNT warheads for our Nike Hercules missiles. The driver parked the truck on a slight slope, away from the bunker, while another truck was loading munitions, and we got out of the truck to stretch awhile and watch the sun rise. Suddenly we heard a scream and metal-to-metal noise, and turning around, we saw where it was coming from; our truck had rolled onto the other parked truck while it was being loaded with ammo. You know, not seeing the truck rolling back makes for a different situation. There was no explosion, and everything was fine, and we went on with our work, thinking what could've happened. No one knew at headquarters about the accident being caused by our driver forgetting to set the emergency brake, allowing our big truck to crash into the truck being loaded and narrowly missed crushing a soldier loading his truck with ammunition.

His Dad's Money

The other curious thing I had in Germany, beside the above truck mishap, was my friend and a model soldier went on a spending spree when nearing his time to leave Germany, and he was nearly court-martialed for being AWOL (absent without leave). What happened was my friend had come into a lot of money before his rotation, and he vowed he would spend it all before he left Germany. He told me that he and his dad never had a relationship, never fished, never played ball, never did anything together; but his father worked two jobs that wasn't absolutely necessary and didn't spend a dime on his family but saved every penny he made. It so happened, months before he was to leave Germany, his father died, and my friend got a large part of his dad's inheritance a month prior to leaving Germany. He was awarded over $20,000 and planned on spending it on German wine, women, and beer. Why spend it all? I asked. Because, he replied, his father never spent a penny on him, and he wanted to enjoy every bit of it, making up for his father not enjoying family life.

Jail Time

The other incident I had in Germany was when I had to transfer a court-martialed private to the US Army Prison in Mannheim, Germany. The private was found guilty of attempting to sell a 50-caliber machine gun to a Russian agent. That was bad stuff, folks; the 50 caliber is the most destructive machine gun in the world, it was then and probably is still today. The gun could wipe out many US soldiers and destroy most equipment in the hands of the Russians. So about half way to the prison in my jeep, he was complaining how the army sucks, and he got a raw deal and blah, blah, blah, blah. I immediately stopped the jeep on the side of the autobahn and gave him an option. I said, I could release him from his handcuffs and would give him a head start count of ten to run and escape, at which time after the count of ten, I would go after him with my 30-caliber rifle. I scared the crap out of him, and he was quiet the rest of the trip. The sad thing was, I truly wanted him to take the escape option.

I left Germany and was transferred to Fort Bliss, Texas, where Barbara and I got married and had our first and second child, Guy and Susan. Soon after Susan was born, I received orders to report to South Korea in October 1963 as a missile crewmen leader. We packed our belongings and traveled to City Island, New York, where Barbara and the kids stayed with her parents while I was away.

Am I a Coward, 1963

This transfer to Korea just didn't sit right with me, something was going wrong with my head, and I was in a cloud, and my thinking ability wasn't there; it just didn't seem real, and maybe I was having a daytime nightmare of sorts. I couldn't go to South Korea was my deepest thought and not to leave my family. Maybe I made a mistake re-enlisting in the Army for four years.

I remember Barbara driving me to LaGuardia Airport with the two kids, sending me off aboard a plane to San Francisco, and as I looked down at Guy before boarding, I could see a confused deep look on his face. I asked myself, *What am I doing, leaving them,* and wondered for a moment, if I deserted the army right here and now, if I wouldn't be better off than going through this emotion of leaving them. Reluctantly I boarded the plane and, in about eight hours, landed in San Francisco and later transferred to the Oakland Naval Base and began the process of preparing to board a troop ship destined for South Korea.

A day went by, and about two to three hundred army and navy Seabees began boarding one of the last transport troop ships for military transportation. And again, I began thinking, *The army can't do this to me,* and, *This may be my chance to desert and get back to New York and take off with Barbara and the kids.* I wondered if I was a coward, not wanting to leave as ordered, but as it was, I didn't desert the army. I kept walking, following the soldier in front of me, toward the boarding ramp, feeling weak and hopeless with my duffel bag on my shoulder. It seemed like hours when I finally stepped onto the portable ramp leading up to the ship, and by then, it was too late. I had to reluctantly trudge the rest of the way up the ramp like everyone else in front and at the back of me.

Well, anyway reluctantly I accepted my plight and settled in. That is, I settled in after the first day at sea. It was dinnertime when we finished boarding the ship, and as we began sailing out to sea, we passed under the Golden Gate Bridge, and like a bad omen, as soon as we were under the bridge, our large ship began rocking from side to side and up and down from the waves and currents that were always there, I was told. At about that time, passing under the bridge, nearly all of the army guys were leaning over the guardrails sick as dogs. However, a few of us didn't have the seasick problem and went to the empty cafeteria to eat dinner.

We got in the cafeteria line in clear view of pork chops being cooked on a greasy grill. However, as hungry as some of us were, we began moving faster in line because of other soldiers quickly leaving the line to go topside and use the rail. What was happening—I think the cooks did it on purpose or at least enjoyed the scene—was the method of how they cooked the pork chops. The meat would slide back and forth on the well-greased grill with the movement of the swaying ship. I didn't have a ruler to measure, but I bet the pork chops slid back and forth up to twelve inches on the grill. I was too hungry to think about my stomach getting queasy and sat down and ate away at the extra chops given to the remaining survivors. Besides before I left New York, Barbara's grandfather, a former English seaman, told me how to keep from becoming seasick. All I had to do was keep as much liquid out of my system as possible and eat plenty of dry crackers. It worked, folks, the entire twenty-six days out at sea, I only felt nausea once during a storm.

Pearl Harbor

Our first stop across the Pacific Ocean was Hawaii, where a soldier actually jumped ship, as the rumor went, and he deserted the army. *What a dummy he must be*, I thought, *to desert now in the middle of the Pacific Ocean and nowhere to go or leave from.* Maybe he walked up the gang plank thinking like I did back in the Oakland Navy Base and not accepting his situation.

Japan Workers

Our next stop, after about twenty days of sailing from San Francisco, was in Yokohama, Japan, where I got a firsthand snapshot look at Japanese laborers and how the Japanese industry would just about eat America's lunch twenty years later in Japan's industrial quest.

It was late in the evening when we docked in Yokohama, and most of us being transferred were in one or more of the large cafeterias passing time. We stayed as long as we could in the cafeterias in lieu of going down into the hot foul-smelling triple-stacked bunk bed areas. I'm thankful I was in the cafeteria and could observe the Japanese's longshore men boarding the ship doing their chores. They were loading and emptying the boat of supplies and looked more like bees in a panic mode, hurrying, doing their work with quick physical jerks of their bodies and voices. They were truly wound up, and I couldn't help but admire them while thinking back just a week passed when the ship had to be hand scraped of loose paint designated for the merchant crew to do. The American unionized merchant marine labors didn't want to do their job, and they convinced their union leader to ask the civilian ship captain to strike a deal with the military commander for the soldiers to do the work instead. Well, all hell broke loose between the ship's civilian captain and our military commander on board. Our commander, a lieutenant colonel, would not allow the military troops to do the work that which the civilian union merchant marines were paid to do. It's too bad, but they weren't receptive toward us after that determination. The union workers ignored us and would not readily do their job if it involved the military problem. You'd think they would have appreciated making the big bucks the way they do and do their job, but then again, our government was setting bad examples and began throwing big bucks at union contractors and education in the 1960s, and nothing proportional in value has come of all the finagling either. Anyway the US Civil Merchant Marine workers weren't happy, and most of their work after their attempted finagling setback was slow, torturous, and poor in comparison to the Japanese workers being viewed on ship that evening.

Japanese Break Time

That wasn't all that the Japanese dock workers did. They not only burned up a million calories when they were doing their job, but they burned up another million when they were on break. I heard their loud lunch alarm sounding, and the Japanese workers came out of everywhere and took over a couple of our long tables and began playing cards with the same intensity and energy as when they were working. I thought what a difference between American workers being paid enormous amounts of money compared to the Japanese being paid much less, and in addition, they had more spirit than the well-paid American worker. I sometimes wonder if those types of Americans weren't partly responsible for businesses being transferred to other countries in several decades to come. Yep, I'm sure it was another reason why when looking back to those days.

You know, I haven't gotten to the "Am I a Coward" subtitle yet, and please keep reading because I think when we fear, you'll see how military cowards are made. For that matter, how any coward is made. And I continue to wonder if I am a coward, not wanting to leave my family and become a military deserter.

Docking in Incheon Harbor, 1963

We left Japan and docked outside of Seoul, South Korea, twenty-four days after leaving San Francisco and began military processing to be reassigned from the now-coastal Korean Incheon area to in-processing areas. Most of us were off the ship in process lines when we began hearing alarms in our administration building that was built on top of a hill, situated not too far from where we disembarked from the troop ship. We were instructed to leave the building, and as we were leaving, I could smell pungent odors and see flames shooting sky-high below us as we were exiting the building.

Freight Train Fire

We could see below, from a hill outside the building about one thousand feet away, in a valley, where six chemical freight train cars were on fire. At about that time, and out of nowhere, a brand-new second lieutenant was scurrying back and forth in front of us, shouting and raising his arms; he needed volunteers to put the train fire out. I looked and sized up the problem pretty fast and determined he was *nuts*. There was no fire equipment around, and all he was able to scramble was about two dozen army volunteers. They began running down the hill toward the fire with nothing—absolutely nothing—to fight a blazing chemical fire with. I was stunned, the *crazy* officer would ask and actually get volunteers to fight the fire and not have any equipment to fight the fire with—absolutely no equipment.

I rushed into the building and found the first sergeant and told him that a lieutenant was outside getting volunteers to fight the train fire with no equipment. He immediately got instructions from the commanding colonel to bring the lieutenant back with the soldiers. From my vantage point, I could see he grabbed the officer by the shirt and started pulling him forcibly away from the flaming train fire with the volunteers following—if not running—past the lieutenant to get back to safety. The first sergeant still had the lieutenant by the shirt when they went into the colonel's office, and all we heard later was that the lieutenant was humbled and alone (*sniff*, too bad, the crazy bastard I thought should be admitted into a mental institution). I wondered later if cowardice prevented me from volunteering or was it just common sense and self-preservation to refrain from a dangerous situation that was too dangerous and a useless cause.

President Kennedy Killed

I had been in Korea for about two months as a section leader of a missile launch platoon, and several episodes had already occurred. During the early part of the two months of duty, President Kennedy was assassinated, causing all NATO troops everywhere on high alert. Several months later, we nearly captured what we think may have been a North Korean spy, and soon after that incident, we went through an air attack alert.

Russian MiG Jets Attack

I remember it was a weekend afternoon, and most of us were on our bunks reading, when sirens began sounding red alert battle stations. We jumped into jeeps and trucks and headed for the missile launch site on top of a nearby mountain to ready our missiles to fire. We were in our below-ground missile control bunker when six Russian jet MiGs, flown by North Koreans, were coming at us located near P'yongt'aek, South Korea, which meant the jets had penetrated one hundred miles into Korean airspace. I was instructed by the radar section a mile away to ready a Nike Hercules missile to be fired from our above-ground launch pad, just above our underground control center. One of our Hercules surface-to-air missiles could wipe out six jets if they remained in formation, but as it were, the South Korean Air Force went up to meet the jets after they entered South Korean airspace and warned them that if they didn't go back to North Korea, they would be shot down by American missiles.

They didn't turn around, and with pleasure, I got the order to count down to fire. And with my finger on the panel, red firing button ready to fire, I began counting with the radar section personnel a mile away—*5, 4, 3*—*but* we lost power to the firing panel before

I could say 2. My first reaction was to send the squad topside to set up our defense with a 50 calibrator machine gun, M60 machine gun, explosives, and personal squad M14 rifles while I tried to gain contact with the radar section using a shortwave radio. We did not hear any gunfire above and assumed we weren't being attacked, and finally our staff sergeant made contact with a shortwave radio with the commanding officer in the radar section. All I heard was a bunch of swearing and "What the hell is going on down there, O'Donnell?" And I could only answer back that the equipment electrical power shut down after the count of 3, and we were not receiving any ground fire as of yet. The next day, we found out what had happened, and it was the beginning of my determination to get out of the military when my enlistment was up.

But first, I'll explain how a missile site is set up so it will be easier to understand what happened above. A complete missile battery site includes a radar section removed from the missile launch section where the missiles are stored, and it being as far away as a mile but in between both sections of the radars and missiles is a relay station. The radars are on a hill, and the missiles on a separate hill with the nearby relay launch station. The relay station was manned by a squirrely staff sergeant who already proved to be an unreliable person. The staff sergeant raped a young teenage girl from the local Catholic orphanage about two months before this incident, and he was still part of our team. I was truly disappointed military justice wasn't initiated due to the raping of a teenage girl, especially an orphan, several months before.[a]

Not a Coward

What caused the electronic blackout preventing us from launching a missile at attacking aircraft was the squirrely staff sergeant. He purposely turned off the panel power from his manned relay station, thereby turning off the power to launch the missiles and preventing the radar site to follow through and destroy the oncoming MiGs.

---

[a] Deuteronomy 10:18.

However, from that near-combat incident, I found the answer to the dark burning question inside of me. Was I a coward? I was elated, assured I wasn't a coward. I found, if I could stand up to life-threatening pressures and not panic, nor *fear* the MiGs coming at us, I was not a coward. Especially when the moment came, I had my finger on the firing button, and the MiGs were headed straight toward us and did not flinch or was nervous. I was seriously disappointed we did not shoot the attacking aircraft down. I'm a good soldier, and from my experiences, I will forever be able to meet challengers of life and not fearing.

It was unknown to us on the missile launch site, when the panel power went off, that at the same time, the MiGs turned back to their air base in North Korea. We were later informed the power was turned off by a cowardly staff sergeant ready to retire from the army who controlled the relay station. His excuse was that he was afraid of starting World War III. No way, I thought, that by blowing the MiGs out of the sky, it would cause a world war. I further thought that the SOB staff sergeant should be put in jail for endangering us and further for raping the Korean orphan girl.

Well, as I always do, I find objectives in my life, and I found my objective as a soldier was to protect America. Life was simple for me as a soldier, especially when I see the objective of why we're here and why we exist. So looking back since that day I was tested, I became more courageous and used that power in me each and every single day of my life to include having the courage to leave a lifelong dream. I left the army in 1966 and began a tough and happy journey as a citizen leader in my community. I missed the army for many years after I got out and often reflected back how even as a ten-year-old boy, wanting nothing else but the army. However, that dream came to a halt when America turned against their military sons in the 1960s. The other entity that turned against American fighting soldiers were former *greedy* CIA (Central Intelligence Agency) operatives stationed in Indochina.

North Vietnam Leaders, 1965

During the middle of the Vietnam War, soldiers heard rumors that the CIA owned and operated poppy plantations in South East Asia. The poppy seeds were reprocessed and smuggled into North Vietnam to weaken their fighting abilities. When the North Vietnam commanders learned of the CIA plot, they began dealing out harsh penalties to their troops that were using the drugs. The North Vietnam leaders remembered what the English did to the Chinese during the Boxer Rebellion and would not allow Americans to do the same to their forces. But nevertheless, several CIA operatives were not about to lose the million-dollar investment, and eventually the drugs found their way into American military camps. The only way for us to remove corruption from among us is to throw up our hands in knowing we can't get it done without asking our Lord for help. Maybe we should organize daily prayers in lieu of the current annual day of prayer. It does appear money rules, but I don't think for long.

Israel's Six-Day War, 1967

All of the Israel people were in despair in 1967, when they were facing an army of 465,000 Arab troops, 2,880 tanks, and 900 aircrafts compared to 264,000 Israeli troops, 800 tanks, and 300 aircrafts. Four nations of Arabs were poised on the borders of Israel, and four other Arab nations as reserves. With no help from Britain or America, they stood alone as so many other times in their history; and so it seemed to the rest of the world, they were alone. But in six days, Israel will quadruple its land and retake many holy sites before the end of the war. And like many other wars in Israel's history, Israel would count their 760 casualties while the Arabs deaths are somewhere around 18,000 men.

Worst-Case Scenario

In the meantime, before the war commenced, Israel was preparing for the worst-case scenario. They began converting national parks into mass burial grounds, expecting mass casualties, while school children were digging sand to fill bags to help protect their homes. And while other defensive Israel activities were going on, the United Nations removed its troops from the Sinai, thereby making Israel truly exposed, standing alone. The Arab armies, not far from Jerusalem, were in position and wanting to make the blue Mediterranean Sea turn *red* with Israelis' blood. What most Arabs did not know is that Jerusalem is God's city on earth ever since King David's reign,[a] and when we look further in the book of Revelation, future armies will attempt to destroy Jerusalem but to no avail. The attempts Arabs made to push Israel in the sea were foiled in miraculous incidents. During the first day, Arabs were in position preparing an attack on Israel's defense positions, when the Arabs noticed *angels* above the Israel positions and would not attack. Also Israel's Army walked unharmed into fortified Shechem, an Arab city, bent on destroying Israel. The Arabs did not recognize Israel as the foe, and they were captured. Other Arab battles, especially losing their air war was due, on their part, to their confusing critical air defense codes that turned disastrous for them.

Late '60s, Nikita Khrushchev

The Russian Communist leader had the audacity, while as an American guest, to say, "America will fall from within." And another quote he made to a Russian assembly was, "We must abolish the Cult of the individual, decisively once and for all." Look around, you'll see attitudes whispering that same message in a not-so-cool Democrat Party. The progressives, socialists, and Communists want to abolish people like me because I am a free person. A person of

---

[a]

God that believes the US Constitution upholds individualism and not organizations, as we're seeing today, beginning to adversely develop. If you *don't mind* being told what to do, disregard this deep and *urgent statement* I convey. Similarly Putin is the Russian leader today but may have a different take on things. Just don't forget he was schooled in Communism, and it should be compensated for. And we'll be able to look back at what the coronavirus fear has done to improve evil movements.

Social Security, 1960s

It was sweet to think I had been paying into the Social Security program since I began working as a teenager during the '50s in Phoenix. And as often as I continue to pay into the social program, there should be a significant amount to retire on. But that may not be the case as I found out in the 1990s. Unbeknownst to most Americans at that time, money was secretly being taken out of the fund. I'll mention who took the Social Security money out in Time Line 2010.

Gripping Welfare

Democrats initiated a stronger and wider welfare system that we would begin to see enslave recipients in the 2000s. By the way, many of us spoke out against the expanding welfare system as becoming a deeper hole that future recipients will not be able to dig out of. And we will see in the 2000s that the observation was true, with the hole getting larger with more dependent people, even noncitizens relaying on it.

FBI, 1968

In the 1960s, Americans began hearing degrading comments about J. Edgar Hoover, the FBI chief. I thought the comments were petty and more of the same negative comments heard from the Vietnam War protesters as being similar to "Hoover needs a night light," "He doesn't know what is going on," etc., etc. "Get him out of being the chief." I've been listening to the radio and reading newspapers for several years now, and certain people seemed organized and outspoken in stepping up the charge against Hoover (later in the 1970s, we find the rhetoric was to gain support to make the FBI into an agency of the government). What a *major* oversight that turned out to be. But most alarming was Herbert Hoover's prediction of what would happen when the FBI began reporting to the government. Hoover was correct in his prediction, and I'll tell you later in the "Time Line" chapter.

I Became a Democrat

I had been out of the service for two years in 1968, and an important primary Democrat vote was to take place that year in the national primary elections. The main issue was yes or no to allow abortion and will take place in about fifteen states. A registered Democrat voter could vote yes or no for abortion. And as you know, I became a Democrat, and from my writings in other chapters, 80 percent to 90 percent of voters voted *no* to abortion. I came away from reading the results a couple of days later thinking Americans rejected abortion as they would reject Nazis' initiatives of WWII. I felt secure that Americans voted for the well-being of our citizens.

Bobby Kennedy Assassinated

As mentioned above, President Robert Kennedy was assassinated in the early '60s, and in the late '60s, the attorney general, his brother Bobby Kennedy was assassinated too, but now in the '70s. Bobby was onto the person or persons responsible for killing his brother but did not live to announce his killer. A lot of activity was centered around the Democrat National Party as being the common denominator in both the Kennedy deaths. You know there is a whole world of monies out there, especially in America, to be made, and men that are justified by power and by money will satisfy themselves accordingly. Look around and see how our history is unfolding, and you'll catch a glimpse of life-threating corruption, nastier than what the Communists portrayed prior to WWII.

Music

"I Fell into a Burning Ring of Fire," "Your Cheating Heart," "Harper Valley PTA," "I Got You," "I Want to Hold Your Hand," "Hey Jude," "I Can't Get No Satisfaction," and "The Twist."

Sayings

"It only takes three generations to lose their faith." "It will only get worse before it gets better." "Spare the rod and spoil the child." "Make love, not war." And last but not least, a Communist saying, "The end justifies the means." "Easier said than done." "If the shoe fits, wear it." "Don't cut your nose off to spite your face."

Time Line: 1970 through 1980

Effects of War

The Vietnam War continues with little sign that Americans are united as we continue to struggle with political and the military advancements. Both military and political functions will soon feel effects in January 1973.

USA Synagogues Protesting

Synagogues were rallying throughout the country, protesting the war but for a different reason other than peace; the National Antiwar people were doing it for Israel's benefits. I remember one evening after college class, I was invited to protest at a local Cincinnati synagogue as my friend explained it to me, "If peace arrives after America discontinues the war in Vietnam, the tax monies will go to Israel for their struggle against the Philistines." I don't have a clue how much—if any—tax money went to Israel, but it will be about five years before the Six-Day War that America and the UN refrained from. Now again and again, hints that maybe government leaders may know a year ahead of time—if not decades—before we go, where we are going. If that is true, do you think government has the insight to motivate themselves to do good for the common good? Can they actually see a pattern of the future? They may see something in the future, but as we would suspect, not everything. And you would think, being so smart, they could see our moral deterioration and help do something about it? You'd think?

Abortion

January 21, 1973, US Supreme Court approved the right to abortion under the Privacy Act of the US Constitution. That was a stretch for a mother when a baby's life is in danger too. However, we'll see later after passing the Obama Health Care Bill and viewing the details, people were already selected to be excluded from the national health care because of age. I'm not alarmed, I'm disappointed that these people have been elected; however, they have been placed by the Father in government. I ask, why do you think they were placed there? They were placed there to honor and obey God to lead His people. Do you think they are honoring Him? I doubt it. But I bet Hitler would be proud of initiating a law in Germany, similar to that of the US Supreme Court, approving abortion, and later congress. Also we'll see in 2020, while the pandemic coronavirus was raging through big cities, the government approved monies for sick people. No way the Obama Health Care system would pay for those without insurance. And most of the old people with issues died as a result of the virus. My question for you is, where was the health care system throughout all this mostly made-up media panic? I'm not angry, I'm concerned for your salvation, and for us to depend solely on a government will make it difficult to find our salvation.

Wise Men

Two middle-age men happen to give their deep impressions to me, one being a black man, a speaker and lover of his community continues. He announced after a church meeting, at which we were discussing problems of the ghetto in Hamilton, Ohio, "What you see here in the black neighborhoods, you'll soon see in white neighborhoods." Yep, the drug, divorce, and single-parent scene was most certainly in the black areas, and in the 1980s, you could certainly see it creeping into white areas, affecting whole communities.

The second person was a chemist in Hamilton, Ohio, I happened to be designing a home for, and of all places, he had some type of an ancient hill on his property. The house I was designing for him was next to that unusual hill. The hill, as it become to be known, was an ancient Indian burial mound. As we were driving back to my home again, after several trips to and from his home, in order to make design changes, he happened to comment to me, "You know, if I had to do it over again, I would be strict with my kids like you are." He further stated that he could always pull back a little strictness in order to teach but cannot presently enforce stricter rules to help them understand responsibility. "I've been too easy with them," he commented. Wow, that coming from a highly educated person was something else. I felt for him deeply and knew of his concerns.

256

The Great American Society

The Great American Society, as was coined by Lyndon Johnson, president of the United States, was indeed coined as he stated Americans were becoming prosperous and beyond the imagination of most of us with change in our pockets. We were becoming the land of plenty, or were we a land of too much?[a]

Food Reserve Sold Out

In the early part of this decade, Americans had *seven years* of emergency food supply with sites throughout America. The emergency food was in case of a national disaster, which was under the control of the government in conjunction with the Farm Bureau. Can you imagine that the government actually helped protect us in accordance with the US Constitution? Yes, we could imagine, but it's hard to conceive it now, most Americans trusted congress to do the right thing. We didn't even think in the 1970s that newspapers were on the road to become major liars. Maybe they developed their own version of lying, but lying is lying, and they seemed to get better at it. Their articles stopped being neutral. So all I can think of is that we didn't shout loud enough to stop the removal of our emergency food supply. The rational excuse said it was better for business and world trade to sell the emergency food storage. Nothing—absolutely nothing—was mentioned about where the money went. Like other incidents occurring as America was getting richer, secrets of our national wealth were becoming prevalent with both parties of congress. Worse yet, a safety net for America was disregarded as other disregards will slowly come about in coming years.

---

[a] Proverbs 30:7–9.

NAFTA

The National Free Trade Agreement was created for North and South America in order for both to prosper. Politicians and finance experts gained experience from it and, years later, incorporated China into an umbrella of high-stakes economic moves while the people were sleeping. Slowly under our noses, our manufacturing equipment was being transferred to China under the calumniation of having cheaper consumer goods that never materialized. Later in the 2000s, we'll see excessive taxes and dangerously high employment rates skyrocketing only to find more Americans out of work and joining welfare ranks. Yet while Americans still out of work, top organizations related to our government, especially the administrations from 2000–2010, were bringing into these country illegal undocumented and sometimes violent immigrants from Mexico, Central America, and not-so-friendly Arab nations. And I ask, what the heck are they doing? What about NAFTA? Wasn't that supposed to be a windfall for Americans? Yes, yes, yes, it was shouted out that way. Again, folks, investigate who the front-runner liars are and continue to be. Don't be blinded by party lines. Are of that lie. A certain party will emerge that claims the other party has all the rich people. It's big business, politics, and the world order which initiated the actions. Can we stop it? It appears to be helping nations that were struggling, and I would say that it is a good thing. I would pray and hope—and I currently do—for fair distribution of the successful endeavor to help nations to prosper. But what sparked Europe and America to accept thousands of people was because we were just about at zero population. Isn't that something! What else can zero population disrupt? The future will tell. And remember, I wrote about zero population beginning to develop while I was in the army in the mid-1960s.

FBI Becomes an Agency

The rhetoric of the day was that the FBI should come under the agency of the federal government. J. Edgar Hoover protested to no avail and warned America that it is easier to *capture and prosecute a criminal than it would to prosecute a politician* if the FBI became an agency of the government. It indeed came to pass that certain political parties of the 2000s–2018 received protection from the FBI as currently noted. Another sad day for American justice, and I wondered if this isn't just another nail in our coffin on the road to decay. This should be on top of our prayer list to rid itself of corruption.

Confirmation Manuals

As a religious teacher these days, in the 1970s, I found the authors of Catholic children and young adult teaching manuals were void of mostly biblical and Catholic Catechism foundations. Soon in desperation, I would read the title of the new religious manuals printed in the 1970s prior to teaching and conduct my entire class from the title only and how I understood Scripture and the Catholic catechist. Later in 2016, I found an answer to why Catholic teaching was being watered down in the 1970s. You know, folks, for centuries, the Catholic Church has kept evil at bay; evil has been unable to succeed as promised by Jesus to Peter, that the gates of the underworld shall not prevail against it, and it hasn't. A lot of bad things have happened in the church since its beginning, but evil has not prevailed. *Amen.*

Music

"The Beat Goes On."

Sayings

"If you can't beat them, join them" (does this saying irritate you? It does me). "I'm not prejudice, I hate them all." Don't forget, these are my observations of the decade. "Can't see the trees from the forest." "Girls are gullible and don't know how to say *no*." "Better safe than sorry."

Time Line: 1980 through 1990

Michael, My Son, Is Born

It was a happy day and a surprise on July 8, 1980, when I arrived at the hospital and was told our eighth child was a boy. Why surprised? We had no desire to know the sex of our babies before they were born. We already had six girls after our first child, Guy, was born, and we developed a recent erroneous mindset from my nurse sister-in-law that the army radars, which I work close with, changed my ability to have more boys. *Ha*, I thought, *I can't wait to get out of the hospital and tell Barbara's nurse sister a thing or two.*

Becoming a Service Nation

In the early 1980s, while in Grand Haven, Michigan, I heard a radio report that America will be a service country someday. Now how do you suppose they knew that (see, I can't help remembering these sorts of things even as a baby)? I brushed it off until years later, in the 2000s, that I understood and related America changing from a capitalist self-sufficient manufacturing nation to one depending on others. It brings me back to when we studied American history in the fourth grade about a colonial settlement that decided to take away all property from the town colonialist and share the work and the proceeds with the whole community. Sounds like the right thing to do, especially to survive the hardship winters they have in New England. However—there is that *however* again—it wasn't long before people began realizing they didn't have to work as hard as others and left it up to their willing neighbor to carry the bigger share of burden. As you may have guessed, the settlement didn't last long, and it dissolved. And as you will know, my architectural training provided real abilities to scale up small things into bigger things. And what I found was that the socialist and progressives are out of their gore and out of touch with common folk ("out of their gore," slang for extremely out of their minds and out of touch). Ha, they've only scratched the surface, reading and making determinations.

Give Away Patents and Processes

I witnessed one company in Kalamazoo and understood there were other companies giving away their manufacturing patents and process documents to Asian markets. What I actually eyewitnessed were defense aerospace documents, classified as confidential, sent overseas to foreign entities, approved by congress in one of those pork bellies deals. I was familiar with classified documents from my former experience in handling military classified documents, to include protecting and assisting in declassifying confidential and secret documents. Maybe the world is headed in the right direction, or America may be setting the scene for its own demise. I find no evidence in world history that allowed great nations to continue prosperity progress forever.[a]

Small Wars Forecasted

A government agency made a startling prediction that small scrimmages of war in various parts of the world were to take place in lieu of major wars occurring as follows: Granada, Falkland Islands, Israel, Cyprus, assorted Russian conflicts, Iran-Iraq War, Iraq assorted conflicts, Panama, American Afghanistan, Ethiopian-Somalia, Lebanon assorted conflicts, Turkey assorted conflicts, and many other regional wars not mentioned here took place around the world during the 1980s. And if you believe small wars don't start big

---

[a] Acts 17:26.

wars, you are sadly mistaken and possibly naive. We may be heading for the big one in 2020's.

Music Hits

"Starting Over," "Endless Love," "Physical," "Billie Jean," "Every Breath You Take," "Where Do Broken Hearts Go?"

Sayings

"An educated society is an informed society." My comment: devious people are educated too and transparency that isn't is devious. Later in the 2000s, transparency is further suppressed, even though it was the same political party platform that lied about NAFTA. What is that saying adults always said in the '50s? "Do as I say and not as I do." "Don't cut your nose off to spite your face."

Time Line: 1990 through 2000

Desert Storm War

Occasionally called the Gulf War, it began in August 1990, and was a reaction of Iraq buildup of forces against Kuwait and Saudi Arabia. A coalition of many nations came in defense of the oil-rich Saudi Arabia and Kuwait nations as Hussein's buildup of his army progressed. The war began when Saddam Hussein, the dictator of Iraq, invaded Kuwait and was defeated by coalition and American forces. Hussein was captured by US forces in December 2003, tried and convicted by a court, and was executed in November 2006. To go back and understand what the root cause was that led up to the war, we will go back to 1980, only when Iraq invaded Iran to destroy its dominance in the region, and in order to do so, Hussein borrowed money from Saudi Arabia and Kuwait to finance the war. For the most part, after the war was over, Kuwait and Saudi Arabia wanted their money back. Hussein refused to pay back the money by giving the excuse that he saved Kuwait and Saudi Arabia from Iranian dominance. Hussein was later inflamed when Kuwait and America were making oil deals, and Israel was involved. It was the same time he invaded Kuwait in August 1990, to get the oil-rich resources himself. He cut his nose off to spite his face too.

Legal Drugs

Someday, maybe tomorrow, people will wise up to what the pharmaceutical industry is doing to our health. It'll come to a head when people begin refusing to purchase pharmaceutical insurance and revert to healthier lifestyles. An example of harm being done to drug-dependent people is to observe them during drug care. The opioid epidemic won't come about until 2018. And when it became known, uninformed Americans were horrified, and today there are more than forty million drug uses in America. I'd say that is a lot of pocket money being circulated.

Divorce Rate

Current divorce rates peaked above 55 percent, and there was no indication it would taper off. However, single parents rose to 75 percent to include both divorced and single parents. Well, it appears again that less children, more materials, and more money still doesn't account for happiness. But maybe I'm wrong to a point about money not buying happiness; we began seeing the US government Welfare system paying single mothers bucks for every child they have without fathers. Is that kindness, golden, or what? Or is it a party scheme to drum up slavery votes? Hindsight is 100 percent, and in 2018, we'll see other situations being used to obtain votes. Note: the divorce rate in the '50s was at 15 percent. And today in 2020, during the coronavirus pandemic, family, wife, and child abuse shoots up 300 percent in some cities.

Music of the 1990s

"I Will Always Love You," "Doo Wop," "Killing Me Softly," "Good Vibrations," and "Everything I Do."

Saying

"Man's economics is prevailing." I say in 2020, what about our spiritual wellness?

Time Line: 2000 through 2010 Decade

The Worst Decade

I believe the decade from 2000–2010 was the worst decade since the early 1940s. We see sides of an American world coalition that were united against Iraq and defeated them but cautiously of questionable Iraq allies that had large armies of their own and were longtime American foes. However, as I go into a future decade below, I am extremely cautious of what North Korea is capable of. This should be top on our list to pray for peace. I wish I had the abilities to hold my hands on Kim's shoulder, pray over him and for North Korea. Keep in mind, we should love our neighbors and for good reason. There is no doubt we have the capabilities to destroy North Korea, but why? There will always continue to be other North Koreans in the world unless we follow God's footsteps. And I ask myself, can we, as a nation, actually pray for an enemy? I think so; with God, everything is possible to do His thing if we ask. If we elect not to, we may see more effects we don't want to see.

Comfort Zone Phenomenon

I found later that what we become accustomed to and familiar with goes deep into our makeup and is often difficult to change. For instance, if you spent many years raising your family and only had $100 in the bank and suddenly you spent it, you would work very hard to get only that $100 back. And if you had $5,000 in the bank and you suddenly got an extra $10,000, you would work getting that money back to $5,000 savings. When people do such things, it's called comfort zone, and just like the people in the Cincinatti flood area, their comfort zone was experiencing annual moving from the flooded neighborhoods to higher ground, and they should not be made to change for another's profit; but then again, that may be progress living in the fast lane. Do you think? It sounds similar to the Indian Wars and agreements made afterward.

Afghanistan War, 9-11

The Afghanistan War began September 11, with the attack and destruction of the Twin Towers in New York City, when three thousand office workers perished and sent world finances into shambles. Bent on a suicide mission, a select group of terrorists flew two passenger jets into the two New York Twin Tower buildings as an act of terrorism. The mission to destroy the office buildings and Pentagon was partly led by the terrorist leader named Osama bin Laden. We soon went to war, destroying Taliban and Al-Qaeda forces, while searching for Osama bin Laden. In May 2011, Navy Seals found and killed (so the story goes) Osama bin Laden, the leader of the terrorist nation, but the world never saw his body. The present administration of that time gave the excuse that to show his body would make him a martyr. The same administration that ran on a transparency platform. Do you believe that? A transparency was avoided again from an administration that vowed to be the hero of transparency. To me, I naturally scale things up in world situations, and I see little kids (politicians) telling fibs to one another. So you see the old saying how "things never change," they just get more volume.

The worst of all excuse of all happened. The administration took sacred constitutional freedom away from us in the name of thwarting terrorisms. So, my friends, "the beat goes on and beat goes on." And watch in 2020 how much more is taken away.

The war effort lessened for American involvement in 2014, but in 2018, it continued to be uncertain after additional troops were sent to Afghanistan.

Gas Prices

Skyrocketing gas prices seemed endless, passing $4.50, but then again, we had to pay for the war, didn't we? However, Barbara and I just paid $2.16 per gallon for gas on November 20, 2018, and $1.70 on April, 5, 20.

How Much
Is Too Much

Since the Afghanistan War, gas prices continue to surge with rumors of hitting $5 per gallon before the end of this summer decade. The price of gas never reached five bucks but came close. To me, after making a basic root cause evaluation, I determined the cost of war was being paid for by gas taxes and oil companies. As the war lessened, the gas prices did too. However, ask your congressman, and he/she will say, "It's complicated."

Move West, Young Man, Move West

Congress enticed US manufactures to relocate to China, and the remaining American businesses were taxed to the hilt. During this time, some manufacturing officers like Gibson Guitar owners were sent to jail by the current administration federal police, only later to be proven wrong from trumped-up charges. But as a result, Gibson lost business in the world market, but its competitor in China suddenly is doing well. Another was when federal police busted into a New England family farm with their guns drawn, confiscating what they thought was an illegal *goat or lamb* brought into this country. It is sad, folks; we may be coming to this. My first inclination, as I wrote above that we were coming into unusual happenings, was in the 1990s when manufacturing gave confidential processes information to foreign nations. The real kicker that hit a sour note with me was the company I was working for actually moved profitable business to China and laid off their current working employees. Remember how I appreciated the hardworking Japanese merchant marine workers in the 1960s? Well, I felt that way with the American workers at the manufacturing plant I was at during this decade. They were hardworking dedicated American workers helping the company achieve its goal. And they were let go.

Banks Failing

A couple of well-documented prominent Democrat Party members made out well financially after bank involvement prior to the banks failing. But as usual, the news media was kind to their kind again and hardly a word written about it (and the impression is that Republicans are the only bad guys).

Social Security

Members of the Democrat Party take monies out of the Social Security account and leave worthless IOUs. Check it out yourself, if it is not unbelievable what corruption can do to people sleeping.

Health Care Bill

Worst conceived nontransparent health care being further exposed that was passed by a political party out of control. They actually passed the bill without knowing what was in it. Included in the details for sure are traces of abandoning the sick and the aging. Why didn't we hear slogans like let's pass a health care bill for the people? Because as we follow the money trail, friends of insurance companies and progressives ensured its passage for their gain.

Spiritual War

It is evident to me, as we understand world news, we are entering into a spiritual war.

Offshore Oil Drilling

One week after President Obama signed an executive order to halt offshore oil drilling, an active production British Petroleum oil drilling rig had underwater piping destroyed in the Gulf of Mexico waters. American or British Petroleum never found what caused the damaged pipes. The oil pollution was around for years, and even EPA didn't say a word. Now isn't that something or what, that they don't know? I'm telling you, we've got to organize a monthly prayer group with American churches first and world churches second. ASAP, after reading this. My phone number is in the back to contact me. I don't know what to do to organize, but it will come after prayer.

Toyota Brake Malfunction

One week after President Obama signed off on purchasing General Motors Corporation stocks to help save them from economic collapse, their competitor Toyota developed mysterious electronic braking problems. Toyota never found the cause of the malfunctions. So they say. Now isn't that something or what? You know, technology was already developed to interrupt various mobile controllers with handheld electronic devices during the Iraq War?

Fast and Furious

The government created a situation to allow our border cops to create situations that would help the administration make America reject individual rights to own guns. They planned this to be by the next presidential 2012 elections. The situation involved the Mexican government to allow the Mexican drug cartel to be equipped with American guns to cross the border and create bloody unrest and cause Americans to take the law into their own hands. The leaders that want to disband guns in America would then demand the US Constitution be amended in order to confiscate our guns. The confiscation would thereby forever prevent us from protecting ourselves with firearms. The scheme failed and not a word printed in the news media could be found. During the Obama term, leaders associated with the Democrat Party worked with the United Nations in an attempt to disband American freedom to own guns. Now isn't that something or what, and gun deaths don't even get close to drug deaths. So what is their objective? I guess politicians would like to change laws to the flavor of the day and not adhere to the US Constitution they erroneously swore to uphold.

World Order Maturing?

The world order leaders may like to think they have a plan by being involved in trading with the world and it bringing world peace. That is a commendable objective, but I ask how many other leaders in the world may think differently that it may be for profit only as the leaders push their own agenda in time? What the world should know is that it isn't their plan but God's plan, and in order to be worthwhile, His footsteps should or must be followed. Do you think it was committee after committee that got the world order where it is today and not God? See for yourselves, written centuries ago, it is God's plan we are to follow if we're to be successful in this life and the next. We are doomed to failure, sooner or later, should we not put our trust in our Lord. And in lieu of thinking it is ourselves that accomplishes our objectives, think again; a hair will only fall out of our heads if He allows it, what does that make Him? I'll say it again in spite of all the good human organizational input we have, it is God's plan and not man's that work properly for us. He knows all outcomes, and man is powerless to change His plan. Man can only change himself to love God. God loves us, and we can't change that.

So let's take another view by attempting to disprove God's plan. If He allows all national leaders—and He does for the good to evolve—what does that mean? In spite of ourselves, we have complete freedom to do whatever we want to do. Should we be resolved not to worship Him and believe in our own devices, He knows that too. And if you come to your senses and asked for forgiveness, He knows that too. The Father already knows if you are going to heaven or hell. And you may say, oh, what is the use, if He knows everything, I'll do whatever I want. If you can ask such a question, think about what you said. He knows that too.

Let me tell you a story of a family experience that is similar to what a knowing God allows. A friend of mine went to college and kept prodding his parents to do things that his parents did not approve of or wasn't in their plan of their experiences. Most of what he asked for, he soon relented and did things according to his parents' advice. However, one day, he wanted to buy a thirty-year-old truck to drive back and forth to school. His father, an auto mechanic, told him not to waste his money, the truck wasn't worth it. But my friend decided to purchase it anyway in spite of what his father wished. As soon as he purchased the truck and drove it, it began breaking down, forcing my friend to be absent from classes and wasting his money on other expenses. His father was there to help him fix the truck problem, but knowing something bad would happen again, something else would break down later.

The analogy of the story I just told is a true family experience, and from it, you may be able to understand a little of what God does with His all-knowing plan. He allows us to make our mistakes and continues to help and nudge us to change ourselves according to the free will He put into us. Had my friend followed his parents' advice, he wouldn't have gotten himself in such a mess. It's the same with God's plan, the world won't get into messes if we follow His footsteps.

War on the Unborn

American internal baby war count since January 21, 1973: abortion providers killed more than fifty-six million babies this decade.

Give Away Six Billion

The administration gave Egypt $6.2 billion for exchange of a few American detainees. Who is worth that much, I ask, or was it corrupt monies? Transparency is nonexistent, and the party involved is mum, and they again, I say, ran part of their campaign on transparency and the news media was mum too. You'd think the news media would wise up and see the forest from the trees and report truth. But then again, the similar Russian news media leaders that helped the Russian's make Russia Communist win power in the 1930s by printing untruths, later certain media voiced their objections and were soon shipped to Siberia. Just look at history to get a hint of the future.

Sayings

"Don't let a good disaster go to waste" (Chicago mayor). "Things never change." "We are in a spiritual war." "You can keep some of the people happy some of the time but not all the people all of the time." "You can bring a horse to water but can't make it drink." "It's like a turtle on its back, face in the dirt, and trying to get traction in the air."

Music

"Gotta Feeling," "Sexy Back," "We Belong Together," "Say My Name," "I'm Real," and "Hung Up."

Time Line: 2010 through 2020 Decade

Obama Health Care—Devil in the Details

The medical concept of aborting the aged is now a reality. An example, if an X-ray is needed to verify your pain of a possible infected colon, but you reached the age of seventy-five, too bad, you won't be X-rayed. And if you are too far gone, and you are an undesirable of some sorts, it is slowly being exposed in the Obama health care, you could be considered dead meat. Details are continually being exposed and understood as we presently speak of that long ago hurry up, forced legislation during a Christmas holiday period. I'll say it again, I think Hitler would marvel at our modern laws to maintain his German image and get rid of the undesirables. So I ask, what's the difference between our political leaders if they don't follow God's footsteps? And today in 2020, we have the Obama health care system not doing a thing to prove it is faulty. The present administration with congress approved separate budgets to care for the coronavirus medical bills.

Teachers Losing Ground

Lower grade school teachers complain of excessive unruly children, especially boys disrupting learning activities in classrooms. We need to take a good look at this situation, find the root cause, and make corrections as a nation. That is if political correctness isn't among us, attempting to shatter our efforts. But for sure, we need both parents with the same dream of their kids succeeding.

Fashion Have Something to Do with Corruption?

We are between a rock and hard place in attempting to survive as a great nation. Trump wants to make us great again, but his direction, it appears, will not materialize. All our, sadly, top leaders and Americans that trust them are not going deep enough and need to get into the heart of understanding that which makes for a prosperous nation if we are to become great again. Or if you'd rather look at the negative side, look at what corruption (sin) does to a nation. As a sidenote, if we continue on the course, we are presently taking with shameful fashion that helps breed corruption, greed, desires, and the other weaknesses that bring nations down into despair, we won't have a chance in hell getting back what we may lose. We allow sex to dominate our lives and conscience, yet when spiritual trouble comes from it, it continues in all walks of American life. Reminder, Israel is the only nation in history to be able to crumble, deteriorate, and bounce back into greatness again. How'd they do that? They began to understand what sin was and asked for forgiveness. If America falls,

I seriously don't think we will be strong enough to recover. There needs to be more God-lovers.

Day of Prayer

March 2 is designated as World Day of Prayer. And today, as I write, it just so happens to be the second of March 2018. I pray and my hope is that we have more people every day talking to God (praying). Let's begin a united Daily National Day of Prayer to start with. I say begin with people in congress to help, it be easier to organize and begin this important endeavor. You, like me, may pray every day, and maybe we can muster more today.

Social Security (Second Notice)

Where did the money disappear to that was taken out by friends of the Democrat Party? The monies went into favorite general public work project fund, then stacked with their Social Security IOUs, never to be paid back. Why hasn't the Social Security been paid back? The IOUs aren't legal, that's why. And *nobody* will make them pay it back. They are above the law and morality. We need to find and expose truth for the nation to understand even those lawbreakers that J. Edgar Hoover spoke about being above the law.

Putin the Russian, Not Playing Ball

So we have a world order that indicates lasting peace through economic equality for the world, yet Russia, North Korea, or Iran doesn't play ball with the New World Order organization, or do they? Sounds crazy, doesn't it, when the three nations could be included in world prosperity? And China is an example, and they seem not to notice. From my mere understanding of history and of people in general, it is like the ole saying, "You can keep some people happy some of the time but not all of the people happy all the time." But what do I know? There are tens of thousands of highly educated people out there that think they know better and know it all. My goodness, what could they lack?

By the way, the Russian leader, Putin, is one of the wealthiest men in the world. You'd think he has everything and would want peace and stability. No, sir, that isn't the way it works. The more we get, the more we want. After all, money doesn't satisfy man. It's finding our Lord Jesus that satisfies us. Putin may have a personality like the rest of the world. I am praying for Putin right now to receive grace.

Transparency

As we know from above, *transparency* was a key word spoken by politicians in hopes of winning the 2012 Democrat election; but transparency never came about from that administration. The news media was politically biased and kept balanced reporting obstructed too. And past president Nixon was a saint compared to Hillary, compared to when the news media crucified Nixon and stayed mum about Hillary. Why are news reporters not willing to do their job correctly? Maybe, just maybe, praying for the news media is a priority. Also pray for the people directing the news media. Wow, I'm praying for the news media half-heartedly because I began to think of them as being the bad news guys. I had to fight off my comfort zone of being angry in order to pray.

Despair

The worst news for this decade was the announcement that suicide was on the rise in our nation. A number of factors was causing the jump, and mental health issues took the lead as expected. Today a report from October 2018, announced that seventy thousand people died from drug overdose. It's sad, very sad, that even one person gets themselves in such a state, let alone thousands. What are the causes?

One problem, when I searched using a root cause method, was the closing of America's state hospitals beginning in the 1970s. The hospitals cared for many abandoned mentally sick disturbed people. So after closing major sections of the hospitals, a majority of those released were given prescription drugs often to fend for themselves.

I think the release of our people is similar to homegrown ISIS Islamists, wandering about without proper care and drugs, and what do they do when faced with loneliness and little hope? They do what comes natural to angry men and women—and that is to destroy. Americans released on the streets unsupervised and not taking the required medicine causes many of them to become homeless. The other clue is to watch simultaneously Michigan's recent voter approval of marijuana and Colorado's prior approval of marijuana. It was proven that Colorado's auto accident rates went up above 30 percent after they approved marijuana, yet over 60 percent of Michigan voters approved the use of marijuana. That midterm election in Michigan had Democrats behind the scenes initiating three proposals to put on the 2018 ballot to help ensure young voters got out and voted for the issues and, while they were there, vote for the party governor that will takes care of their wants. The people who voted for the drug cared for themselves in lieu of educating themselves of the problems known about marijuana. No matter, if you agree or disagree, the damage is done; and who and what is responsible, and I know you care. All of us better care, it's your future—a better quality or not quality of life.

And what motivates the Democrat Party to want abortion, divorces, drugs on the streets, laced foods, the health care system, and/or welfare? It is power control or make slavery of people, similar to the Nazi and Communist Parties striving to have the world populace under their control. Also another control is the food industry lacing our foods by adding not good chemicals into the soil or food mix in order for you to crave more to eat. Look what happens when deceitful manufacturers add bad stuff into our food to make us seek more pleasure, eat more, make us fat? Or help change our attitude and spend more for that pleasure. However, the dollars made from excessive dollars to the perpetrators is easy money. Case in point, do you know that some commercial farmers will not allow their families to eat the food grown from their farms? Now we begin to understand the soil worldwide is being contaminated by no other than us—the highly educated. So the big question I have these days, is what is meant by being better educated? Has it made us better off? We need a moral twist to make it perfect. Did you know that there are pharmacists that use health foods and natural plants in lieu of consuming their medicines for their families? Why are we slipping off the good track? Is it because we don't follow God's footsteps? Yes, indeed it is.

So where does all this education take us? Are we really smarter? Ask college professors what it means to be better educated and perform a root cause analysis of it. You will be shocked at the fluff you have to put down in the analysis. Keep on asking basic questions and watch them start frigging. Then the most important question, if they believe in the one God Almighty; and if they don't, ask, what do they believe in?

The World Will Begin Crumbling

So I ask, will the Russians or North Koreans attempt to pound us into oblivion? Not at first, they would not be able to pound us until we and the world have the appearance of the present-day South American Continent. You may see for yourself, South America got themselves into a world of hurt, and the hurt is spreading in other areas of the world. My grandson, Mitchell Kovacic, a high school junior, spoke at a mock model United Nations conference, sponsored by Mattawan High School on November 30, 2018, and the following is his first discourse sample of how we can become similar to Latin American politics, and the second discourse is concerned with world nationalism.

Rising Nationalism and Political Extremism
Mitchell Kovacic

For years now we have seen a rise in nationalism, while it may not have been as popular back in the 18th century it was still a relevant political stance that some people practiced. Nationalism, like all political stances, has those that oppose it and those that embrace it. Today we can see a rise in nationalism as never before. Nationalism is the strong belief in one's country. Nationalism has taken a rise, especially with the rise of national issues such as immigration. We can see members of certain countries showing nationalism in their nation. Nationalism is a very broad belief; some are extremely radical while others are just showing patriotism.

Napoleon Bonaparte, a well-known French military leader, was a big supporter of nationalism. Napoleon used the excuse of the French Revolution to bring his country together as one and to fight alongside him. Nationalism was used by Napoleon to get his country to spread the idea of French Revolution across Europe. We see nationalism happening not only hundreds of years ago, but also today. After the September 11th Islamic Terrorist attack against the United States many Americans showed nationalism toward their country. Ready to fire back against those extremists the very next day. Even the Islamic Terrorist are nationalist. They show large amounts of support for their belief in their religion. While Islam may have been against al-Qaeda, the Islamic Terrorist group still showed much nationalism toward their own group, to the point that they would even kill themselves to make a point/statement. Nationalism is not something you can eradicate; nationalism is a feeling of pride one feels toward their nation. And trust me, you nip any nation in the butt they will bite right back. Nationalism can be blamed on national leaders of the present or past. But the truth is that it's not the leaders nor the events faults, those events just give a nation's followers the little push they need to show their patriotism.

Political extremism however is a different subject. While political extremism can be branched off of nationalism, it is not directly related. One can be politically extreme yet still show hatred toward their nation. For example, al-Qaeda (An Islamic Terrorist group) is not exactly on great terms with their nation, yet they are extreme when it comes to their political/religious stance. We can see many examples of those that are politically extreme, yet show no patriotism toward their nation whatsoever. Democratic Liberals in the United States have been known to constantly whine about their country they live in, even threatening to leave. But they still will say they are a Democratic Liberal because they are proud of their political stance. Both nationalism and political extremism can be dangerous. But just like a gun, it is only dangerous if the person practicing these values are dumb and is willing to do something drastic. If it's someone from al-Qaeda it will end drastically, but it it's just an average citizen of a nation showing patriotism and where they stand politically then it's harmless.

Mitchell was in high school when he presented the above nationalism to a Model United Nations panel, and hopefully, his observations are positive improvements over my observations. I wonder because this month alone in August, 2020 Democrat mobs in large USA cities are organized, and a few hoodlums use guns to make their point.

RAYMOND T. O'DONNELL

Grass Man: Angel or a Man?

June 24, 2020

It was about 8:30 a.m., and it was getting hot working outside in the sun that morning. It was just too hot to finish watering the elderberry orchard out back, and I decided to go into the house and cool off a little before starting back up again. As I was walking toward the house to turn the water valve off, I looked up and a blurred figure was walking on the other side of a thick bush toward the front door of the house. The main front door was opened in order to get fresh air into the house this warm morning. All that remained between the inside and outside was a flimsy wood screen door that protected my wife, Barbara, who was recovering after three months from six different ailments. Barbara was in a state of weak physical condition, and her abilities to walk through the house was even a task.

When the blurred figure caught my eye on the other side of a thick bush, I looked over to my left, where we had a customer parking lot, and there were no extra vehicles in the lot where the trotting figure may have come from. Most friends out here in the farmlands come to the back door and this figure was moving fast toward my front door. All I thought about was Barbara was alone with our watchful female German Shepherd. The Shepherd would certainly sound the barking alarm, but I'm not sure she would attack an intruder. As I began a faster pace to get around the bush and meet up with the figure, I took my three-inch farm pocket knife out of my pocket, opened it up, and put it back into my pocket opened.

I got around the bush and headed straight for the front door and up on the porch near the door area was, and a man with a red shirt on bent over, looking at our Shepherd and talking softly to her from the outside of the screen door. I eased up a little from being tensed, thinking his posture was not aggressive; he wasn't attempting to get into the house, and the Shepherd was just turning her head a little sideways, looking at him as if she was trying to understood him. As hot as it was, the man didn't give any indication to get into the house.

As I walked nearer to the front door, near to where he was and asked him in a military type command voice, "What do you want?" the short skinny figure did not appear frightened when he stood up looking at me and said he was looking for the homeless shelter. Nothing in his eyes indicted alarm. As he stood up, it appeared some of his teeth were missing, as if drugs took a toll on him. But because I didn't sense a fear alert from him, I believed he truly wanted the homeless shelter. He was informed that there is no homeless shelter for at least twenty miles from here in Kalamazoo or in Chicago. I began questioning him and asked him to come in the back of the house where we can discuss the shelter. Even though the walk to the rear of the house was only a few seconds, the time was needed to think and get away from the flimsy screen door and ask more questions as to what was going on. (Unbeknownst at the time, my daughter, Ann, went by the house earlier as she does most mornings traveling toward Kalamazoo to work. As she drove further down the road past our house is when she observed a man with a red shirt on the side of the road rolling in the high grass.)

My main intent now was to ask him questions and catch him in a lie that would nail him to the wall. All the questioning and answering information seemed to come from an honest and sincere person. But my experience told me not to let my guard down. By now, we were back of the house with the homeless guy sitting down on the wooden deck steps in-lieu of the picnic table nearby. He was looking up now, and his clothes that seemed to be unkept were not dirty. His name is Aric he said, and it was a nice and clear voice. He mentioned his last name, and it sounded as being of Spanish heritage, but for the life of me, I cannot remember what his last name was. No matter at this time, Aric projected his self-respect and helped to ease tensions.

As he was sitting on the deck steps, he mentioned that he was thirsty, and that all he had this morning to eat was grass (hence Grass Man), and he would lick the grass to get the dew off of it from the side of the road because he was thirsty. He began talking about eating grass when I felt an old melt inside perk up. His statement reminded me of the stories my grandfather spoke about when the Irish came here and had green-colored teeth and lips from eating grass to ward off starvation. I told Aric that story, and he didn't seem to be moved and seemed poker faced.

Aric was thirsty, and we offered him a sixteen-ounce plastic cup of water, which he immediately drank down the hatch. I went inside again while he sat on the steps to make a favorite ham and cheese and mayonnaise-on-flat-bread sandwich for him. He downed the sandwich almost as quick as he did the water. I went inside again for another sixteen ounces of water, and he downed that just as fast as the first one. Barbara was up at this time and got a good glimpse of Aric walking past our kitchen windows, just prior to him sitting on the deck.

We continued talking, and I was ever watchful for a lie when he told me he was a foster child and came from upstate New York. His father would not admit that he was Aric's father, and his mother said she did all she could to raise him. I didn't ask how he got into the foster-care system, and it started becoming clear that Aric had cousins near the Michigan Thumb area. He went to the thumb area the other day from New York to contact them, but no one answered his calls or was at home. He left the area and traveled south, searching for a homeless shelter and came to our home instead. We began to run out of things to say, and there wasn't any known lies. He was asked if he would like to go to the homeless shelter in Kalamazoo, and he accepted. He seemed anxious to get there.

I grabbed my pocket gun, just in case, and truck keys to transport him to US 131, just seven miles east of here, but as we got into the old farm truck, I realized I grabbed the car keys instead. Oh well, I didn't really want him in my car, but I don't want to run back into the house, leaving him alone. So, with the car keys in hand, we got into the car and headed toward 131. Before getting into the car, I thought of a safety plan in case Aric tries to take advantage of the situation and goes a little wacko. Part of the plan was to ensure our seat belts were fastened, and there was easy access to the hidden gun if needed. All the way to 131, we discussed various subjects, and before long, we were there. As we approached the intersection, my thought was to drop Aric off there and he can find his own way to the shelter.

But I asked him (Why? I don't know why.) if he wanted me to take him further? His answer was an absolutely surprised, and it set me back a little. He said, "Whatever you want to do." He said it in a soft forgiving do-as-you-wish tone.

It was difficult to drop him off at the intersection; even though it was a busy highway, he could easily hitch a ride into Kalamazoo. Besides, he doesn't seem to be a threat, and what surprises me is that, for being a homeless person traveling all this way, he doesn't stink. He doesn't even look dirty or unshaven; he looks unkept and is intelligent and not purposely attempting to be someone; he isn't or try to hustle the situation. He is real, with a real problem. Or maybe I have the problem, not fully trusting him? I could have prayed sometime during this time and ask God for help, but the situation was too distracting and wasn't thinking of God during this whole episode. However, I thought about God the second I dropped him off in Kalamazoo.

We got onto 131, traveling north from "U" Avenue and discussing his life in general, and before we knew it, we were at the Stadium Drive intersection, about seven miles from the shelter. I told Aric we would go further east from here to the Hilton Hotel and hopefully the shelter would be near the drop off. On the way to the hotel, I wanted more information, and especially how deep his faith was after he said, "Whatever you want to do." So I told him a story about us needing six girl coats for the up-and-coming winter. We did not have enough money to buy six coats, and credit cards were not popular back in the 1970s. Barbara and me did the only thing we could do, and that was to ask God for the coats. The next day, a wealthy woman from our church gave us six wool coats. Again, no response from him either one way or another, so the religion conversation was dropped, and we went with small talk, driving the rest of the way to the Hilton. And as the car slowed and stopped to allow Aric to step onto the sidewalk, he turned around, and reaching his hand toward my hand, held it and said, "God bless you." I was taken back in shock; his eyes were made of crystals; both his eyes were sparkling with gratitude and happiness. As I began driving back to Lawton, I was in a daze and barley noticed passing the homeless shelter a couple of blocks away.

By this time, Barbara and my daughters, Ann and Janine, were frantic. Unbeknownst to me, my daughters were tracking me on their phone through my phone. They could see I turned around in Kalamazoo and was headed back to Lawton. They waited at the intersection of 131 and U Avenue for maybe fifteen minutes, and I finally rounded the corner and spotted them. They were besides themselves when I left them alone and travelled with a homeless man to Kalamazoo. Well, anyway, I told them the complete story when we got home, and I think it will leave an impression on them. After all, what just happened would not have happened if God didn't allow it. And why did he allow it? Maybe to repeat the story to you in hopes of you knowing another wonder of God.

Continuation: The hard questions/comments and looking back at what just happened today is part of God's plan for us and the following comments and observations are included:

1. Barbara's comment of Aric was when she looked out the window, he wasn't carrying anything. She felt all homeless persons carry something while traveling. I think she was right. Aric was wearing shoes, pants, and a shirt. And his shirt was red, absorbing the sun's heat. Aric didn't have any extra clothes for cool nights either. But then again, angels don't feel weather conditions.

2. How could Aric not find the Kalamazoo homeless shelter when traveling south from the thumb area? It sounds like his trip to our home was planned.

3. Aric didn't seem anxious to get into our house out of the heat. After all, Ann seen him rolling in the grass down the road as she left for work. He had to have been retaining the sun's heat from walking up the hot road. Angels aren't affected by heat or fire either.

4. Aric didn't show regrets toward his father whom rejected him. Where did he get that strength from? Or was his comment meant to be passed onto us?

5. How did Aric know his mother did all she could? (Opps, it just dawned on me that the message may have been for

me.) He was telling me it seems what my own mother insisted that she did all she could too, and the suffering all these years thinking and saying she failed. Maybe we all fail each other.

6. Aric may have thanked me for the sandwich. However, the sandwich was the best-tasting sandwich made, and Aric didn't say it was good or bad. Angels just appear to eat and probably can't taste, and maybe the angel slipped up again by being silent.

7. How did this skinny young person chug down thirty-two ounces of water in a five-minute span? He didn't even belch or cramp up. He isn't who he is supposed to be.

8. Aric didn't demand or hustle me to take him into Kalamazoo while at the intersection at 131 that hot day. I can't imagine any human not being additionally assertive in getting someone to drive them in an air-conditioned car in-lieu of walking. No, he said, "Whatever you want to do."

9. And to top it all off, when I got home, I couldn't stop thinking what just happened when Aric reached over at the Hilton sidewalk and held my hand and made good eye contact and said "God bless you," and his eyes appeared to be made from fifty or more crystals. The crystals were small, probably one-eighth-inch square, making his white eye crystals sparkle with different lite colors. Aric's eyes were supernatural, and I want to remember them forever.

Note: I was too busy attempting to figure Aric out while we were together and not thinking of anything else—his situation or if he was a safe person. Until we shook hands at the Hilton and we looked each other in the eye, there was no thought he may be an angel. Also, some background information, several months ago before this incident, I asked God for more faith and further said to Him, "If need be, I would and fight an angel for more faith, similar to Jacob's fight with an angel (Genesis 32:23–32), except it would not be a physical fight but a spiritual fight. END.

Sayings

"Wealth and lack of teaching, causes a third generation to lose its faith." "Education will set us free." "Money talks." "Thirty million Americans may die resisting political change." "Misery loves company" (this was a saying in the 1940s and is a saying for the 2020 coronavirus people coughing on others). "Good is Bad and Bad is Good."

Summary Since the 1940s

Undesirable:

1. Divorce rate from 15 percent to over 55 percent in America. Can it be, we are not happy but we became a richer nation, so how can that be? Isn't everything supposed to be hunky-dory (great) when we have riches?
2. Killing the unborn from a few to over sixty million in America. Have we become like the past world regimes, killing undesirables? Congress would not halt the destruction and instead passed it onto the supreme court.
3. A few welfare and dependent recipients to start to over forty million in America. Is this a form of government slavery for power or kindness? You know we should have the power as written in the US Constitution and the politicians are to be the people's servants.
4. A few druggies multiplied to millions in America. Could it be the high rate of druggies began with the divorce rate going wacko in America and/or the higher economic standard we have?
5. Irresponsible people grew to millions in America. Look to reading chapter 9, "A Saint Is Born," and see how a

low-educated, poor, and powerless priest was treated badly and became a true lover of God. Maybe American Catholic bishops should change their colorful garments to drab tunics or sackcloth and see for themselves their real worth.

Note: Just a small exercise to determine why Costa Rica hasn't improved since their last earthquake. Conduct a root cause analysis of Clinton's collection of donations for the Costa Rica disaster. It is a shame that people of Bill Clinton's caliber have been around for centuries, and the news media of today refuses to investigate certain political parties. Could George Soros be calling the shots of what is printed and what is not? Why doesn't George want the *truth*? Maybe he is afraid of it. If that is true—and I think it is—it could be just as alarming to our freedoms as economic corruption is. You know, he collaborated and turned his own Jewish relatives over to the Nazis when he was a teenager in Austria during the German occupation of World War II. I hope many Jews have forgiven him, but did he ask God for his own forgiveness? If he hadn't, what is he afraid of? *Fear* is not what God wants of us, and I see that what He wants of us is a higher priority. Could this book be a shadow for George? I hope so, and I hope he is blessed and finds peace someday. We should find a way to stop the influence of misinformation being given in American and world politics.

Michigan Election

I did a root cause analysis on a Democrat candidate running against Republican Upton in 2018. The Democrat had MD inscribed after his name during the political campaign and claimed to be a medical doctor. However, his opponent, Fred Upton, called him out several times and stated he wasn't a licensed doctor and that he was going against Michigan State law claiming to be a doctor. The false doctor came back with a quick TV response, showing the public a one-second caption that should prove Upton was lying, they said. What I saw during that brief second was a copy of a college graduation degree, and it did not indicate a license but instead it was a degree from a medical college and not the doctor's license the caption was intending for you to believe. Viewers had to be quick to read the deceptive message lacking the word *license*. I was happy for Upton winning 74 percent to 58 percent, or somewhere close to that, but you have to wonder what kind of people supporting the Michigan candidate could not see it was not a license but an attempt to deceive you and me.

However, the biggest deception of all was the candidate himself having the audacity to call Fred Upton a liar. For a moment, I didn't care what party Upton belonged to; he was a good person, and that was all that mattered concerning this issue. Oh, by the way, several national elections ago, the campaigning ad tactics were considered negative and made many voters angry, but now worse yet, campaign ads are growing into bigger lies. Maybe lying is common with the fake political doctor and the current news media, then I wondered if the fake political doctor's life is full of falsehoods too, and I further wonder if the news media isn't full of falsehood. The other big deception is the governor of California stating that the worst fire in California history, killing over eighty people and over two hundred missing, was caused by *climate change* (global warming). No, that isn't all of it; it is the political elect and the people that work for him that are responsible. They did not take proven forest fire preventative maintenance action beforehand, like initiating control fires as other states in the West perform beforehand. Again it is the political establishment's fault for not taking the proper action and not solely the climate, and also the news media allowing fake news to convince the nation. You should wonder why Oregon and Washington wasn't in flames too; they have the same forest and weather as Northern California. Maybe Oregon and Washington aren't in the world's climate change. Ho ho.[a]

---

[a] First Kings 18:21.

Looking Ahead at 2020 through 2030

Will This Be the Decade of the Big War?

I think North Korea will most certainly fire their missile in defiance of the New World Order that is appearing, unless America, China, and/or Russia influences the North not to take such action. I think most people in the world want a piece of the freshly baked economic pie that is appearing on the horizon, but Kim, I don't know about him. I don't have a warm fuzzy feeling he is straightforward. Russia and Iran may not want to share or have the will to fit into the world community.

Time Line Ends

Family Health Initiatives

When Barbara and I retired on Social Security in 2004, we had to make choices or spend extra dollars we didn't have in order to purchase pharmaceutical insurance. We couldn't afford the insurance nor did we have good reasons to purchase it after watching other people's lifestyles deteriorate while relying on legal and or illegal drugs. We felt the drug industry was greedy, and worse, the drugs they produced were not healthy. As shown later in the 2018 opioid epidemic, we had good reason not to depend on drugs as we watched other prescription drug users from various ages succumb to utter dependence on prescriptions. I watched, especially my healthy mother, in 2005, deteriorate in a nursing home after what appeared to be prescribed drugs for her to be calm. Barbara and I soon related the bad side effects of prescription drugs to be extraordinarily harmful. No matter, too-big-to-fail government and greedy pharmaceutical businesses kept pockets filled in order to continue high pharmaceutical health care sales and quick returns on investments. So our question was, do we want to depend on what the drug company claims to cure or not? Well, maybe occasionally we'll use their prescription drugs, but not entirely. So we kept our distance from purchasing the insurance. We looked for natural foods to maintain our health. Barbara began a journey on the Internet.

I'll tell you another story about our grandson Vincent, as mentioned above, when he was going through leukemia treatments. Myla, his mother, knew, without a doubt, the drugs that were given to Vincent had ingredients harmful to her son but could not reject the treatment without serious consequences from the medical staff. *So* she did the next best thing and began to counter the hindering medicine from doing further harm with her newly acquired knowledge of healthy foods.

First and foremost, the easy task Myla found was to feed Vincent carrots, broccoli, and wheat grass, followed up with fresh juices. The rubber hits the road when Myla developed a fierce determination to save her boy. Myla was still angry that God allowed this to happen to her firstborn child, and I guess a lot of that angry energy went into determination to research various problems with leukemia and what chemo and other medical drugs caused problems from the high-tech medicines given to Vincent. Myla wasn't at all happy finding what was being given to her son and the after effects of fragile bones, losing his hair, and his skin color. She pushed herself onto a quest to counteract everything that would bring Vin-Ray's health down any further using the prescribed medicines.

Myla was more determined during the research period, finding the immense problems caused by the drugs, nonphysical activity, and the lack of medical research countermeasures for them. If the medical field wasn't going to close the loop fighting the bad stuff, then she would find it. She began to dig deeper, understanding what caused the disease, what medicines did harm, and spend more time finding absolute solutions. She was relentless, and of course, Barbara and I were relentless at prayer and continued knocking each evening, asking God to cure Vince and to keep Myla from becoming frazzled. We didn't know for sure who was the focal point at this time, Myla or Vin-Ray; both had to be saved, but Myla worried us more.

It came to pass that Vincent would be cured from all the death-causing problems, and Myla would catch a breath, but not completely relaxed, knowing Vin-Ray could relapse during the five-year waiting period to declare him cured. Just the same, Barbara and I were thankful for having Vincent and Myla back to normal with our family, and we continue asking our Lord each evening, before our meal, to continue keeping him healthy, even to this day. And looking back, God knew we would continue asking Him.

You see, through Myla's determination, she was able to stop the bad effects of prescription drugs. We, as a people, can stop the bad drugs and cancer in America too. Maybe we can get enough people together to knock until God answers. You must and should keep knocking until God answers.

Flu Shots

These days, Barbara and I don't spend extra getting flu shots because of a whispered fruit and vegetable we found to thwart off the virus. We found through various Internet locations that we could slice an onion and place it somewhere in the kitchen, which is near the center of our home, and let it do its thing—fighting off viruses. We don't have any verification or proof that the onions prevent viruses, but we slice them just the same in case this ole wives' tale works. Besides it only cost pennies, and the house smells like something good is cooking. However, later on the Internet, we found an absolute flu prevention cure from the elderberry fruit that prompted us to grow our own trees and developed a process with the fruit and other natural ingredients processed in canned vacuum jars. We consume the homemade mixture during the winter influenza seasons, and to this date—knock wood—we haven't even gotten a long-lasting sore throat or cough. Which by the way, I coughed hard enough each fall and spring while in Michigan to hurt my stomach and chest for hours, every year up to nine years ago. Now it is eleven years ago when it stopped after I began using the homemade elderberry tonic. Also, it kept our twenty grandchildren healthy during the flu season. And that, my friends, is when the pedal hits the road in success.

Bronchitis

Let me back up to eleven years ago when I went to the doctor for the last time concerning head and chest congestion. Each year, until about eleven years ago, I would come down with deep painful coughs that eventually caused bronchitis or pneumonia. In frustration, I asked the doctor what it was that made me come back year after year, feeling weaker and weaker? He simply said it was allergies, and his answer stunned me to thinking all this sickness was caused from allergies. The next emotion I had was removing my contempt and anger for modern medicine curing all, and Barbara and I began finding a cure for the allergies ourselves.

We began searching for allergy cures on the Internet, and two natural solutions for allergy cures were elderberry and honey. We decided elderberry was the prime cure and picked up an ounce bottle at a natural health food center store in Kalamazoo. When I got home, we took a small amount of elderberry extract, and within two hours, my awful congestion was cleared and allowed my strength to eventually improve too. By the way, we haven't taken a flu shot in over eleven years and have been flu-free that entire time, just from taking the elderberry and eating healthy; the extra nutrients we ate affected us as if we were younger. Also we developed our own slight version of the elderberry process and found it is good for not only congestion but small infections, energy loss, fighting cancer, sleep disorders, and the down and outs for our children and twenty grandchildren.

The berry process we developed several years ago included elderberries, raw honey, ginger root, cinnamon, and whole cloves. And a few years back, we were able to begin growing our own elderberry shrubs and begin a business, selling by word of mouth to moms, athletes, nurses, farmers, teachers, and—absolutely—doctors. Also we have a small patch of land to grow onions and cleared land for more elderberry shrubs. If you are interested in how we make the elderberry tonic, e-mail me using the address at the back of this book. Good luck.

Review of Chapter 9

A Saint Is Born

My son-in-law Guy Miller called and said he bought four tickets for us to go to Detroit's Ford Field in November 2017, to attend the beatification of Father Solanus Casey. Father Casey was declared venerable for sainthood in 1995, and then in November of 2017, he was beatified. It will bring him much closer to sainthood through the church's official process. I was ecstatic to be invited and happy to know that Father Casey, the one Christian I admired most of modern times, will hopefully become a saint.

A Capuchin Franciscan (priest), Father Solanus Casey was a humble friar in the Catholic Church who simply embraced the will of God and became a righteous person of our century and is on his way, at that moment, to be declared a saint in the church. Hurray for the world! He was declared a saint. Thank God

He was born on November 25, 1870, the sixth of sixteen children to Irish immigrant farmers that lived in Oak Grove, Wisconsin, in a twelve-by-thirty-foot cabin on the banks of the Mississippi River.

I remember saying to myself a long time ago that embracing the will of God should be easy, but the more I found the things that lingered in my heart, in my thoughts, and all the pressures developing in me, I realized I was far from being the person I ought to be.

Hopefully I can convey how Father Casey embraced the will of God and became a healer too.

Chapter 9

A Saint Is Born

A saint was and is now being declared.

What was I doing on July 31, 1957, the day Father Solanus Casey, a Capuchin Catholic friar, died? I was fifteen years old in 1957 and have slight recollections what I was doing at that time, but for sure I did not know of Father Casey. I do remember about that same time my uncle Ryan owned a rental house on Maricopa Street in Phoenix, Arizona, and my mother and father helped take care of the building. At that time, it was rented out to a drifter family from Oklahoma. They were considered to be "Okies" by most people of the Southwest. Maybe it was another convenient negative name like Shanty Irish. They were economically strapped migrant people from Oklahoma, attempting to find farm work in Arizona or California and were called Okie for short, suggesting a lower class of people.

As a fifteen-year-old, I heard the term *Shanty Irish* being used and a couple of times directed toward me but didn't give a hoot because I knew who I was, and I wasn't anything like what was suggested. Whatever it meant, I would let it slide if an adult said it, but I would physically challenge anyone my age that dared call me a Shanty Irish. What am I getting at? Solanus was born in a shanty, and I guess maybe the Okies were too. We'll see in this chapter what a great person Solanus and his siblings became. Oh, by the way, I lost all contact with the Okie family in Phoenix, but I hope that they became prosperous and close to our Lord. I enclosed a short story of their down-and-out life in hopes of comparing a minor segment of our society back then in the 1950s.

The story begins when my mother and I were about six miles away from collecting the rent from the Oklahoma family when suddenly, I had a weird thought and knew the father of that family just died, and I told my mother. I told her that the Okie father just died, and she never said a word. When we got there, the father indeed just passed, and his wife and kids were there. I especially noticed his son, Bob, seemed bitterly happy his father was dead. I looked at him; he was about my age, and as usual, he was wearing a dirty stained T-shirt and clearly communicating how negative he was about life in general but happy that his father was dead. I wondered how he could be so bitter and happy when his father just passed away on a bed in the next room. I still wonder to this day what made him tick. Could he be as angry as terrorists seem to be these days? But then again, I see anger in many places today, or is it just me being over sensitive? I often ask myself what the difference of anger today and yesterday is?

Now I wish to show you some of the things going on during Casey's spiritual life and how a few Catholics, especially Catholics in clashes of cultures on the American scene, may have influenced Solanus during his lifetime. During the early 1800s, Catholics weren't thought of by many as true Americans but thought of as people only devoted to Rome. So consequently feeling they weren't accepted, many Catholics continued living in familiar neighborhoods, clinging to their own kind, and paid more attention to what achievements Catholics were accomplishing. As a result, we see below, under "A Saint Born," many Catholics became part of American achievements.

Just so you know, I'm a person who considers confirmed saints in the Catholic Church as being a good example of those persons. I know there were thousands of people who were saints in the past without going through the sainthood recognition process as mentioned in the New Testament. However, like the early Christian saints, Casey deserves to be known for the hardships he suffered within certain church hierarchies and how his faith overcame those diversities and later became a healer. Amazing enough, though, he was considered a simplex priest, and in his appointed ministry, he became a door porter, opening the monastery doors for visitors. However, this ministry put Father Casey, as was his vocation, in touch with the real problems and situations of ordinary people coming and going. He easily forged relationships and was known for his wise counsel, humor, and gentleness.

A Saint Born

We'll begin the saga with the year Solanus Casey passed in 1957 and work backward to 1870. I'll show you what was happening in America to American Catholics during his time on earth too. As I mentioned, many new American immigrants stayed with their own nationally when they first relocated to America until later generations became situated in melting pots of sorts and began moving their tight communities away from immediate families. But in the meantime, those Catholics that surrounded each other built schools for the remaining Irish, Italian, German, and Polish sons of the nationalities that lived in the immediate areas. As you go through the chronological order below that begins with his death, you'll see the influence of American Catholic communities had in his eighty-seven-year-old span.

Chronological Order

America's Great by Thomas J Craughwell.

- 1957—Before passing, most of Casey's priesthood was spent as the monastery's porter. Serving at monasteries in New York City as well as Detroit, that constantly put him in touch with real problems and situations. His reputation for the supernatural as a wonderworker grew thanks to his generous intercession and miraculous healings. Because of his renown and reputation for the supernatural, his superiors, not being familiar with his supernatural happenings, attempted to distance Casey from the crowds and eventually assigned him to retirement at the remote Capuchin home in Huntington, Indiana. But communication, correspondence, and miraculous activities continued. By the way, it was ten years later, after Vatican II, in 1968, that Pope John said to "open up the windows of the Church and let in the fresh air." That fresh air he spoke about was the Holy Spirit.

I had watched a documentary about Father Casey several years ago of his ill treatments by fellow priests and was enthralled at how he was misunderstood. I understand the oppressed becoming the oppressor. The Catholic Church, from the mid-1400s (Reformation) had time to become defensive; but today it is a different story, the church is looking back and removing those shortfalls (good for all the world, but bad times aren't forgotten so easily).

- 1957—Baseball slugger Hank Aaron was honored as the National League's Most Valuable Player as a Yankee the year Casey died. He was foremost in breaking the color barrier in sports, and you could tell many Catholics in New York admired Hank for being Catholic too, even if they were Dodgers' fans. Many Christians accepted Hank as a great baseball person able to get past color barriers.

- 1950—Father Kapaun, an army chaplain, was captured with 1,200 troops during the Korean War and sent to a North Korean POW camp where he would sneak out of his barracks and steal food for his fellow prisoners. The army honored Kapaun by naming our Seventh Army Barracks in Kaiserslautern, Germany, after him. I was stationed there in the 1960s.

- 1942—The five Sullivan brothers are lost aboard the USS *Juneau* during a naval battle in World War II. The brothers were just like other large families of brothers I knew about in New York when I was a kid. The brothers fought each other growing up but let no one step in to hurt one of them, without all of them taking up the fight. They were thought to be together on a ship in the Pacific during a WWII naval battle when it was destroyed and sank. The story later told was that they were all together during that last moment, as they always were protecting one another. The story of their last moment together may be fictional, but another story of them meeting God in their last moment is true, and maybe they all were together.

- 1937—Margaret Mitchell wins the Pulitzer Prize for *Gone with the Wind*, featuring a Catholic heroine, Scarlett O'Hara, who catches every twinge of conscience she feels as a result of her Catholic upbringing. I was embarrassed for Scarlett when I was a young man but later realized Scarlett went through hard times and acted like a person without emotional control. But later in our own lives, sometimes we lose control a bit, and we too are forgiven, and after seeing the weakness of the world around us, we don't glee over it.

- 1928—Alfred E. Smith, a Catholic, was nominated for president of the United States by Franklin D. Roosevelt. His nomination inflamed various people across America and the determined Ku Klux Klan went so far as to burn crosses alongside of the railroad tracks he was traveling on, and consequently Smith lost the election by six million votes.

- 1920—Babe Ruth was raised in an orphanage for wayward boys, and later he became the greatest baseball home run hitter of all time and was sold by the Red Sox to the New York Yankees and became what he is known for today. My father often reminisced about the Babe when he visited the orphanage he himself lived in.

- 1918—Maryknoll's first missionary priests arrive in China, and later some were expelled, killed, or imprisoned by Communists. The church, I think, was patient and later contacted the Catholic lay people remaining in China and began evangelizing again. Maybe like America, China is changing too. Let's pray we all change for the good.

However, we hear today about the Catholics in China going underground. China may want to control Catholics as the Russians controlled the Orthodox Catholics in Russia. I can image how strong their faith is by even thinking of going underground.

Even though Chinese government workers cut down church crosses in Eastern China's Zhejiang Province recently, I wondered about a friend who lives nearby, just north of Hangzhou, in a town called Jiaxing, how he may be affected by the ordeal. The backlash that came later throughout China was written in the religion section of the *Kalamazoo Gazette* on August 13, 2015. It was written in the fifth paragraph, and the photo caption illustrated a Protestant lay leader on his church's roof with the cross cut down. And another parishioner who wanted to remain anonymous, saying, "We have violated no law. We do not oppose the government." Later even the Chinese semiofficial Christian associations—which are supposed to ensure the ruling Communist Party's control over Protestant and Catholic groups—have denounced the campaign as unconstitutional and humiliating. Well, after more than three decades, the Christians of 100 million outnumber the Communist Party of nearly 88 million today. I can't help but be reminded of the Egyptian Pharaoh that was fearful of the growing number of sons of Israel.[a]

- 1917—Father Edward Flanagan opens his first home for boys in Omaha, Nebraska, obtaining custody of five boys who had gotten into trouble with the law. His famous saying was, "There are no bad boys."

As a teenager in Phoenix, during the '50s, I felt the sting of being thought of as a bad boy, when a friend's mother would not allow her son to be friends with me because I was not of their faith. And there was another time with two Mormon friends, we were rid-

---

[a] Exodus 1:8–22.

ing our bikes in a white neighborhood and two black kids stopped their bikes right in front of us, trying to prevent us from going further. They said they were going to kick our asses, and my two friends turned around and left me with them. The colored kids looked at me with a grin and said, "It looks like your friends left you." But that was when we met one another's eyes, and I knew I was going to beat them into a pulp instead. I told them what I was going to do, and they both turned pale as I got off my bike to proceed with my threat. "Hold on!" they shouted nervously. "We're just trying to scare white folks and didn't want to fight." I stopped going toward them in a threating manner, and soon we became friends.

The worst part in those days was that my two friends who left me went home and told their father what had happened, and he forbade them to hang around with me again. So much for many of those attitudes in Phoenix back growing up. I hope all of us, through our short time, have matured and changed for the better. It is our Savior that truly wants unity.

The irony of the above story was that I was a Catholic in name only. Their rejection of me gave me a resolve that continues today. Well, that was a start. I had to go through hellish times and back to become what I've become.

- 1916—Archbishop George Mundelein brings German-speaking Catholics into the American mainstream. He mandated that English be taught in all of Chicago's parochial schools. I think German immigrants came from a proud and hardworking culture, and they assume others were like them too. So I think as a result, the German culture breeds high achievers, and when someone like Solanus, an Irishman who doesn't speak German, attends a German-speaking seminary was over his head, and he got kicked out. However, I think leaders weren't able to or didn't care to see his spiritual strengths. That was too bad at the time, but good for humanity later, that we can now see a comparison of good and of achieving something better through his sainthood process. Of course, only a few will take on understanding and read about Father Casey; but those few, I think, will impact many more.

- 1916—Eastern-rite Catholics reacted against the Latin-rite Catholic Church (mainstream Roman Catholic hierarchy) because of hostility toward their customs and later joined the Orthodox Church in America. The church seems to take two steps forward and one step backward through history. I guess that is what man does. It isn't until we have examples of looking back do we get a better self-awareness of history. Maybe, just maybe, the making of saints are somehow tied to doing just that.

Hmmm, my whole life has been looking back and making corrections.

- 1914—In the beginning of World War I and the next several years, Americans saw the New York "Fighting Irish of the Sixty-Ninth Regiment" battling across France into Germany. I loved America, I loved it because of the constitution and the justice that it communicated to us. And as a kid, when I heard stories of the Fighting Sixty-Ninth, I was proud of those men having risked their lives for what I believed was our inspired country, and they were also like me—Irish—and this is their country, and this is my country.
- 1912—Jim Thorpe, a Catholic and a magnificent athlete at the Stockholm Olympic Games, won the pentathlon and decathlon events. It'll be an additional forty-five years before Hank Aaron, a baseball Hall of Famer, helped break American color barriers.
- 1912—Mary Rogers and five fellow Catholic women formed the missionary religious community that became the Maryknoll's Sisters. They would risk their health and lives for their faith, as did many people of faith.
- 1900—One hundred thousand Italian immigrants arrive in the United States. There were very few priests in America that were fluent in Italian or familiar with their religious cus-

toms. However, decades later, the descendants of the Italian and Irish immigrants became America's top-noted minority leaders. How did that happen? I asked. It was found that the progression was similar to that of the South Koreans emerging as world leaders in the 1990s, first educating their children and continue to do so. Note: the American Catholic Church built schools and educated the sons of immigrants in those early years, and thus they became prosperous and highly educated Americans for decades. I wondered if being highly educated and prosperous could be a crutch, especially when we drift from our roots.

- 1898—Rose Lathrop opened a clinic for cancer sufferers in a slum neighborhood in New York City, and later they founded the Dominican Sisters of Hawthorne. The sisters became a nursing order, caring for cancer patients, and those women who were handed that baton continue today.

- 1893—As a young man, perhaps twenty-two years of age, Casey considered the priesthood after he witnessed a brutal murder of a woman while operating a streetcar. Wanting to make a difference in the world, he decided to become a priest and joined a German-speaking seminary in Milwaukee. But because of his poor grades in German, as well as other subjects, he was dismissed from the seminary and marked as a simplex. Too bad, but that was a standard for the majority, and the nonmajority may get caught between the cracks. And he did, but he had other gifts.

- 1892—Boxing champ John L. Sullivan loses the world heavyweight bare-knuckle boxing championship fight in the twenty-first round.

- 1891—The first black priest, Father Charles R. Uncles of Baltimore, was ordained a priest in the United States.

- 1890—Mother Mathilda Beasley, Georgia's first black nun, operates an orphanage for black children.

- 1887—Anne Sullivan arrives in Tuscumbia, Alabama, to tutor Helen Keller who could not see or hear. I remember thinking, after watching a documentary about Anne

Sullivan, that she wasn't just educated but much more. She knew tough love and had a faith of high magnitude. Tough love is something I see the upstart Israelites had in their many rises into prosperity and, later, many losses during their downfall. And again, I don't know of any nation in the past that was able to come back into God's graces as I see Israel did. I found that if a great nation loses their greatness, it stayed lost. However, we can see Israel changing for the better and asking forgiveness and God's favors. I see bits and pieces of present-day America losing vital community values it takes to guide a nation into prosperity. But we as the children of God can find favors.

- 1885—The *Baltimore Catechism* was published, featuring 421 questions and answers about Catholic doctrine and practice. For the next eighty years, millions of Catholic children learned the fundamentals of their faith through the catechism. I was one of those kids who couldn't memorize and was bored from the lessons. I learned to daydream or sleep with my eyes open during most religion classes. Except one day, a visiting nun came into the classroom and put her Bible on the desk and began telling us the story of Jesus curing the blind man. The blind man story was part of my soul, and I fell in love with the nun speaking. Her voice and story touched my heart, and I became curious and learned to love Jesus ever since. The practical lesson I learned from that experience of the nun teaching was she spoke from her heart, into my heart, with her book at her side. I loved her being capable of speaking, and when I first began teaching during military active duty, I rarely read from a book; and likewise when I taught teenagers religious lessons, I refrained from looking at a book.

- 1870—Born Bernard Francis Casey to Irish immigrants in Wisconsin, in a family of sixteen children in a small 12×30 bungalow, Bernard grew up with loving parents and siblings.

In summary, Casey overcame adversity. We too, sooner or later, will overcome adversity.

Architectural Indicators of Failed Nations

DORIC   IONIC   CORINTHIAN

Three Life Phases of a Nation

Corinthian-Doric-Ionic are Roman column examples

When I was at the University of Cincinnati in the 1970s, studying architecture under the GI Bill, I discovered a fantastic secular period in the life of all great nations through architectural building designs. There were three architectural column designs at different times, supporting the roof, indicating the beginning of the Greek nation. They were called, in their beginning, Doric, the middle is called Ionic, and the final period was called Corinthian, the truly final period of Greek and Roman history as an example. But wait, that isn't all. A more fantastic revelation was found—all great nations had three design periods as the Greeks did of their buildings, but of course, with various names and styles but similar. So like clockwork, you could follow the time and rise and fall of each great nation in its architecture. At that moment, in the1970s, I began several years of searching for architectural designs that may indicate America's progression in history and at what stage America was in.

I found American beginning designs and even the middle but could not find the final period. But by the twentieth century, I would think architects were aware of the design periods and purposely stayed away from public controversy. However, I did find an obscure final design that appeared in its infancy of the third order. I was astounded that I found the design, mainly because America wasn't readily seen as being in a downward spiral in the late 1970s, and America was still thought to be a place of opportunity. But quite by accident, I found what may be the beginning of the last and final phase of America. When I discovered it, it wasn't a building design, and I questioned the validity of my findings, especially since it wasn't a building design or column. It didn't take long, and I began seeing a tinge progression toward that final phase after the US Supreme Court made a law permitting the killing of unborn babies in January 1973. After that timing episode, I thought our government was capable of conspiracies against us. And years after the 1973 supreme court decision, I confirmed a national design of what could be the last phase of a great nation. It wasn't a building as mentioned above; it was a photograph of NASA's rocket to the moon, with its boosters alongside of it appearing like the last Corinthian column phase with leaf-like rocket-propelling fire and smoke.

By the way, Nazi Germany's beginnings were in the late 1930s and ended in 1945, according to their own designs. During those years, all three architectural designs were observed. The beginning, middle, and final designs of Nazi Germany.

Chapter 10

Questions and Thoughts

I could not read the Bible without writing serious questions below, and after reading Psalms, I was driven to write cogitate *thoughts*. Most of the questions and thoughts were answered.

Cogitate Questions

1. Can God really do anything and everything?
2. How is it that a lying spirit can lead to mischief?
3. How is it that God made us a little less than a god?
4. How can loving others keep bitterness away?
5. Why is the Sabbath important to adhere to?
6. Why does sleep elude us?
7. What makes great nations come and go?
8. Why is heaven eternal?
9. What does it mean that the end may be here soon?
10. Is it only God that allows a tree leaf and/or a person's hair to fall?
11. Will a hair fall out of our head without God willing?
12. Can God see our hidden sins and good as well?
13. Was the law and God's love implanted in us when we were born?
14. What are results from turning away from the needy?
15. Can we have a déjà vu without God's plan?
16. Why was man made to be above animals?

17. How can other people suffer from my sins?
18. Do shadows come from God?
19. Can animals cry out to God?
20. Does all spilled blood cry out to God?
21. Can we win over evil if we're insincere?
22. How does forgiving a scoundrel benefit all of us?
23. If it doesn't rain in heaven, why does it rain on earth?
24. How could sandals last the Israelites forty years walking through the desert?
25. Can love be the only language we use in heaven?
26. Will man destroy the world or cause it?
27. Should the end of the world be fearful?
28. Will most people go to heaven at the end?
29. What is love? Is God love?
30. Why when two or more pray, it may come to pass?
31. Can we find God by searching our heart?
32. Are angels all around us?
33. Why were Jews called God's people?
34. Do Jews have a free pass into heaven?
35. Can perseverance alone eliminate sins?
36. How come all sin doesn't motivate us?
37. How come all good doesn't move us?
38. Where were we when God made the world?
39. Will following our conscience always be correct?
40. Will we have to account for our sins someday?
41. Can animals and trees have souls?
42. Can creatures go to heaven?
43. Why must we be united as one in Christ?
44. Why did Jesus send the Holy Spirit?
45. Is wisdom worth all the gold and silver on earth?
46. Why is God the fullest in me when I'm in my lowest?
47. How can a person be free in prison?
48. Why does God protect widows and orphans?
49. Why, when a Bible book is coming apart, its owner is not?
50. How can a weak person be stronger?

51. How can a virgin have a baby?
52. Why did Mary have to be a virgin?
53. Where is the ark of the covenant located?[a]
54. Why could only certain persons carry the ark?
55. To live, why do we need every Word of God?
56. How can God breathe life into us?
57. What is the bread of life?
58. Why are we here, in this place, right now?
59. Why can't we know everything?
60. Did Israelites go to heaven before Christ came?
61. Why are childbearing women saved through childbirth?
62. Are we completely saved before we get into heaven?
63. Will our biggest surprise be when we're in heaven?
64. Is it better to pluck out our eye rather than to go to hell?
65. Can love cope with severe hardships?
66. Why are the Three Wise Men wise?
67. How did the bright star of Bethlehem show the way?
68. Can science see planet/star lineups from the past when Christ was born?
69. Why can't I get into heaven by my own accord?
70. Will we meet our relatives in heaven?
71. Does God want us to honor our relatives and parents?
72. Will we receive new bodies at the end of time?
73. Why does God hold children in high esteem?
74. Can loving really be a great achievement?
75. Do I need to go to a university to obtain wisdom?
76. Are we, this very moment, in a spiritual war?
77. Were angels sighted during the Six-Day War?
78. How can we eat the body and blood of Christ?
79. Darkness comes to man, but is God always light?
80. What kind of mark do we get from baptism?
81. Do we have the sign of the cross on our foreheads?
82. Do we need the cross mark to enter heaven?

---

[a] Second Maccabees 2.

83. Will others not having the cross on their head receive the mark at the end?
84. Are angels messengers of God?
85. Do trees and men have souls?
86. Why was Jesus sent to forgive our sins?
87. Is sin a lack of God?
88. What does "You shall not kill" mean?
89. Is anything and everything against and not of God a sin?
90. Can living in comfort be vain?
91. Does *reborn* mean a physical event?
92. Is there one God and/or three persons in one God?
93. Does Islam have the same God as the Jews?
94. What is love? Is it liking someone?
95. Can we be void of love?
96. Was God alone when He created the universe?
97. Did God say, "Let us make man in our own image?"
98. What is God's image?
99. What does it mean to be fruitful and multiply?
100. Are there processes for boy babies to be conceived?
101. Does God dwell in us and/or in heaven?
102. Can we breathe without God?
103. How can the good and/or bad receive grace?
104. How can I be down and out and still be close to God?
105. Can man achieve world peace alone?
106. Is history a barometer of current world events?
107. Does history repeat itself?
108. How can we break from a repeating history?
109. Can an apple fall far from the tree?
110. Can the saying "do as I say and not as I do" be good?
111. Is a bad apple always a bad apple?
112. Did it take 10 percent of Russians to start Communism?
113. Why do we prompt war? Psalm 120:6–7.
114. Do the rich really get richer?
115. Why is there either good and/or evil?
116. Why is there rich and poor?
117. Why is there LIFE AND Death?

118. Why is there either wisdom or foolishness?[a]
119. Could Israel's Sheol be similar to purgatory?[b]
120. Why does day and night exist?
121. Why are we either happy or sad?
122. Why do sinners want others to sin?
123. Why do people who suffer want others to suffer?
124. Why do those who love God wish it for others?
125. Why does love make for a better world?
126. Does love cause happiness?
127. Does sin cause anger and wars?
128. How can we stop sinning?
129. Is Jesus a reflection of the Father's love?
130. Do people who search their heart want good?
131. What is the advantage of loving?
132. How can a Bible help us in daily life?
133. Does God want all to be prosperous?
134. Is lasting prosperity achievable?
135. Why do we take the good with the bad?
136. Why is everything light or dark, good or bad?
137. Why is there male and female?
138. Can perfection be a form of love?
139. Why did God create us?
140. How can God love us when we are imperfect?
141. Why does Jesus want all men with Him in the end?
142. Why can't man achieve peace alone?
143. Can we achieve world peace by being nice or by loving?
144. Is it costly having children, and could it be its own treasure?
145. Did the staff sergeant in South Korea truly want peace?
146. What good is it to us to repent?
147. Can I become more fulfilled, putting trust in God?
148. Did angels fight some of Israel's war?
149. Is the whole Bible inspired by God?

---

[a] Ecclesiastes 8, 9.
[b] CCC 633, 1030–1032.

150. Can God cure sin from us?
151. Can we win a spiritual war with evil intensions?
152. How do we become stronger spiritually?
153. Do dark clouds mean rain?
154. Does forgiveness give us a lease on life?
155. Is the pope God's prince on earth? Isn't he a man too?
156. Why do we have obstacles?[a]
157. Is complaining a sin?[b]
158. What is sin?
159. Is sin anything that doesn't come from God?
160. Is sin the opposite of love?
161. Does a lying heart damage us?
162. Can worshiping idols hurt us?[c]
163. Are monsters real and can God keep them at bay?
164. When did man begin inventing?
165. Did man invent idols?[d]
166. Who made the atom?
167. Should we turn everything over to our Lord?[e]
168. If we sleep, Lord, will we miss you?[f]
169. Are angels servants of God?[g]
170. Are angels among us?

For answers and comments concerning the questions, please contact me at (1-269) 624-6971.

---

[a] Matthew 18:7.
[b] Wisdom 1:10.
[c] Wisdom 14:12–31
[d] Wisdom 14:12–31; man invented idols near the beginning and will be gone in the end.
[e] CCC 215.
[f] Mark 13:33–37.
[g] CCC 328–336.

Collection of Modern Thoughts

1. Father, animals do what you say (CCC 339).
   Trees do as you say.
   Yet man, whom you love more than animals, don't.

2. Why were we born?
   Why do we cause trouble?
   Was it to experience what trouble was?
   Trees and animals don't perpetrate trouble.
   Yet man causes trouble.

3. Lord, how do you do it?
   How do you cope with us?
   I am afflicted, my body is an annoyance.
   Yet you allow me to breathe.

4. You put us above the animals and trees.
   You'll put us above the angels.
   You forgive our trespasses.
   Yet you made animals and trees without sin.

5. Scripture seems to be three phases:
   Where we were with God.
   Where we are with God.
   Where we are going with God.

6. You want perfection?
   Yet how can I be perfect?
   You always raise the bar?
   Will I ever be perfect?

7. Will you let me know when I'm perfect?
   Is there a guide for me to look at?
   Will someone tell me when I'm perfect?
   Is it written for us to know when we're perfect?

8. Should we not close our eyes to see evil?
   Do we see evil in order to reject evil?
   Is comparing what you want of us to see?
   Yet you don't want us to judge?

9. Is wisdom your gift?
   Is wisdom truly my friend?

Will wisdom help me conquer my sins?
Does wisdom know about our innermost?

10. Does a lying heart hurt?
Does a lying heart keep wellness away?
Do lying hearts maintain a sick world?
Can lying hearts and mouths bring death?

11. How can my efforts help others?
How can it not be wasted time?
Does feeling good make physical good?
What does that mean, you will heal us?

12. Will the earth become lawless?
Will the earth become ruin?
Will evil bring disaster upon itself?
Will we see the armies of the Almighty?
Will you create a new Earth and Universe?

13. Why can't inspiration be forever?
Why do we fluctuate so much?
Is it because we're here, inspiration is sporadic?
Will inspiration ever be permanent?

14. Like I'm crippled with sin, and you watch me.
Like it takes so long, but you wait.
Like bit by bit, you help me.
Like good or not, you love us.

15. What do you mean by opposites?
Are all things opposite?
When I believe truth, is nontruth near?

16. Are there coincidences?
Is a coincidence when feathers fall from birds?
Is it a coincidence when a hair falls from us?
Are all coincidences in your power?
Do you really control feathers and hair from falling too?

17. You love me.
Do I love you?
How do I love you, do I follow your commandments?
If I persevere, will I find your love?

18. How do I persevere in truth?
    I don't think I can persevere.
    But somehow, you helped me manage truth.
    Can I honestly say I love you?
    How do I know when I love you?

19. Why does opposite exist?
    What is heaven opposite with?
    Will my memory wash away from me in heaven?
    Will I remember something of the past?
    Will I be with my family and relatives in heaven?

20. I read and read, and I listened, and I live.
    I become more faithful and loving.
    I become more of the remnant of Israel.
    I'm more Catholic, I'm universal, I'm happier.

21. It's difficult.
    Sometimes preferring my deceased son to be near.
    Sometimes preferring my Lord Jesus Christ to be near.[a]
    It's hard not talking to my son.

22. Israel's mileage has been high many times in the past.
    What does America's odometer say?

23. Do I obtain lottery tickets to be prosperous?
    Why does the lottery make you distant?
    Why am I at peace when I rely on you?
    I know it is up to you if I'm to be rich or poor.
    I know you want everyone to be prosperous.

24. When my sweet dreams fail, do I give up?
    Was it God's will that my dream failed?
    God wants us all to have good dreams.
    Should I continue to pray and rely on you?
    Oh yeah, I can see good in truth.

25. I know my angel buzzed into my ear twice.
    I don't believe it was to save my life.
    I know God has our life span planned.
    Was the buzzing a message for everyone?

---

[a] Matthew 10:37–38.

26. When did I exist?
    Did I exist when I was born?
    Did I exist when you created man?
    Yes, I think I existed when you created man.

27. A man said there are no rights or wrongs.
    But there are rights and wrongs.
    Was he trying to be kind or intelligent?
    You cannot be kind if not telling the truth.
    Can a person be kind by telling the truth?

28. What did my son see on the road before he passed?
    What did my sister-in-law see in hospice before she passed?
    Both my son and sister-in-law indicated they saw something.
    My son took a photo only seconds away from passing.
    My sister-in-law lifted her arm up toward heaven only seconds away.
    The hospice staff verified they've seen people lifting their arms up.

29. Why, Father, did you allow me to miss death many times?
    I missed death at least five times, why?
    Why do you love me, a sinful person, and live?
    Are you keeping me here until I finish what I am supposed to?
    Yes, indeed I think so, your plan is forever, without change.
    What appears to man as a change, you've known from the beginning.

30. Can a person be saved by calling on your name one day?
    Can that same person be saved not calling on your name?
    What will the biggest surprise of our lives be?
    Will our biggest surprise be when we are with you?

31. Is tough love part of your reign?
    Is sacrificing considered tough love?
    Is it a sacrifice to love others?
    Should I love God first, man second, and myself third?

32. Is nice the same as love?
     I don't think being nice is love.
     Love comes from our heart.
     And nice seems to come from our head.

33. How come love doesn't come from our head?
     Did you make our hearts different from our heads?[a]
     How we recognize God? Is it from our hearts?
     How do we get to our heart to recognize you?

34. How come each time I do good, there is evil around?
     Is good and evil always here to compare?
     Do all men have both evil and good?
     Does fighting evil ever end?
     Is it only in heaven we no longer have to fight evil?

35. Is Kim, the North Korean leader, out of touch?
     Or are we of the world out of touch?
     Do we just sit back and point a finger at Kim?[b]
     We do as Jesus teaches us; we reach out to Him.
     And God does the rest?

36. I sinned, and I didn't die?
     I was dead and walked around places.
     I asked Jesus for life.
     He forgave my terrible shortcomings.
     I'm alive, and my hope is for eternally being with you.[c]

37. Lord, how can more of you come into me? I feel
     uncomfortable.
     My heart rang with your words forty-five years ago.
     Today it is fantastically growing and happy, it is becoming better.
     Your word keeps filling up in me?
     How do you do it, Father, allowing my heart to be filled?
     Yes, that's it, the same words of forty-five years ago is
     getting stronger.

---

[a] Romans 2:13–16.
[b] Romans 2:1–2.
[c] Romans 5.

38. Father, how many times must I forgive?
    Seven times seven or seventy times seventy?
    It is difficult to forgive a person sometimes.
    But I see in forgiving, I become stronger.
    Oh yeah, I see now forgiving makes loving you easier.
    Send more for me to forgive. *Bring it on.*

39. It seems there are two more final *TWOS.*
    Is your Second Coming a final *two?*
    Yes, your Second Coming, is it?
    But what else is the other final? Is it my death?
    Should I be afraid or ask you for help?

40. Are we dead when declared brain-dead?
    Do we continue loving while our heart beats?
    Are we in heaven before it stops beating?

41. What do you mean, happy is the poor in spirit?
    Will the poor in spirit really inherit heaven?
    Is there a special place in your heart for the poor?
    Yes, yes, and I can see it. *It is better to be poor.*[a]

42. What is that old saying?
    Don't criticize the other guy until you walk in his shoes.
    Does that mean don't judge? Amen.

Answers: call me at (269) 642-6971 for answers and comments if I can.

---

[a] Matthew 5:3.

Summary of *TENDERNESS, KINDNESS, FORGIVENESS*

So what did I intend to communicate as mentioned in the "Introduction"? The need to focus on what was real and true and what I observed was: what man has to offer, is only temporary puff. Stop to think for a moment how man has not changed their hearts, and on and on, the world has been the same all these centuries, and we've only come a little way. It's an old worn method that man doesn't seem to learn from their mistakes, and because we don't learn, we continue destroying one another.

Now you see why I hint that animals know God? It's not that I think they are intelligent or better. It is for sure, God made animals to behave like they do and know Him, and He made man to behave like sons of God, but they have to search. Man has free will and a soul, and animals have souls and haven't free wills, and animals don't destroy themselves unless diseased, and you have to wonder if we have a touch of that disease. From here, it appears evil is the disease and a lack of spiritual gifts. Spiritual gifts are indispensable to our health and growth and help us to connect to tenderness, kindness, and forgiveness as we in our life journey.

So what can we do? We continue communicating the Word and pray to the Father that the world will see and understand that God can and will give us rest, if we only ask.

Thanks to Him, all ends well, and all things
hold together by means of His Word.
—Ecclesiasticus 43:28

Acknowledgments

Most thanks go to Jody and Ann Michaels, Tony Karsen, Ann Nesbitt, Myla Kovacic, Guy and Denise Miller, Guy, Maureen, and Patrick O'Donnell, Mitchell Kovacic, Bruce Wiegand, and the McFall family for their kindness and assistance. To my dear friends who further assisted me in helping with the completion of this book: Mary Boff, Dan Wahmhoff, Joe Magalski, and Jack Butler.

Addresses:

Raymond T O'Donnell
24974 County Road 354
Lawton, Michigan, 49065 9800

Send your return e-mail address or a self-stamped envelope for a no-cost list to you of the *TWOS*, other questions, or for an elderberry recipe.

Capsule

Have you ever heard from inside of a large masonry building, the blasting of horns, babies crying, and viewing the world sporadically from being upside down? I remember, for only a moment, being tossed around and suddenly seeing hard objects spinning while feeling a burning sensation. I have, and it was when I was born in New York City, March 22, 1942. Was it dreams I had as I got older? I don't think so, only because I recalled many other insightful instances when I was a youngster. I even remembered being in an underground NYC subway train station with my mother and seeing armed navy police, carrying rifles and wearing white leggings over their boots. That was during World War II, and I had to have been between one and three and a half years old with Mom holding my hand. And I certainly remember the awful first air raid drill we ever had while living in a Bronx, New York, apartment building. I remember the end of the war when seeing and hearing car horns blowing, people were going out into the streets, shouting and dancing. I remember my surroundings for years and how our country got the way we are today. It really matters that I remembered those things; they pertain to us, and *I have* to convey my experiences to you, or I will certainly burst.

I hope you see family, religious and political comparisons of what makes us what we are today. Little by little, from within you, you'll see my insignificant footsteps; you'll see inside yourself when love began in order to forgive and become kind and tender. It takes a powerful God to begin changing what was deep inside of us. I had a mountain of frustration and turmoil, attempting to rid my mother and father's DNA from within me. The beatings and violent behavior of my father coming back during World War II and the turmoil from his violent behaviors made life unbearable and, later, desperately attempting to thwart their DNA from my own DNA. I was convinced the mountain could not budge. The mountain did budge, and I was on level ground.

References

1. Artwork by author.
2. *Baltimore Catechism and Mass*, no 2 (out of print).
3. *Catechism of the Catholic Church*, 2nd ed.
4. Metropolitan Master Plan Study Cincinnati, 12/1947 (out of print).
5. Pope Benedict XVI. *Jesus of Nazareth*. Doubleday.
6. *The Coup at Catholic University*. Ignatius (in the '60s we can see our culture changing too).
7. The Jerusalem Bible, Reader's Edition. Doubleday. The Jerusalem is referenced throughout this book and should be similar in meaning as other modern Bibles. However, it contains more original books than most other Bibles.
8. Thomas J. Craughwell. *America's Great.*

About the Author

The author, born in New York City during the beginning of the Second World War, begins to tell his story of the adults and events he remembered from his early childhood. He noted various accounts of the war effort affecting people's emotions around him as a child, especially his mother's emotions. He remembers the churches being overcrowded and worshipers standing in aisles. He remembers lingering memories during those days, even from the day he was born and two sailors standing with rifles and wearing white leggings in the underground subways. A memory persisted that led him to write about his surrounding observations as an infant and a child. Later he used the same alerted memory aptitude to communicate his adult happenings during military service, and even later, on January 21, 1973, clearly seeing the beginnings of a world in a self-destructive angry mood.

As he questioned others concerning their childhood memories, there were a few pleasantly surprised by his questions. They were all too willing to convey the year and circumstances of their being less than a year old and their memory of an exact event(s) they remembered. It was exciting to learn that others recalled past experiences at an early age when he decided to write this book.

The firsthand memories of his surroundings, personal relationships, world events, and understanding how the Old and New Testament of the Bible relates favorably to living in a better world prompt the writing of this book.

CPSIA information can be obtained
at www.ICGtesting.com
Printed in the USA
BVHW092058311021
620415BV00014BA/208